Transforming Defense Capabilities

TRANSFORMING DEFENSE CAPABILITIES

New Approaches for International Security

EDITED BY
Scott Jasper

Viva Books
New Delhi | Mumbai | Chennai | Kolkata | Bangalore | Hyderabad | Kochi | Guwahati

First Indian Edition 2010

VIVA BOOKS PRIVATE LIMITED

- 4737/23 Ansari Road, Daryaganj, New Delhi 110 002
  E-mail. vivadelhi@vivagroupindia.net, Tel. 42242200
- 76, Service Industries, Shirvane, Sector 1, Nerul, Navi Mumbai 400 706
  E-mail: vivamumbai@vivagroupindia.net, Tel. 27721273, 27721274
- Jamals Fazal Chambers, 26 Greams Road, Chennai 600 006
  E-mail: vivachennai@vivagroupindia.net, Tel. 28290304, 28294241
- B-103, Jindal Towers, 21/1A/3 Darga Road, Kolkata 700 017
  E-mail: vivakolkata@vivagroupindia.net, Tel. 22836381, 22816713
- 7, Sovereign Park Apartments, 56-58, K. R. Road, Basavanagudi, Bangalore 560 004
  E-mail: vivabangalore@vivagroupindia.net, Tel. 26607409, 26607410
- 101-102 Mughal Marc Apartments, 3-4-637 to 641, Narayanguda, Hyderabad 500 029
  E-mail: vivahyderabad@vivagroupindia.net, Tel. 27564481, 27564482
- Beevi Towers, First Floor, SRM Road, Kaloor, Kochi 682 018, Kerala
  E-mail: vivakochi@vivagroupindia.net, Tel: 0484-2403055, 2403056
- 232, GNB Road, Beside UCO Bank, Silpukhuri, Guwahati 781 003
  E-mail: vivaguwahati@vivagroupindia.net, Tel: 0361-2666386

www.vivagroupindia.com

Published by arrangement with

Lynne Rienner Publishers, Inc.
1800 30th Street, Suite 314
Boulder, Colorado 80301
USA

ISBN: 978-81-309-1244-8

Published by Vinod Vasishtha for Viva Books Private Limited, 4737/23, Ansari Road, Daryaganj, New Delhi - 110 002. Printed and bound by Anand Sons, Delhi - 110 092.

Contents

Foreword

Dick Bedford

Why is this book so important? In the twenty-first century, international military decisionmakers have lacked easy access to a detailed reference for common and accepted principles and practices that can be used to implement transformational concepts and procedures. In response, academics and practitioners from leading transformation directorates and educational institutions have collaborated to produce a volume that examines explicitly the process of defense transformation. By capturing practical insights and proven methodologies generated over years of study and application, they offer a comprehensive guide to the implementation of a capabilities-based approach for defending national interests and contributing to collective security arrangements.

Transformation requires a radical shift in the cultural mind-set. The transformed mind accepts risk and embraces strategies of change that support the common goal of security. Strategies that promote transformation usually combine emerging technologies, effective organizational structures, and trained personnel in novel ways to develop powerful concepts and capabilities designed to defeat current and future threats.[1] In the case of the North Atlantic Treaty Organization (NATO), transformation is an issue of maintaining relevance and pursuing new opportunities in the post–Cold War era. As Admiral Sir Mark Stanhope eloquently stated, "New times and capabilities call for new approaches. Nations need to re-examine the ways in which they use national power, as well as other national instruments, to maintain peace, security and prosperity."[2] This vision of transformation is guided by continuous learning and vetting of innovative concepts through scientific experiments that illustrate the potential effects of actions never before taken.

At the Bucharest Summit in April 2008, the heads of state and government of the member countries of the North Atlantic alliance reviewed "the significant progress we have made in recent years to transform NATO, agreeing that this is a process that must continue." They recognized that "today's security challenges cannot be successfully met by NATO acting alone. Meeting them can best be achieved through a broad partnership with the wider international community."[3] Thus, the expansion of cooperative arrangements, such as the Mediterranean Dialogue and the Istanbul Cooperative Initiative, and the active engagement of partners across the globe, like Australia, Japan, New Zealand, Singapore, and the Republic of Korea (all supporting the NATO-led mission in Afghanistan), are important to the process of transformation.

For a single nation, much less an alliance of nations and its global partners, to transform is considered by many to be a monumental task. Fielding effective capabilities through the transformation process depends on a critical and exacting analysis of the evolving security conditions, potential adversaries, anticipated range of military missions, and desired end state. An alliance or partner that is intent on transforming aspires not only to do things right but also, and more important, to "do the right things."[4] This requires a transition in military thinking from a doctrinal focus toward a creative visualization that contemplates how problems may be solved as well as how conditions might be shaped—in other words, a comprehensive approach. For this transformational process to be successful, planners must understand the threat environment; determine the effects that will be required to defeat adversaries or prevail in crises; consider the contributions of all major actors, including nongovernmental organizations and relevant local bodies; and equip forces with the capabilities they will require to accomplish a range of military operations.

The security of Western civilization in this post-9/11 era of globalization will be tested by an increasingly volatile and chaotic world. Foremost, these tests will be measured by our ability to contend with ideological groups that are transnational, inimical to Western ideals, and striving to develop and use a hybrid concept of warfare that combines easily procured conventional capability with asymmetric tactics in a global effort to destroy the core of the very societies we strive to protect. Other issues that complicate the problem include the continued proliferation of weapons of mass destruction (WMD), the declining efficacy of governments in the face of opposing groups who reject the laws of armed conflict, failing states incapable of invigorating their economies by providing a secure environment that protects and promotes democratic values, and radical developments in technology that provide sophisticated weapons and tools on the open market.

Simultaneously, ballistic missile proliferation and cyber attacks pose increasing risks.[5] These global trends threaten Western society by empowering and invigorating our adversaries.

To establish security in this environment, we must develop the capability to launch and sustain concurrent, major joint operations and smaller contingency operations, including crisis response, on national territory, at its periphery, and at strategic distances—all on short notice. To achieve this end, a transformed force must have the ability to

1. Train and educate multinational forces to make them interoperable
2. Deploy and tangibly contribute to collective security arrangements
3. Work in concert with nonmilitary entities in a mutually supportive fashion
4. Establish networks that rapidly collect, analyze, and disseminate information
5. Adapt to counter conventional, asymmetric, or evolving threats in a joint manner

Nations can realize these capabilities by continuing to adjust their force structures to maintain deterrent power and respond to challenges with speed, precision, and flexibility. Forces must be able to adapt and respond rapidly, swinging from support of provincial reconstruction teams and infrastructure projects to military combat with an adversary employing asymmetric methods. They will have to be rapidly deployable, sustainable in austere environments regardless of the duration and rate of operations, and supported by a just-in-time system of logistics that is increasingly reliant on local infrastructure and serviced by the private sector—all in a networked environment. Using NATO as an example, if there is one thing the alliance has learned in Afghanistan, it is that expeditionary forces demand scalable command, control, and communication assets that can span ever greater distances between nations and the area of operations.

Even as NATO works hard to create and build these and other advanced combat capabilities, it is important to note that this volume is not intended as a guide to procuring sophisticated military hardware. Rather, its purpose is to guide a methodical transformation process that uses rigorous experimentation to evaluate creative concepts as potential solutions to security challenges. The authors describe how to employ capabilities-based approaches to solve operational gaps or shortfalls, often by implementing combinations of enabling technologies, innovative processes, organizational improvements, and personnel development initiatives. Ultimately, the volume seeks to broaden the view of international defense policymakers: to better prepare them to balance national agendas with collective security arrangements, weigh the risk of interdependence against the expense of unilateral capabilities, and find the right proportion between civil domestic concerns and an adequate military budget. In doing so, this work should better prepare decisionmakers to think and act in new ways to counter formidable challenges to national and collective security.

Notes

1. "Military Transformation: A Strategic Approach," US Office of Force Transformation, Washington, DC, 2003: 10, www.oft.osd.mil/library/library_files/document_297_MT_StrategyDoc1.pdf.

2. Admiral Sir Mark Stanhope, deputy Supreme Allied Commander Transformation, address at the Athena Crisis Management Centre, Athens, Greece, 30 June 2006, http://www.act.nato.int/multimedia/speeches/2006/060630dsactathena.html.

3. Bucharest Summit Declaration, 3 April 2008, http://www.nato.int/docu/pr/2008/p0-049e.htm.

4. James J. Townsend Jr. remarks at the Atlantic Council of the United States, Rome, 25 September 2006, http://www.comitatoatlantico.it/forum/articolo/171/Remarks-before-the-Rome-Atlantic-Forum.

5. Sally McNamara, "NATO Backs Washington's Missile Defense Plans: A Victory for U.S. Diplomacy," Heritage Foundation WebMemo number 1884, 4 April 2008, http://www.heritage.org/Research/Europe/upload/wm_1884.pdf.

Acknowledgments

I was first inspired to study, practice, and teach in the field of defense transformation while attending the US Naval War College. Professor Mackubin Owens taught me unique perspectives on the synergistic power of force planning across multiple dimensions. Later on, during my assignment to US Pacific Command, I was privileged to witness the remarkable courage displayed by Admiral Dennis Blair as he worked to effect changes in military operations on a grand scale. Without their example, this project might never have borne fruit. I am deeply thankful to Richard Hoffman, director of the Center for Civil-Military Relations at the Naval Postgraduate School, for his unstinting support of this analysis of defense transformation, which, I hope, adequately reflects the vision and fortitude of these extraordinary men.

I would also like to thank each of the contributors for taking the time to share their insights and experiences, garnered over years of study and practice. In particular, I am grateful for the sage advice of Professors Tom Bruneau and Harold Trinkunas of the Naval Postgraduate School. The book benefited greatly from Scott Moreland's exhaustive literature research. Elizabeth Skinner's exacting copyediting and insightful comments throughout the project made the final product much better than it would have been otherwise. My sincere appreciation additionally goes to Lynne Rienner and her staff for their professional guidance and precise technical editing.

Most important, I would like to thank my lovely wife, Annie, and our wonderful boys, Christopher, Kevin, and Brian, not just for their patience and support in my academic pursuit of this passion for defense transformation, but also for their many sacrifices made during my demanding naval career.

—*Scott Jasper*

1

The Capabilities-Based Approach

Scott Jasper

> We are all vulnerable. We're in this together. From the point of view of the Islamic terrorists, New York is a target and Washington, D.C., is a target, Los Angeles . . . London, Madrid, who knows where else, Rome, Paris.
>
> —*Former New York mayor Rudolph Giuliani*[1]

The terrorist attacks on New York City and Washington, D.C., on 11 September 2001 marked the entrance onto American soil of ruthless transnational terrorism. Devastating subsequent attacks against commuter networks in Madrid and London confirmed that this unanticipated threat extended to European societies as well. While the horrific attacks against tourist facilities in Bali (October 2002), Jordan (November 2005), and Egypt (October 2006) displayed the global influence of these unpredictable adversaries, they also galvanized world resolve to defend national populations and common values. At the Riga (Latvia) Summit in 2006, the North Atlantic Council reaffirmed that resolve in declaring that "we confront complex, sometimes inter-related threats, such as terrorism, increasingly global in scale and lethal in results, and the proliferation of Weapons of Mass Destruction and their means of delivery, as well as challenges from instability due to failed or failing states."[2] At the Bucharest (Romania) Summit in 2008, the North Atlantic Council declared its members will "ensure we have the right kind of capabilities to meet the evolving security challenges of the 21st century, and to do so, we will transform, adapt and reform as necessary. Transformation is a continual process and demands constant and active attention."[3]

The capabilities-based approach to defense readiness, used by the United States and the North Atlantic Treaty Organization (NATO), provides a deliberate and universally applicable means to turn transformational concepts and operational requirements into fielded capabilities that can meet current and future security concerns. It focuses more on how adversaries may challenge us than on who they might be or where we might face them. This planning approach identifies a broad set of capabilities that international military forces will need to deter and defeat adversaries who will rely on surprise, deception, and asymmetric warfare (the use of dissimilar means or methods to circumvent or negate an opponent's strengths while exploiting weaknesses to obtain a disproportionate result) to achieve their objectives.[4] The approach aims to determine capability requirements for preparing joint operating concepts and executing tasks across a broad range of scenarios and missions, and to suggest prototype solutions to be assessed through joint experimentation.

This chapter will begin by exploring the changing nature of warfare and crisis, defining the overarching need for international defense transformation, and describing the shifts in defense policy that are necessary to accommodate it. The chapter then offers examples of methodical, capabilities-based means to identify and field the assets needed to maintain a competitive advantage over adversaries. Finally, the chapter will propose a broad set of necessary capabilities worthy of consideration in international defense transformation plans.

Compelling Need to Transform

> We must recognize that new asymmetrical threats call for different kinds of warfighters, mission systems and strategies. We need to be smarter, lighter, more agile, and more lethal. Only by applying our own asymmetric advantages—our people, intellect and technology—and by maintaining a force correctly shaped, sized, trained and equipped can we adequately defend the nation.
>
> —*Admiral M. G. Mullen,*
> *chairman of the United States Joint Chiefs of Staff*[5]

Defense transformation at its best uses forward-looking techniques that strive to anticipate future threats and create capabilities that will meet future conditions. *Transformation* is defined as a continuous process that shapes the nature of military competition and cooperation through new combinations of emerging technologies, streamlined organizational structures, innovative processes, and adaptive personnel developments that exploit national advantages and protect against asymmetric vulnerabilities. By definition, transformation has no end state.

The principles of transformation originate from the proposal for a new revolution in Soviet military affairs, which first appeared in the writings of Marshal N. V. Ogarkov in the early 1980s. Ogarkov based the imperative for revolution on the inadmissibility of a limited nuclear war and the qualitatively new combat characteristics of precision conventional weapons and microcircuitry that the United States was beginning to field. Ogarkov wrote that the "creation of non-nuclear means of armed combat with great destructive force . . . is sharply changing the nature of war, the methods of unleashing it, and its possible consequences."[6] The realization of this forecast came quickly in Operation Desert Storm (1991), where the synergistic use of precision-guided weapons, global positioning systems, and the Internet codified what was being called the ongoing American revolution in military affairs (RMA).[7]

Skeptics questioned whether an actual change in the nature of war occurred in the 1991 Persian Gulf conflict or whether the swift victory was really caused by Iraqi tactical errors in cover, concealment, suppressive fire, and combined arms.[8] While the Gulf air campaign, by proving mechanized ground forces can be destroyed at long ranges from the air, met the criteria that an RMA should either render obsolete or create a core competency in some dimension of warfare, the German blitzkrieg of World War II, in which highly mobile armored forces rapidly broke through enemy lines to change the paradigm of static defense of prepared positions, might provide a more exact example of an RMA.[9] The blitzkrieg model also demonstrates how combinations of tactical concepts (offensive shock), organizations (combined arms), and technologies (radio communications and internal combustion engines) can be used to solve strategic problems.

The United States used cutting-edge technologies that seemed to presage an RMA to maintain air superiority in operations in Bosnia and Serbia (1992–1999), but ground failures in Somalia (1993) and Kosovo (1999) yielded the realization that Cold War structures did not fit emerging operations. Defense planning shifted from the "threat-based" model that had dominated past thinking to a "capabilities-based" model for the future. The less unsettling term *transformation* replaced *revolution in military affairs* to characterize the planned extension of asymmetric advantages well into the future.[10] Early advocates of twenty-first-century transformation pushed the notion that advances in information technology could create a new theory of war in which networked forces would predictably outperform forces that lack network capabilities.[11] The concept was undeniable, but its advocates suffered from overzealous implementation of network centricity beyond its utility for fighting the predominant kinds of war.[12] Today, therefore, transformation is recognized to be more than just net-centric-type technologies; it must encompass combinations of operational, organizational, and personnel changes that exploit technological innovation. Transformation is intended to improve "the capability of units to conduct full spectrum operations" as evident in military service plans for "transforming to meet the challenges of the new security environment characterized by an era of persistent conflict with adaptive enemies in complex environments."[13] Simply stated, the overall goal of defense transformation is to shape the conduct and character of warfare and crisis resolution to sustain or create superiority across all defense operations.

Those operations take place in a world embroiled in continuous change and widespread instability. The fascist and communist states that were defeated in the twentieth century engaged in traditional forms of conventional military and, in some cases, nuclear competition. Today, the strategic environment is beset with violent political visions and extremist ideologies that generate a new array of challenges to national interests and power. Terrorist and insurgent opponents use increasingly sophisticated irregular methods of attack to erode national influence, patience, and will. Some of these hostile forces and problem states seek catastrophic means to produce calamitous effects that could paralyze national power.[14]

State competitors are trying to develop disruptive technical capabilities in key areas, such as biotechnology, cyber operations, space, and directed energy weapons, that could offset the advantages enjoyed by today's preeminent militaries.[15] Meanwhile, rogue states that sponsor acts of terrorism and undermine world order continue to obtain sophisticated conventional military capabilities.

States that have failed or are failing as a result of political disorder, resource corruption, ideologically centered mismanagement, economic collapse, and ineffective social infrastructure generate threats by their very instability.[16] Weak law enforcement institutions, lax financial regulations, and limited economic alternatives for citizens tend to foster transnational organized crime, such as illicit drug trading, trafficking in persons for prostitution and forced labor, intellectual-property counterfeiting, and money laundering.[17] Lack of effective governance in failed states also affects maritime security; violent piracy has soared in underpatrolled coastal waters, including attacks on merchant vessels, cruise line ships, and even supertankers.[18]

To compound the precarious security situation, devastating natural disasters and pandemic diseases can overwhelm fragile nations in the world's most turbulent regions. Only an international response could cope with the enormous loss of life and shelter that followed the massive tsunami in the Indian Ocean in December 2004, the mammoth earthquake in South Asia in October 2005, and the cyclone that smashed Myanmar in May 2008. Entire societies are at risk of panic, disruption, and suffering by the global transmission of infectious diseases, such as a mutated avian influenza virus that acquires the ability to transmit rapidly from human to human and becomes a worldwide pandemic.[19] Although international partners might perceive the severity of these various threats differently, the enormity of these events becomes universally apparent when they converge in crises.

These challenges to national and collective security bring into stark relief the compelling need for international defense transformation. Modern adversaries threaten domestic security with kinetic strikes or even nuclear, chemical, and biological attacks, potentially delivered by ballistic missiles. Increased human mobility and porous international borders, the by-products of the interconnected effects of globalization, facilitate the movement of transnational factions; the transfer of sensitive technology, hazardous material, and advanced weapons; the conduct of illicit trade; and the spread of pandemics. Falling barriers to competition in the Information Age allow adversaries to equip themselves with advanced technologies that were previously unaffordable to all but the most advanced militaries. As of this writing, distributed (noncontiguous) enemies have access to key information domains through commercial innovations such as the Internet, cellular networks, global positioning systems, high-resolution imagery, and digital mapping technologies.

If the international community fails to transform defense capabilities, we risk the loss of competitive advantage over complex and adaptive adversaries employing the full range of traditional, irregular, catastrophic, and disruptive methods in an unstable world. This creative and continuously evolving threat to security is dispersed and unpredictable in nature. An effective response to how adversaries may challenge us demands a capabilities-based force that is integrated seamlessly across joint, multinational, and interagency partners.

Defense Policy Shifts

> Future NATO forces must be agile, joint and expeditionary in character and design. They must be capable of integrating operations across the spectrum of conflict.
>
> —*Admiral Sir Mark Stanhope, British Royal Navy, former deputy Supreme Allied Commander Transformation*[20]

Most of the methods that adversaries are likely to use threaten national and collective security interests. Ideological targets include domestic security, democratic development, human dignity, rule of law, economic liberty, and energy security. In order to secure its country's vital interests, a nation's defense policy must set priorities for defense transformation agendas. Appropriate defense objectives might be to

1. Guarantee territorial integrity, sovereignty, and political independence.
2. Provide capacity for crisis response across the spectrum of operations.
3. Secure strategic access and freedom of action in the global commons (space, international waters and airspace, and cyberspace).
4. Strengthen integration into international collective security structures.
5. Promote international order, peace, stability, and security.

A capabilities-based force is the means to achieve defense objectives. To ensure forces are optimally sized, shaped, and postured to support national and collective operations, defense policy must shift its emphases across the following broad areas:[21]

1. From single-focused deliberate threats to complex crisis response;
2. From solely nation-state threats to those including decentralized nonstate network threats;
3. From conducting war against nations to conducting war in safe havens;
4. From major conventional combat to multiple irregular, asymmetric operations; and
5. From static-defense, garrison forces to mobile, expeditionary operations.

The capabilities-based force must have the ability to defeat any adversary or control any situation across the range of military operations. The spectrum extends from collective defense to counterterrorism and consequence management, from counteraggression and peace enforcement to humanitarian and military support operations. Future forces must be able to conduct operations whenever and wherever they occur, even in complex urban settings, congested littorals, or remote, austere locations. To ensure operational effectiveness, the conduct of joint warfare and crisis resolution must undergo the following changes:[22]

1. The customary process of top-down sequential planning and controlled execution shifts to top-down guidance with bottom-up collaborative planning and execution, where multiple networked

components apply decentralized initiative to react faster than the enemy's decision process or faster than crisis conditions deteriorate.

2. Sequential and pulsating pressure against an enemy force or objective shifts to simultaneous and continuous pressure in nonlinear and distributed operations, by which interdependent forces dispersed throughout the battle space attack directly and concurrently at enemy centers of gravity from multiple directions.
3. Deconflicted operations by multinational or service forces employed in their own dimensional area shift to self-synchronized operations guided by commander's intent, so that interoperable tactical-level units integrate activities based on shared information and a common operating picture.
4. Service-platform-centric operations shift to fully integrated network-enabled operations, whereby networked sensors, decision-makers, and shooters are able to increase combat power through improved speed of command, lethality, and survivability.
5. Massed forces shift to massed effects, by which instruments of national power (political, economic, military, and civil) apply a common focus and a holistic understanding of the operational environment to collaborate on actions that influence or change adversary behavior.

Examples of the Capabilities-Based Approach

> Transformation, irrespective of the level it occurs at, can be carried out only if it is understood and accepted in terms of necessity, opportunity and effective commitment of all who are in charge with implementing it.
>
> —*General Eugen Badalan, Ph.D., chief of the Romanian Armed Forces General Staff*[23]

A *capability* can be defined as "the ability to generate a desired effect" in a military operation, under a set of conditions, and to a specific standard. A methodical capabilities-based approach will enable planners to identify and field broad capabilities that counter adversary methods. Following are two examples of ongoing collaborative processes.

Capability Development Process: The NATO Approach

Allied Command Transformation (ACT), NATO's agent to force change, formulated a systematic methodology for moving from threat-based to capability-based planning it calls the Capability Development Process, shown in Figure 1.1.

Figure 1.1 NATO Capability Development Process

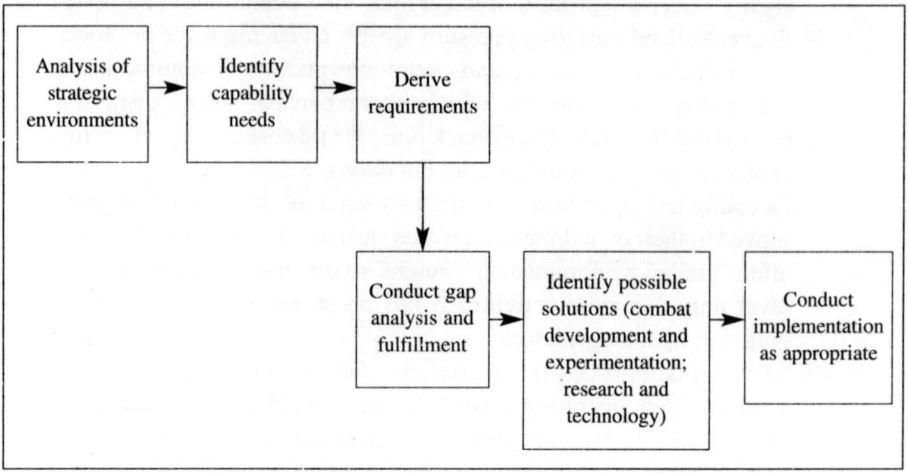

Source: "A Framework for ACT Capabilities Management Organization and Processes," Allied Command Transformation, Annex A to ACT Directive 80-7 ("Managing Transformation"), 20 April 2005: 4–17.

The first step in capabilities development is an analysis of the strategic environment, which includes a description of the predicted security environment and identifies potential types of military missions. The next step is to identify capability needs; these are generalized descriptions of known or desired capabilities necessary to accomplish particular missions. This step applies transformation concepts that offer an idea of how to solve a problem or create a certain effect. They elucidate a set of key attributes that shape desired capabilities, such as agile, joint, expeditionary, interoperable, networked, collaborative.

The third step, to derive requirements, refines capability needs to produce tangible capability requirements, expressed in Doctrine, Organization, Training, Material, Leadership and Education, Personnel, and Facilities (DOTMLPF). A systematic assessment of needs will produce requirement details such as how much, how far, how fast, and how many. The determination of requirements starts with the development of "planning situations" that capture all aspects of NATO mission types.[24] Planning situations are examples of various collective defense and crisis response operations that could occur within the planning period, and within the possible geographical areas. The planning situations are selected to ensure that there is a mix of mission types, terrain, and climates, at suitable distances from alliance nations. These are used to identify the minimum military requirement to satisfy the alliance's level of ambition.[25] Planners perform a mission-to-task assessment, using the projected situations to determine operational objectives and key tasks and thus identify qualitative and quantitative capability requirements.

In the fourth step, which is to conduct a gap analysis and fulfillment study, overall requirements are translated into generic forces and units that can be compared to national inventories and armaments programs. The outcome of this assessment is a clear understanding of fulfilled capability requirements, shortfalls to be addressed, or recommendations for excess inventories reduction. The penultimate step, to identify possible solutions, uses approaches such as the assessment of prototype military utility in realistic experimental settings, for instance in operational exercises or on the battlefield itself. Finally, the implementation of DOTMLPF configurations, the last step, can be conducted with tools such as Force Proposals for national contributions or Capability Packages for NATO common funding.

Joint Capabilities Integration and Development System: The US Approach

The US Joint Staff developed a concept-centric capabilities identification process that will allow joint forces to meet the full range of military operations and challenges of the future: the Joint Capabilities Integration and Development System (JCIDS). Within the Top-Down Capability Need Identification Process, depicted in Figure 1.2, the Capabilites-Based Assessment (CBA) identifies capabilities, gaps, and redundancies as well as potential means to solve problems.

The mandate for the CBA is guidance on the country's defense interests, objectives, and priorities, as provided in national strategy documents. The guidance is further refined at the operational battle space level by Joint Operations Concepts (JOpsC), which provide a common vision of how forces would like to operate in the future, along with their desired attributes.[26] For example, the Capstone Concept for Joint Operations describes the key attributes of joint forces: knowledge empowered, networked, interoperable, expeditionary, adaptable or tailorable, enduring, precise, fast, resilient, agile, and lethal.[27] A CBA may also be based on a joint, service, or agency Concept of Operations (CONOPS) that covers the problem, the mission, and intended effects.

The CBA methodology starts with a Functional Area Analysis (FAA) that identifies the operational tasks, conditions, and standards needed to achieve military objectives for joint, coalition, and allied operations. Sample scenarios that depict a wide range of relevant military situations provide

Figure 1.2 US Top-Down Capability Need Identification Process

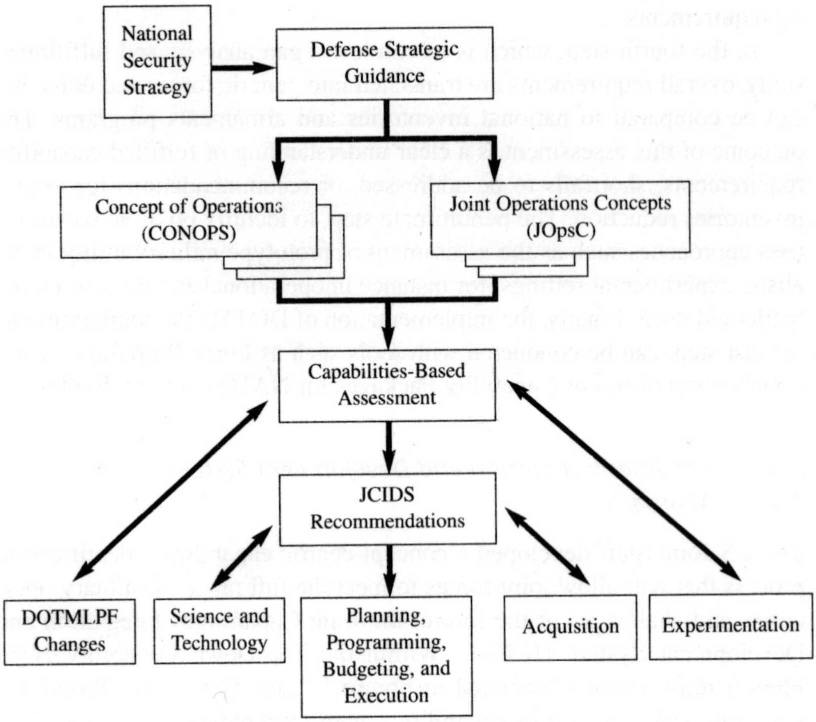

Source: Office of the Joint Chiefs of Staff, "Joint Capabilities Integration and Development System," Chairman of the Joint Chiefs of Staff Instruction 3170.01F, 1 May 2007: A1–A10.

a means to assess capabilities and attributes. The scenarios represent defense strategy guidance and portray the spectrum of anticipated conditions, such as enemies, environments, and access challenges. The military objectives of the scenarios are used to develop a list of desired capabilities using the common lexicon established in the Department of Defense Joint Capability Areas. Tasks that describe doctrinal approaches for providing these capabilities are drawn from the Universal Joint Task List (UJTL) to create an overarching task structure. Standards for these tasks can be used to assess capabilities. Standards are a quantitative or qualitative measure to specify the acceptable level of performance of a task. Relevant attributes in the concepts are used to develop an appropriate set of measures with criteria for determining adequate mission performance.[28]

The next CBA step is a Functional Needs Analysis (FNA) that assesses the ability of current and planned force and system capabilities to meet the military objectives of the scenarios. Using designated tasks, conditions, and standards, the FNA evaluates whether there are capability gaps or redundancies, and assesses the risk any capability gaps might pose to the mission and to the force. Performance data are analyzed to see how well force elements and systems operate within the scenarios and why some outcomes might not be acceptable according to criteria specified in the FAA measures. Capability gaps could simply reflect a lack of needed assets, but they might also be due to limitations in proficiency, sufficiency, or policy. The output of the FNA is a prioritized list of pressing gaps that are linked to force priorities identified in the strategic guidance.

The final step is a Functional Solutions Analysis (FSA) that assesses potential approaches to solving or mitigating the capability gaps. The scope of approaches encompasses changes in existing DOTMLPF, policy, or CONOPS alternatives. Proposals must meet the criteria of being strategically responsive (deliverable when needed), feasible (with respect to policy, sustainability, personnel limitations, and technological risk), and realizable (affordable within the required timeframe). Various alternatives can be grouped into sets of options portfolios related by a common theme, such as total solution cost, strategic risk guidance, or employment domain. The portfolios for each framework can then be analyzed within the scenarios for effectiveness and risks using designated measures. The outputs of the FSA are JCIDS recommendations, which can be converted to acquisition programs or treated as candidates for joint experimentation assessment.

Future Character of Warfare and Crisis

> In the face of US superiority in conventional, high-technology warfare, potential adversaries are developing strategies designed to counter or circumvent vital US operational capabilities and to undermine strategic political and public support for military action.
>
> —*Dr. Mathew J. Burrows, National Intelligence Council*[29]

Asymmetric warfare by smart and adaptive enemies is the hallmark of how adversaries may challenge us in the early twenty-first century. With such an approach, the adversary avoids direct force-on-force tactical engagements. Instead, he employs an oblique strategy that uses unconventional equalizers to achieve disproportionate effects. A low-end example is the use of shoulder-fired, heat-seeking missiles to shoot down a low-flying tactical helicopter or a cargo aircraft on takeoff. A more technologically advanced example would be the use of a shore-based surface-to-surface missile to destroy a high-value unit such as an aircraft carrier. Cross-domain asymmetric approaches could include cyber attacks aimed at networks critical to military or commercial information systems, or space attacks on satellites by kinetic kill vehicles launched aboard ballistic missiles.

"Fourth generation" warfare uses primarily asymmetric methods to achieve political outcomes. The first generation of modern warfare encompassed massed manpower and the line and column tactics of the Napoleonic Wars, the second was dominated by massed firepower in the heavy artillery barrages of World War I, and the third was characterized by nonlinear maneuver starting with the German blitzkrieg in World War II. Fourth generation war focuses on the use of all available networks—political, economic, social, and military—to convince enemy decisionmakers that their strategic goals are either unachievable or too costly for the perceived benefit.[30]

Fourth generation warfare seeks to collapse the enemy from within by destroying public support and political will. The whole of the enemy's society becomes a target. Small groups of combatants operate flexibly to carry out mission orders based on their commander's intent, using methods that differ substantially from an opponent's usual mode of operations.[31] Fourth generation warfare looks like an evolved form of insurgency, a type of conflict not necessarily new to global societies, given that over 200 insurgent-state dyads have occurred in the past sixty years.[32] While insurgency strives to defeat or displace the state, however, fourth generation warfare directly targets the will of the enemy (and its allies) to continue the war.

One distinctive characteristic of fourth generation adversaries is the manipulation of modern media to erode the support of the enemy's public for their government and policies. The media have become a powerful mechanism to conduct psychological operations through intimidation and instilling a sense of futility, intended to discourage rivals from committing combat forces. Digital cameras or camera phones provide vivid images of atrocious acts or perceived injustices that are instantaneously broadcast by twenty-four-hour news outlets. Media-produced propaganda scenes amplify the horrors of war and influence domestic and world perceptions. For example, the Al-Qaida-affiliated television station Al-Zawraa promoted violence against the United States in Iraq by broadcasting images of destroyed mosques and dead children to the Islamic community.[33]

Cataclysmic Terrorism

Islamic extremists seek to impose a radical ideology and political tyranny on the world through terrorist methods that reflect fourth generation warfare tenets. Al-Qaida-affiliated or -inspired terrorist networks have conducted dramatically destructive acts against innocent people across the world, using fear of unpredictable violence as a means to change political or social positions. Although terrorism is certainly not unique to the modern era, the global ascension of liberal democracies has provided a vast new array of largely indefensible targets. Localized cellular terrorist networks exploit those vulnerabilities inherent in free societies to attack from within by the ultimate asymmetric weapon, the suicide bomber. Rigorous adherence to legal due process and zealous guarding of civil liberties inadvertently obscure the embedded terrorists' identities and intents. Democratic demands for open society and trade, fair multiethnic treatment, porous borders, and unfettered access to information and technology leave infrastructures and populations open to sensational attack by human-transported bombs, worn in explosive vests, driven in cars, or hidden and detonated by timers or remote control.[34]

In Madrid on 11 March 2004, for example, an Islamic extremist faction called the Moroccan Islamic Combatant Group attacked four commuter trains during the morning rush hour. They used ten mobile phones to detonate explosive devices hidden in rucksacks, killing 191 people. Two days later a videotape by a purported Al-Qaida spokesperson in Europe linked the attacks to revenge for Spain's "collaboration with the criminal Bush and his allies." On 14 March, Spain's Socialist Party, which pledged to bring home troops from Iraq, scored an upset in the general election over the Popular Party, which backed the Iraq War and had been stung by charges of government mishandling of the bombing investigation.[35] The brutal nature of these politically charged attacks supports the assertion that radicalized terrorist factions do not appear to possess empathy for the suffering of others and therefore would not hesitate to use weapons of mass destruction to achieve ideological objectives. In fact, Al-Qaida's leader in Iraq called for nuclear scientists to join the jihad and test unconventional weapons against American bases.[36]

Cross-Cultural Conflicts

The deterioration of the situation in Iraq after the conclusion of US-led combat operations was the result of sectarian violence superimposed on a tenacious insurgency.[37] Sunni Arab insurgents seek to restore Sunni control, and Al-Qaida fighters want to defeat Western forces so they can spread their radical version of Islam throughout the Middle East. The insurgents employ guerrilla tactics (bombings, assassinations, kidnappings, and infiltrations) to disrupt the establishment of effective governance and the reconstruction of economic independence. Acts of seemingly indiscriminate violence contributed to an astonishing death toll of more than 34,000 Iraqi civilians during 2006, further undermining attempts to establish centralized democratic governance.[38] To complicate matters, rogue Shiite militiamen from the Mahdi Army joined the fight against US and Iraqi troops,[39] while, in contrast, some Iraqi Sunnis turned against the mostly foreign-composed Al-Qaida in Iraq because of its extreme tactics and attempts to impose restrictive Islamic law.[40] To limit Al-Qaida's influence, they created "Awakening Council" movements or became "Concerned Local Citizen" fighters to protect their communities, and in turn suffered heinous reprisal attacks by jihadists.[41]

Insurgents and militants defeat Western coalition conventional superiority by exploiting force vulnerabilities, preferring to operate in congested urban terrain where overhead sensors, long-range precision weapons, and rules of engagement have limited value against an elusive and embedded enemy. The insurgents' asymmetric weapons of choice against coalition forces are the dreaded roadside improvised explosive device (best known by its acronym, IED) and the more sophisticated explosively formed penetrator (EFP), which have caused over half of the American combat casualties in Iraq. Persistent media reporting of the mounting death toll and extended military commitment contributed to the erosion of American public support for the war, first evident in the Republican Party's loss of Senate control in the November 2006 elections, in which Democratic Party candidates seeking to change the administration's Iraq policy defeated six incumbents to gain a majority.[42]

High-Technology Warfare

Nation-state competitors realize that the use of asymmetric tactics, including anti-access measures, could create opportunities to exploit the weaknesses of a militarily superior opponent. An anti-access measure is any action to slow deployment of forces or to compel opponents to operate from distances greater than normally preferred. Hostile regimes could use modern weapon systems to strike quickly, even preemptively, and inflict large numbers of casualties, creating a traumatic experience that undermines the friendly population's will to continue in the conflict. Asymmetric attacks could occur upon aircraft carriers, information systems, space-based assets, logistics systems, air bases, and ports, blurring the location of the combat zones and logistics staging areas.[43]

Key point strikes by the adversary are not necessarily designed to achieve a total military victory but to accomplish limited political goals in a local war. This high-technology version of fourth generation warfare aims to attain the desired political outcome by convincing decisionmakers in the friendly population that the risks and costs of the war are too great. Even if the conflict continues into total war, unbearable economic and social pain inflicted from loss of trade in consumer goods or natural resources could mean loss of the war "on the empty shelves of Wal-Mart," as business lobbyists clamor for the government to negotiate a compromise to end the conflict.[44] The United States recognized this challenge to security in the 2001 Quadrennial Defense Review Report, which identified "defeating anti-access and area-denial threats" as one of six critical operational goals for focusing transformation efforts.[45] Thus, the improvement of high-intensity conventional capabilities is an important aspect of transformation. This type of scenario has justified production of advanced weapon systems, such as the US Air Force F-22A Raptor for long-range air defense, heralded as key to defeating future air-to-air and surface-to-air threats.[46]

Most Dangerous Adversaries

> We have to confront not single, easily identifiable threats but flows: that is to say terrorism allied to drug profits or cyberspace; or small arms allied to militias and to illicit diamond trading; or organized crime networks allied to nuclear proliferation.
>
> —*Jaap de Hoop Scheffer, NATO secretary-general*[47]

Nearly half of global terrorist networks are tied to narcotics trafficking, including the terrorists behind the 2004 Madrid train attacks, who dealt hashish and ecstasy to pay for explosives.[48] Jihadist cells in Europe have become racketeering syndicates that engage in low-level fraud. Lucrative scams include credit card fraud, identity theft, sham life insurance claims, and pirated multimedia sales. In North Africa, radical Islamists and Al-Qaida affiliates partner with criminal organizations to profit from human smuggling into Europe. In Asia the Al-Qaida affiliate Jemaah Islamiyah engages in bank robbery, and the latter used profits from jewelry store robberies to finance the 2002 Bali nightclub bombings that killed primarily Australians.[49] Insurgents in Iraq also have used the criminal playbook to become financially self-sufficient, raising tens of millions of dollars a year from oil smuggling, kidnapping ransoms, counterfeiting, and corrupt Islamic charities.[50] Insurgents have additionally financed their war effort by extorting from Iraqi contractors cash payments in exchange for safe passage of supply convoys.[51]

The goal of modern adversaries, no matter whether terrorist, insurgent, or hostile regimes, is to dissuade, delay, disrupt, or make ineffective military intervention in their activities. In designing a capabilities-based force that can achieve competitive advantage over these enemies, it is imperative to understand succinctly how adversaries may challenge us in twenty-first-century operational battle space. Among many options, the most likely adversarial strategies for using the full range of traditional, irregular, catastrophic, and disruptive methods are

1. Terrorism, atrocities, and asymmetrical strikes that have shattering effects and surprise opponents' intelligence, like liquid explosives or biological agents on airliners, or long-range ballistic missile systems.
2. Protracted conflict campaigns that exploit misinformation and produce calamitous human suffering, like indiscriminate bombings on marketplaces, religious sites, workplaces, bus stations, or police recruiting centers.
3. Infrastructure attacks that disrupt financial, information, and transportation networks or energy, food, and water sources, such as kinetic destruction of gasoline distribution facilities or electrical power stations.
4. Counterairpower superiority methods that deny precision targeting and attack, like hardened underground facilities, concealment and deception tactics, advanced surface-to-air missiles, and counterspace weapons.
5. Anti-access capabilities that deny force embarkation, like multiple warhead ballistic and antiship cruise missiles, high-speed torpedoes, swarm missile boats, diesel submarines, and rocket-propelled mines.

A Broad Set of Capability Needs

> Australia cannot and will not abandon Afghanistan. We need to remain committed to supporting this fledging democracy. The struggle against extremism continues.
>
> —*John Howard, former Australian prime minister*[52]

In military operations, capabilities allow forces to set the conditions (ensure access and freedom of action), control the situation (stop the killing, suffering, or dying), and achieve decisive resolution (dispose of regimes, establish a secure environment, or restore vital services). Australian reconstruction teams working in southern Afghanistan are an example of how combat engineering and security capabilities can assist the nation to achieve a stable future, despite persistent opposition from the Taliban-led extremist insurgency.[53] Given the need to sustain preeminence over twenty-first-century threats, and the wide range of probable scenarios and mission types that may emerge, the capabilties-based force must have the ability to

1. Express a compelling set of goals for military, interagency, and multinational partners, and define comprehensive effects that will achieve the desired outcome;
2. Share a complete understanding of the full dimensions of the operational environment and of all partners' equity or influence in the conflict;
3. Establish an accessible and user-friendly common operational picture, and a collaborative strategic-to-tactical environment supported by standing operating procedures;
4. Deploy persistent, enduring, and stealthy intelligence, surveillance, and reconnaissance systems and other appropriate means to identify hostile elements;
5. Field compatible, culturally aware forces, with the greatest practicable interoperability and standardization, that can effectively conduct operations in demanding geographical and climatic environments;
6. Project joint forces directly to the objective, in a position of advantage, from intertheater and intratheater distances;
7. Employ adaptive, modular, and mission-oriented expeditionary forces throughout the battle space;
8. Develop procedures and systems to generate lethal and nonlethal effects through fully integrated combat fires, maneuver of forces, and information operations, while limiting collateral damage;
9. Provide layered security for populations, territory, forces, and systems, including critical infrastructure, information, and space assets;
10. Sense, detect, identify, defend against, and recover from chemical, biological, radiological, nuclear, and high-yield explosive attack;
11. Establish and operate an adaptive, timely, distribution-based support system with improved commonality, reliability, maintainability, and survivability;
12. Integrate military support with government, nongovernment, and civilian capabilities in stabilization operations, reconstruction efforts, and humanitarian relief operations.[54]

Conclusion: An Adaptive Enemy

> This year [2007] will prove to be the bloodiest for the foreign troops. It is not just a threat, we will prove it.
>
> —*Mullah Dadullah, senior Afghan Taliban commander*[55]

> I'm not convinced we're winning it in Afghanistan [in 2008]. . . . The Taliban and al Qaeda have grown bolder in launching ever more sophisticated—even infantry-like—attacks against fixed coalition positions.
>
> —*Admiral M. G. Mullen, chairman of the US Joint Chiefs of Staff*[56]

Our adversaries are tenaciously devoted to their cause. They are smart, adaptive, and constantly seeking new ways to challenge us. For example, the Taliban in Afghanistan have adopted Al-Qaida-style tactics, such as suicide bombers who achieve spectacular effects; one such attack during a diplomatic visit by the US vice president made a dramatic geopolitical statement.[57] The insurgents in Iraq implement new tactics in a campaign to provoke fear, such as combining tanks of toxic chlorine gas with explosives to make chemical weapons.[58] This menacing actualization of fourth generation, or irregular, warfare has garnered tacit international cooperation to improve collective defense capabilities. At the other end of the spectrum, potential international military competitors are fielding advanced systems for attacking asymmetric vulnerabilities—systems such as long-range ballistic missiles,[59] anti-access cruise missiles,[60] and counterspace antisatellite missiles.[61]

As disruptive technologies become cheaper and more readily available, enemies could exploit coalition force, site, and system protection vulnerabilities with directed energy weapons, multimedia information operations, electromagnetic pulses or high-power microwaves, or other "weapons of mass effect." A shift in capability portfolios must replace comfortable legacy programs focused on traditional threats with capabilities packages that are relevant to current and future challenges. Capabilities-based planning addresses the ramifications of how adversaries may challenge us in the twenty-first-century complex security environment. This systematic approach is ideal to identify required capabilities, analyze gaps, and determine excesses as well as potential solutions to mitigate capability shortfalls.

In the capabilities-based process, innovative thinking results in prototypes derived from concept development and experimentation, and embodying desired shifts in the conduct of joint warfare and crisis resolution. Creative combinations of transformational elements, like networked sensor-to-shooter packages, knowledge fusion centers, joint interagency coordination groups, and humanitarian relief support packages, are examples of force multipliers. As the enemy adapts to challenge the world's societies through asymmetric techniques, so must international military forces adapt if they are to prevail in conflict and crisis resolution. The capabilities-based approach provides a deliberate means for turning transformational concepts and operational requirements into fielded capabilities that can sustain a competitive advantage over twenty-first-century threats.

Notes

1. Rudolph Giuliani, remarks to the NATO Supreme Allied Command Transformation Seminar, Norfolk, Virginia, 11 October 2007, http://www.joinrudy2008.com/article/pr/891.

2. Riga Summit Declaration, issued by members of the North Atlantic Council in Riga on 29 November 2006, http://www.nato.int/docu/pr/2006/p06150e.htm.

3. Bucharest Summit Declaration, issued by members of the North Atlantic Council in Bucharest on 3 April 2008, http://www.nato.int/docu/pr/2008/p08-049e.html.

4. North Atlantic Treaty Organization, "AAP-6 (2008)–NATO Glossary of Terms and Definitions," NATO Standardization Agency, 1 April 2008: 2-A-20; "Military Transformation: A Strategic Approach," US Department of Defense, Office of Force Transformation, 2003: 10, http://www.oft.osd.mil/library/library_files/document_297_MT_StrategyDoc1.pdf.

5. Admiral M. G. Mullen, US Navy, "CJCS Guidance for 2007–2008," Office of the Chairman, Joint Chiefs of Staff, 1 October 2007: 3.

6. Mary C. FitzGerald, "Marshal Ogarkov and the New Revolution in Soviet Military Affairs," research memorandum, Center for Naval Analyses, January 1987: 1–5, http://handle.dtic.mil/100.2/ADA187009.

7. Admiral William A. Owens, US Navy (retired), "The Once and Future Revolution in Military Affairs," *Joint Forces Quarterly* 31 (Summer 2002): 55–61.

8. Stephen Biddle, "Land Warfare: Theory and Practice," *An Introduction to Strategic Studies* (New York: Oxford University Press, 2002), 104–107.

9. Richard O. Hundley, *Past Revolutions, Future Transformations,* report, (Santa Monica: RAND Corporation, 1999), Chapter 2, 7–20.

10. Donald H. Rumsfeld, US secretary of defense, "Quadrennial Defense Review Report," 20 September 2001: iv.

11. "The Implementation of Network-Centric Warfare," US Department of Defense, Office of Force Transformation, 5 January 2005: 3–24.

12. Major General Robert Scales, US Army (retired), "Transformation," *Armed Forces Journal* (March 2005): 23–25.

13. Lieutenant General Stephen M. Speakes, US Army, "2008 Army Modernization Strategy," 25 July 2008: B-6, http://www.g8.army.mil/G8site_redesign/modStrat.html.

14. Paul Richter and Greg Miller, "CIA to Describe North Korea–Syria Nuclear Ties," *Los Angeles Times Online,* 23 April 2008, http://www.latimes.com/news/nationworld/world/la-fg-norkor23apr23,0,3070215.story.

15. Donald H. Rumsfeld, "The National Defense Strategy of the United States of America," Office of the Secretary of Defense, March 2005: 2–3.

16. US Joint Forces Command, "Joint Operating Environment—Trends and Challenges for the Future Joint Force Through 2030," December 2007: 19.

17. John R. Wagley, "Transnational Organized Crime: Principal Threats and U.S. Responses," Congressional Research Service, report for Congress no. RL33335, 20 March 2006: 1–6.

18. Associated Press, "Pirates Seize French Yacht," reported on CNN.com, 4 April 2008, http://www.cnn.com/2008/WORLD/africa/04/04/cruiseship.pirates.ap/index.html; Barbara Surk and Tarek El-Tablawy, Associated Press Writers, "Somali Pirates Hijack Saudi Tanker Loaded with Oil," reported on iht.com, 17 November 2008, http://www.iht.com/articles/ap/2008/11/17/news/ML-Piracy.php.

19. Associated Press, "WHO: Human Flu Pandemic Inevitable," reported on CNN.com, 7 November 2005, http://www.cnn.com/2005/HEALTH/conditions/11/07/bird.flu.who.ap/index.html.

20. Admiral Sir Mark Stanhope, British Royal Navy, deputy Supreme Allied Commander Transformation, "Information Sharing Is the Key to True Effects-Based, Operational Capability," *Defender* 2, no. 3 (2005): 4.

21. Donald H. Rumsfeld, "Quadrennial Defense Review Report," 6 February 2006: vi.

22. General Peter Pace, US Marine Corps, vice chairman of the Joint Chiefs of Staff, "An Evolving Joint Perspective: US Joint Warfare and Crisis Resolution in the 21st Century," 28 January 2003: 18–39.

23. General Eugen Badalan, chief of the Romanian Armed Forces General Staff, "Transformation and Responsibility—Assuming Responsibility for Transformation," *Romanian Military Thinking—Military Theory and Science Journal* (January–March 2006): 15.

24. Ron Wilder, wing commander, British Royal Air Force Defence Planning Coordination Cell, Allied Command Transformation, "Transformation of Capabilities," lecture for an International Defense Transformation course, Naval Postgraduate School, Monterey, California. 31 October 2006.

25. According to an official explanation of the NATO Defence Planning Process, posted in July 2005, "Political guidance sets out the overall aims to be met, including NATO's Level of Ambition that establishes in military terms the number, scale and nature of operations that the Alliance should be able to conduct." From the NATO website, http://www.nato.int/issues/dpp/in_practice.htm.

26. US Office of the Joint Chiefs of Staff, "Operation of the Joint Capabilities Integration and Development System," Chairman of the Joint Chiefs of Staff Manual 3170.01C, 1 May 2007: A-1–18.

27. US Department of Defense, "Capstone Concept for Joint Operations, Version 2.0" (Washington, DC: Government Printing Office [GPO], 2005), 20–23.

28. US Office of the Joint Chiefs of Staff, *Capabilities-Based Assessment (CBA) User's Guide, Version 2,* Joint Staff Force Structure, Resources, and Assessments Directorate (JCS J-8) (Washington, DC: GPO, 2006), 28–60.

29. Mathew J. Burrows, director, Analysis and Production Staff, National Intelligence Council, "Intelligence Community Perspective on the Maturing URW Threat," in *Proceedings on Combating the Unrestricted Warfare Threat: Integrating Strategy, Analysis, and Technology* (Baltimore: Johns Hopkins University, 2007), 97, http://www.jhuapl.edu/urw_symposium/Proceedings.aspx.

30. Colonel Thomas X. Hammes, US Marine Corps, "Fourth-Generation Warfare: Our Enemies Play to Their Strengths," *Armed Forces Journal* (November 2004): 41.

31. William S. Lind et al., "The Changing Face of War: Into the Fourth Generation," *Marine Corps Gazette* (November 2001): 65–68.

32. Gordon H. McCormick, Steven B. Horton, and Lauren A. Harrison, "Things Fall Apart: The Endgame Dynamics of Internal Wars," *Third World Quarterly* 28, no. 2 (2007): 321–324.

33. James Phillips and William L. T. Schirano, "Stop the Broadcasts of Al-Qaeda's TV Propaganda," Heritage Foundation WebMemo no. 1312, 16 January 2007, www.heritage.org/research/MiddleEast/wm1312.cfm.

34. Steven J. Lambakis, "Reconsidering Asymmetric Warfare," *Joint Forces Quarterly* 36 (2005): 102–103.

35. "Timeline: Madrid Investigation," BBC News Online, 28 April 2004, http://news.bbc.co.uk/go/pr/fr/-/1/hi/world/europe/3597885.stm.

36. David Rising, "Al-Qaida Wants Nuclear Scientists to Join Jihad," *Monterey County Herald,* 29 September 2006: A6.

37. Kenneth Katzman, "Iraq: Post-Saddam Governance and Security," CRS report for Congress RL31339, 10 January 2008: 28–30.

38. United Nations, "Human Rights Report," UN Assistance Mission for Iraq, 1 November–31 December 2006: 2–3, http://www.uniraq.org/FileLib/misc/HR%20Report%20Nov%20Dec%202006%20EN.pdf.

39. Kim Gamel, "Militia, Security Forces in Battle for Basra," *Monterey County Herald,* 27 March 2008: A1, 9; and "Al-Sadr: New Force to Fight U.S. in Iraq," CNN news online, 13 June 2008, http://www.cnn.com/2008/WORLD/meast/06/13/iraq.alsadr/index.html.

40. Sudarsan Raghavan, "New Leaders of Sunnis Make Gains in Influence," *Washington Post,* 8 January 2008: A1, http://www.washingtonpost.com/wp-dyn/content/article/2008/01/07/AR2008010703514_pf.html.

41. Leila Fadel and Nassan al Jubouri, "Headless Corpses Found in Iraqi Province," *Monterey County Herald,* 30 January 2008: A5.

42. "Senate Passes Iraq Withdrawal Bill; Veto Threat Looms," 26 April 2007, CNN news online, http://www.cnn.com/2007/POLITICS/04/26/congress.iraq/index.html.

43. Roger Cliff et al., "Entering the Dragon's Lair: Chinese Antiaccess Strategies and Their Implications for the United States" (Santa Monica: RAND Corporation, 2007), 1–50.

44. Ralph Peters, "The Counterrevolution in Military Affairs," *The Weekly Standard,* 6 February 2006: 18–23.

45. Donald H. Rumsfeld, "Quadrennial Defense Review Report," 30 September 2001: 30.

46. General Hal M. Hornburg, US Air Force, commander, Air Combat Command, "Why We Need the Raptor," *New York Times,* 3 November 2004: A18.

47. Jaap de Hoop Scheffer, NATO secretary-general, keynote speech to the Atlantic Council Conference, Riga, 28 November 2006, http://www.nato.int/docu/speech/2006/s061128a.htm.

48. David E. Kaplan, "Paying for Terror," *U.S. News and World Report,* 5 December 2005: 2, http://www.usnews.com/usnews/news/articles/051205/5terror.htm.

49. Ibid., 2–4.

50. John F. Burns and Kirk Semple, "Insurgents in Iraq Finance Themselves," *New York Times,* 26 November 2006, in the *International Herald Tribune* online, http://www.iht.com/articles/2006/11/26/news/insurge.php.

51. Hannan Allam, "Iraqi Insurgents Extorting U.S. Funds from Contractors," *Monterey County Herald,* 28 August 2007: A6.

52. "Australia to Send More Troops to Afghanistan," *Agence France-Presse,* 10 August 2006, http://www.defencetalk.com/news/publish/index.php.

53. "ISAF Constructs Police Check-point in Uruzgan," ISAF news release no. 2007-596, 15 August 2007, http://www.nato.int/isaf/docu/pressreleases/2007/08-august/pr070815-596.html.

54. US Department of Defense, "Major Combat Operations Joint Operating Concept," version 2.0, December 2006: C1–4.

55. Saeed Ali Achakzai, "Afghan Taliban Say Rearmed, Ready for War," Reuters, 23 February 2007, http://today.reuters.com/news/CrisesArticle.aspx?storyId=SP100413. The Taliban threat continues in 2008; see "Hundreds of Taliban Occupy Afghan Villages," CNN news online, 16 June 2008, http://www.cnn.com/2008/WORLD/asiapcf/06/16/afghan.villages.ap/index.html.

56. Quoted in Luis Martinez, "Military Brass: U.S. Running Out of Time in Afghanistan," reported on abcnews.go, 10 September 2008, http://www.abcnews.go.com/print?id=5769529. Also see Jason Straziuso, Associated Press, "US Deaths in Afghanistan Make 2008 Deadliest Year," reported on abcnews.go, 11 September 2008, http://abcnews.go.com/print?id=5778769.

57. Aryn Baker, "A Taliban Message to Cheney," *Time,* 27 February 2007, http://www.time.com/time/world/article/0.8599,1594097,00.html?cnn=yes.

58. Kim Gamel, "Three Suicide Bombers Attack with Chlorine," *Monterey County Herald,* 18 March 2007: A8.

59. Joseph Bermudez, "North Korea Conducts Major Missile Exercise," *Jane's Defence Weekly,* 12 July 2006: 5–6.

60. Alon Ben-David, "West Doubts Iran Missile Claims," *Jane's Defence Weekly,* 12 April 2006: 4; and Robert Hewson, "China Rolls Out Z-9 Helo Naval Variant with Anti-ship Missile," *Jane's Defence Weekly,* 6 August 2008: 8.

61. Craig Covault, "Chinese Test Anti-Satellite Weapon," *Aviation Week and Space Technology,* 17 January 2007, http://www.aviationweek.com/avnow/news/channel_awst_story.jsp?id=news/CHIO1177.xml.

Part 1

Thinking About Transformation

2

On Military Revolution

Daniel Moran

In January 1955 the British historian Michael Roberts delivered a lecture at Queen's University of Belfast entitled "The Military Revolution, 1560–1660." In it he proposed that changes in European military institutions, connected with the advent of firearms and the consequent reorganization of armies, gave rise to a strategic and social transformation extending well beyond the military sphere, which "stands like a great divide separating medieval society from the modern world."[1] Roberts was not the first to apply the concept of revolution to the study of war. He began his essay by admitting that it was already commonplace for historians to note the "widely ramifying consequences" that can result from changes in military technique. He offered as an example the adoption of the stirrup in the sixth century A.D., which made heavy cavalry the dominant arm on European battlefields for centuries afterward. Nevertheless, his work was a challenge, in two respects. First, there were the dates, specifying a period that did not feature any terribly striking technological novelties, merely an enormous amount of fighting arising from quarrels over religion. And then there was the definite article: not *a* military revolution, but *the* one—the one that counts.

The Transformation of War

The revolution that Roberts identified was rooted in what he described as "a perennial tactical problem: . . . how to combine missile weapons with close action."[2] The lethal effect that archers had exercised on the battlefields of the Hundred Years' War—think of the "arrow storms" at Crécy

(1346) and Agincourt (1415), by which French chivalry was decimated—had left European armies in a tactical limbo. The perceived value of cavalry had declined, and the weight shifted toward infantry. Infantry in turn had come to be deployed in extraordinarily deep, unwieldy formations; but these great blocks of soldiers also made the use of missile weapons prohibitively difficult, except in the incidental role of providing protective and harassing fire to facilitate the advance of the massive squares.

Firearms had appeared on European battlefields about 200 years before this state of affairs came to pass. Their presence had transformed siege warfare by rendering the curtain-walled fortifications of the medieval castle obsolete, but their impact on battle in the open field had been limited by the small number of guns available, and by the difficulty of employing them in a tactically coherent way. A longbow is a far more formidable weapon than an early infantry firearm, being superior in range, accuracy, rate of fire, and striking power. Yet it was easy to see that archers would never predominate among the armies of Europe, because the use of such weapons required great individual strength and skill. Any weakling half-wit could be a gunner. It was this fact that brought gunpowder weaponry to the forefront of modern war.

Once guns were sufficiently numerous, it became worthwhile to take tactical risks to bring them more fully into play. As the risks began to pay off, the blocklike columns of pikemen dissolved into attenuated lines of musketeers, extending over hundreds of yards and firing their weapons in unison. For the gunner, the linear tactics demanded discipline rather than skill; even in Napoleon's time, the average foot soldier was not taught to aim his weapon, merely to hold it level and fire it on command. Discipline required constant drill and standardized equipment, which soon extended to the clothes on a man's back. Military uniforms made their first appearance during the period of Roberts's study as potent symbols of the tactical and political subordination that the new art of war required.

Warfare of this new kind also entailed dramatically increased social costs, which meant that it could be waged only by large territorial states whose governments were vigorous enough to secure the taxes—and, if need be, the conscripts—required to keep up with the need for ever-lengthening lines of gunners. Armies became larger, and the organizational demands of sustaining and training them made it easier and cheaper to maintain them all year round. Larger armies also required more robust logistics and more complex methods for bringing them into action. These placed an increasing premium on skill and initiative among the officer corps, which began to evolve from a hereditary elite into a professional class defined by technical and managerial expertise. And from there, as Roberts proposed, "the way was clear for the armies of the nineteenth century: it remained only for the twentieth to complete the process by replacing dolmans, busbies, eagle's wings, and all the flaunting *panache* of Cossack and Hussar, by the flat uniformity of field-grey and khaki."[3]

The Rhetoric of Revolution

The literature on military revolution has grown enormously since the appearance of Roberts's celebrated article, and with it our understanding of the history of European society between the Renaissance and the Enlightenment. But Roberts's work also reveals how limited the idea of revolution is for analytic purposes. Virtually all of the work that his argument stimulated has been devoted to loosening his grip on this particular word. Some have taken issue with Roberts's claim that military changes in his chosen period were more seminal than those that came earlier or later, and have sought to shift the chronological boundaries of the time when the "military revolution" occurred. Others have raised doubts about technical issues, shifting the argument away from the conduct of pitched battles toward naval warfare or the new architecture of fortifications—which again alters the temporal and geographic dimensions of the problem. Still others have denied the revolutionary element altogether and portray the military history of the period as derivative of social changes whose impetus lay outside the realm of war.[4]

Clearly, there is no generally accepted standard for what counts as "revolutionary" change. This is especially true in the case of revolutions like the one Roberts proposed, which had no one to proclaim a new dispensation or announce the death of the old order. Like the industrial and commercial revolutions, which were well-established historical concepts at the time Roberts wrote, the military revolution of the seventeenth century is a retrospective academic construction, an interpretation of events according to criteria that were not always apparent to contemporaries.

There is, in other words, good reason to suspect that, as a critical concept, the idea of revolution may be more trouble than it is worth. It is really in the context of mobilization—of inspiring consensus and stifling doubts—that the rhetoric of revolution comes fully into its own and deserves to be taken seriously, which includes being wary of inflationary pressure. To declare a change "revolutionary" may merely mean that the change is supposed to be a big one. Such claims are designed to resist the well-recognized tendency of modern times to normalize change as such.[5] All technologically and socially complex societies share a willingness to anticipate a future that is different from the past. And commercial democracies, as Alexis de Tocqueville wrote of the United States, having organized themselves to promote the pursuit of every possible advantage, are inclined to "love change" as such, and produce enormous amounts of it. Yet he also suspected that such societies would "dread revolution" and become skilled at avoiding it.[6]

Not everyone has felt this way, however. In the late 1970s, military planners in the Soviet Union began talking about what they called a military-technical revolution, arising from improvements in sensor and information technology. This idea first made its way into print in an interview by Marshal N. V. Ogarkov, chief of the Soviet general staff, which appeared in the military magazine *Krasnaya Zvezda* ("Red Star") in 1984. He proposed that advances in sensors, guidance, and communications systems were "[making] it possible to sharply increase (by at least an order of magnitude) the destructive potential of conventional weapons, bringing them closer, so to speak, to weapons of mass destruction in terms of military effectiveness."[7] Ogarkov expected the United States to master such technology and believed the Soviet Union should do so as well, rather than relying upon nuclear weapons to counter a potentially decisive conventional superiority.

Here one sees the rhetoric of revolution in its truest form, as the language not of analysis but of action, in which claims about the past serve as platforms from which to launch claims about the future, along with demands that steps be taken now to make sure the future turns out as expected. Such arguments are always worthy of close scrutiny, and not just because they cannot be resolved by direct appeal to the evidence (the future being an ever-receding thing, even for revolutionaries). It is probably not by chance, for instance, that the popularization of the idea of military revolution first arose among soldiers ideologically predisposed to view revolutionary change as inevitable and positive in historical terms—or that it occurred in extremely discouraging circumstances for the practitioners of conventional warfare.

By the 1970s, nuclear weapons, which had numbered in the low hundreds (or, in the Soviet case, the dozens) twenty years before, had metastasized into arsenals more than sufficient to annihilate the inhabitants of both superpowers many times over, and much of the rest of the planet in the bargain. The institutionalization of overkill cast a pall over other forms of fighting, by making the consequences of inadvertent escalation so high that any degree of prudential restraint would be warranted to avoid making that one fatal error. The prospect that a new generation of weapons might be developed that would rescue conventional operations from the dustbin of history was one that those committed to execute these operations were eager to seize, and with it the possibility that history, having changed course with the onset of the nuclear era, might be getting ready to change again.

For our purposes it is the logic, rather than the merit, of this argument that is worth pondering, since it points toward what might be thought distinctive in any claim that a given change is revolutionary. To be worthy of the name, a revolution should entail not merely an alteration in the pace or scale of life but also an element of reversal, of things being turned upside down, so that formerly secure assumptions and advantages are cast into doubt. That is the core meaning of the word, after all, and it is worth clinging to, if only to restore some analytic usefulness to a term that has proved all too handy for purposes of marketing.

Once the idea of reversal is taken to heart, two other propositions follow. The first is that revolutionary change will indeed be rare. Bringing it about requires not just that something new happen—a commonplace feature of modern life, as Tocqueville foresaw—but that, too, institutional, political, or social interests accumulate around the new thing that are sufficiently distinctive to resist assimilation by established methods, and sufficiently weighty to develop an independent, countervailing momentum of their own. The second is that such conditions are likely to be brought about by a series of incremental challenges to conventional practice, whose cumulative revolutionary implications may become only gradually apparent. In the history of war, as of politics and society, even the most dramatic and transformative episodes can be fully understood only if they are recognized as symptomatic of revolutionary circumstances, whose original creation will often be half mysterious to those directly involved.

A profound reversal of fortune is apparent in the revolution that Roberts identified. However much his conclusions may have been modified by subsequent research, few would now deny that the changes in warfare that he described were implicated in a basic shift of political and economic advantage in favor of the bureaucratically centralized territorial states of northern and western Europe, at the expense of the city-states and ecclesiastical polities that had set the standard for European civilization in the Renaissance. In conceptual terms his revolution remains *the* military revolution—the exemplary case—because the process he identified demonstrates the possibility that modest changes in military tactics can set in motion, or lend new impetus and energy to, far-reaching shifts in the international system as a whole.

Whether the military-technical revolution promoted by Soviet planners, and subsequently embraced by their Western counterparts as a "revolution in military affairs," will rise to this level of significance is hard to say. That information technologies have changed the face of the tactical battle is incontestable; but then the tactical battle has been changing pretty steadily in one way or another for at least a century and a half now, and there are many who argue that the ostensibly revolutionary innovations that arose toward the end of the Cold War, however impressive at first glance, represent no more than an acceleration of an established evolutionary process, in which case one would not anticipate the kind of strategic reversal that Roberts's revolution exemplified. The point is strengthened by the fact that the revolutionary vanguard in this instance is being led by the armed forces of the United States, the strongest military power on earth, and the one that should be least likely to contemplate a genuine turn of history's wheel with equanimity.[8]

Nevertheless, such questions are inherently difficult for contemporaries to judge. Even the most sophisticated military organizations can become caught up in changes whose direction and outcome may be hard to anticipate, despite a serious effort to master them. As of this writing, such prospects, linked especially to the sudden appearance of some new technology, call to mind "tipping points" and the "butterfly effect," in which the movement of a butterfly's wing is imagined to set storms brewing on the other side of the world, owing to some critical instability among the forces of nature. This is an outlook more useful to mathematicians than to those concerned with human affairs, in which "sensitive dependence upon initial conditions" is unknown.[9] In the history of war there are no initial conditions, no pure immovable moments from which subsequent events can be judged with confidence. Students of military revolution will do better to ponder the proverbial wisdom that great oaks from tiny acorns grow. In practice, the study of military revolution is about learning to recognize acorns and figuring out what makes them grow.

This sort of dynamic is well illustrated by one of the most frequently cited examples of military transformation in modern times: the rapidly unfolding mechanized operations, popularly known as blitzkrieg, by which German armies swept across Europe in the early years of World War II. The new art of war that the Germans unveiled in 1939 is best understood as a climactic crisis within a broader framework of revolutionary circumstances, in which long-accumulating pressures finally burst forth in radical, and for a time deeply disruptive, innovation. The new German methods exemplified the tactical extremism that is a characteristic feature of revolutionary change. Yet they failed to resolve all the contradictory forces that had inspired them. Except in some matters of detail, the blitzkrieg cannot be said to have embodied the future as we have come to know it. Nonetheless, its brief history can tell us something about how that future, which is our present, came to be born, and about the perils that revolutionary conditions may present for even the boldest and most determined military organizations.

The New Art of War

The destruction of Poland's armed forces by those of Germany in September 1939 came as no surprise to knowledgeable observers. Poland had 1.3 million men under arms on the day the war began, against 1.5 million Germans, an imbalance that many doubtless hoped might be made up by the advantages of fighting on the defensive. But the Germans were far better equipped, and when this factor was added to the traditional excellence of German training and tactical leadership, the outcome was never really in doubt. Hitler had taken the additional precaution of partitioning Poland between Soviet leader Josef Stalin and himself at the end of August, which eliminated whatever possibilities for prolonged resistance might have existed once the initial German attack had been absorbed.[10]

The cascading power of the German offensive, and the prominent part played in it by armored vehicles and ground-attack aircraft, contrasted sharply with the pace of operations during the Great War of 1914–1918, when people had learned to think of modern armies as vast, ponderous beasts grappling blindly with each other. Tanks and airplanes had played a part in that conflict, too—there where thousands of tanks on European battlefields when the fighting ended, and the air war had gripped the public imagination from the start—but the results had been nothing like this. *Time* magazine reported:

> This was no war of occupation, but a war of quick penetration and obliteration—*Blitzkrieg,* lightning war. Even with no opposition, armies had never moved so fast before. Theorists had always said that only infantry could take and hold positions. But these armies had not waited for the infantry. Swift columns of tanks and armored trucks had plunged through Poland while bombs raining from the sky heralded their coming. They had sawed off communications, destroyed stores, scattered civilians, spread terror. Working sometimes 30 miles ahead of infantry and artillery, they had broken down the Polish defenses before they had time to organize. Then, while the infantry mopped up, they had moved on, to strike again far behind what had been called the front. By week's end it mattered very little whether Warsaw stood or fell. The Republic of Poland, aged 20, was lost.[11]

Still, there was no way at that moment to be sure how far this appalling scene was a reflection of anything other than Polish weakness. With the fall of France nine months later, however, there was no longer any question that something terrible had been let loose in the world. The difficulty was to figure out what it was.

It is almost impossible to overstate the shock and dismay that accompanied the French defeat in 1940. On paper the combined forces of France, Great Britain, and the Low Countries were broadly equal to those of Germany in terms of manpower and equipment.[12] They had also had months to prepare, in contrast to the Poles, who were thrown into the maelstrom almost overnight. Their preparations, however, had taken the form of a plan to push British and French troops rapidly forward into Belgium and the Netherlands. This vaguely offensive scheme was supposed to bring the anticipated German advance up short, before it could build serious momentum. But it also deprived the Allies of the reserves required to attack the flanks of the salient created by the initial German breakthrough at Sedan, France, an area that had been lightly held on the strength of its formidable terrain, and in order to conserve forces for the blow that the Allies were hoping to deliver farther north.

The effect of this miscalculation on the subsequent course of events was considerable, though it is difficult to say whether, had the French adopted a more authentically defensive posture, they could have succeeded in establishing a stable front in northwest Europe, as they had done twenty years earlier. To do that, they would have needed more than the strategic reserves that they had squandered in an ill-conceived maneuver. They would also have had to overcome a pronounced tendency to interpret tactical setbacks, like that suffered at Sedan, as strategic defeats, from which no recovery was possible. All accounts of the atmosphere in French governing circles and senior military headquarters during the opening phases of the campaign suggest unusual psychological disorientation, which was clearly connected to the speed and violence of German operations, the same factors that had so impressed *Time*'s correspondents in Poland.[13]

Yet the fact remains that in strategic terms the fall of France was overdetermined. Germany was then and had been for some time a significantly stronger country than France. German armies drove pell-mell across the Rhine three times within a span of seventy years, and on two of those occasions, in 1870 and again in 1940, the French army collapsed in a matter of weeks. In such circumstances it is usually the exception that proves the rule, and in this case the exception came in 1914, when successful French resistance condemned the Germans to ultimate defeat. It is in that campaign that the acorn of blitzkrieg can be found.

Military planning before World War I was dominated by the twin problems of increasingly lethal military technology, which the Industrial Revolution had made possible, and the mass armies that were required to survive the resulting increase in firepower. All the Great Powers had concluded before the war that their best chance to win was to mount a major offensive at the outset, in the hope of catching the adversary before he had fully mobilized. The emphasis on speed was redoubled by concern about the social consequences of stalemate, which seemed sure to follow once armies numbering in the millions became locked together along fortified fronts. If the war did not end in rapid victory, it was feared, it would end in revolution instead, as the strains of prolonged fighting ate away at the fabric of modern societies, which professional soldiers of that era were inclined to regard as exceptionally fragile.

In 1914 the outstanding embodiment of these assumptions, in which the spirit of the blitzkrieg is perfectly apparent, was the so-called Schlieffen Plan, by which Germany sought the rapid defeat of France, before shifting its armies against the more slowly unfolding threat posed by France's ally Russia. Most versions of the plan envisioned an immediate, massive wheeling offensive in the west, aiming to envelope Paris itself within about six weeks of mobilization.[14] The unrealism of this expectation has been much remarked upon. Yet it is a fact that German armies had already done it once before. In 1870, Helmuth von Moltke the Elder led the forces of Prussia and its allies in a two-pronged assault through Alsace and Lorraine, which surrounded and destroyed two French armies seriatim and then proceeded to besiege the French capital, all within forty-seven days of mobilization, and only twenty-eight days after first contact with the enemy. *Time* magazine was wrong about the unprecedented speed of the "lightning war." If anything, German armies in the twentieth century would struggle to maintain the standard that was set in the nineteenth.[15]

The German advance on Paris in 1940 was not faster than that of 1914. Its tactical character was different, though, and this helps explain the panic of the French leadership. Such reactions are never easy to understand. This one had something to do with the despairing tone of French politics in the interwar years and also with the personalities involved. Chief of the French General Staff Joseph Joffre, who commanded in 1914, was a phlegmatic character even by French standards, which could scarcely be said of his counterpart in 1940, the ostensibly brilliant but febrile General Maurice-Gustave Gamelin. Yet some credit, and perhaps most of it, must also be given to the disruptive, penetrating attacks conducted by German armor and aircraft. The French army in 1914 retreated en masse and at enormous human cost, but nevertheless as an intact force, which retained control of its communications and logistical base (upon which it was being driven backward). French infantry in 1940 was broken by the sudden appearance, in its own rear areas, of armored fighting vehicles that they had no means of resisting, apart from calling in artillery fire or aircraft. But the available guns were not organized to acquire such rapidly moving targets, and there was no way for engaged forces to communicate with Allied aircraft. French and British armor were dispersed in support of the infantry, and those not deployed forward in Belgium and Holland were unable to concentrate against the heavy armored columns that led the German advance.[16]

At a minimum it seems fair to conclude that traditional German tactical excellence, leveraged and amplified by the new technology of the internal combustion engine, had created a puzzle to which Germany's opponents had no immediate solution, in circumstances in which only an immediate solution mattered. German air and armor sowed chaos along with destruction and made it easy for French senior officers to accept a defeat that many had quietly been expecting for some time. These results, as has long been recognized, were more in the nature of a discovery than an invention. There is nothing in contemporary German doctrine that describes the heavily armored formations that wrecked the French defenses. The initial scheme of maneuver by which the Germans tore into France in 1940 was also markedly more conservative than what Schlieffen had proposed a generation earlier.[17] But the results, conceived and then successfully extemporized by soldiers whose supreme wish was to avoid the horror and futility of the trenches, may nevertheless count as a vindication of Schlieffen's vision, in which agility and ferocity were supposed to prevent the attritional character of industrialized warfare from asserting itself.

Indirect Fire and the Mechanical Battle

Yet it would soon do so anyway, on terms all too familiar to those who had survived the Great War and struggled to learn its lessons. The dominant weapon in that conflict had been artillery, employed for the first time on a large scale as instruments of indirect fire. This was unexpected. From biblical times to the Battle of the Marne, wars had been fought between combatants who could see each other. In 1914 that ceased to be the case. Warfare in the nineteenth century had pointed toward the ascendancy of infantry, whose weapons had improved so rapidly that they seemed on the verge of driving artillery off the battlefield entirely. Between the American Civil War (1861–1865) and the Russo-Japanese War (1904–1905), artillery accounted for no more than 10 to 15 percent of casualties, and gun shields had become the norm, to protect the operators from the fire of rifles whose range now approximated that of cannon.[18] From the 1890s onward, however, the guns had begun to catch up, owing to improvements in engineering, chemistry, and metallurgy, and to the development of recoilless gun carriages that allowed higher angles of fire and permitted gunners to strike targets repeatedly and reliably without having to re-lay their weapon after every shot. Between 60 and 70 percent of the 30 million casualties (killed and wounded) suffered in the Great War were inflicted by artillery, nearly all of it delivered by indirect fire at ranges out to 20 miles or more.[19]

These facts are worth recalling because they created the revolutionary conditions to which the blitzkrieg would provide a stunning but ultimately inadequate response. It was the failure of the Schlieffen Plan that had given the guns their chance, after all. Indirect fire made the trenches necessary—there was no other way to stay alive in its presence—but it had also threatened to make them permanent, since the weapons that so dominated the battlefield were barely able to move across it. Here again, *Time* magazine's attempt to explain the blitzkrieg to a bewildered world includes an illuminating error; it is most definitely true that "only infantry can take and hold positions."[20] The bulk of the German army, in 1939 and throughout the war, consisted of unmechanized infantry divisions intended precisely for this purpose. The point of the blitzkrieg was to find a way for that infantry to advance swiftly enough to prevent the war from turning into a trial of economic strength, of which the great guns were merely a military expression. That was why Germany had lost the last time. And that is why it would lose this time, too.

It is only when set alongside the long-term ascendancy of indirect fire (which continues to this day, in the guise of the long-range strike systems that dominate every aspect of contemporary warfare) that the revolutionary features of blitzkrieg can be fairly weighed. To do that, one must begin by recognizing that, for all its tactical audacity, the blitzkrieg was in many respects an expression of strategic weakness. Germany's need for a swift military result, lest its exposed position in the middle of Europe begin to tell against it, was no less pressing in 1940 than it had been in 1914; it had, indeed, been apparent since the days of Frederick the Great. The concentrated armor formations that were one of blitzkrieg's hallmarks were in turn a reflection of the speed of German re-armament, which had proceeded at a furious pace since the mid-1930s but was still incomplete by the time Hitler's policies had brought on the war.[21] Germany's opponents had done no better, of course; but their governments were not bent upon war, hoping instead to avert it. After the fall of France, the Nazis tried to take credit for the blitzkrieg by claiming that it represented an adaptation, in the military sphere, of the revolutionary dynamism of National Socialist ideology.[22] This is nonsense, but it points toward an aspect of the general situation that cannot be overlooked. German soldiers from 1933 onward were called upon to supply military methods capable of supporting a political leadership that was manifestly determined to run colossal risks. They breathed the same air as their masters, and the results are apparent in their work.

The decision to concentrate what limited armor was available into large independent formations, in the expectation that, once through the crust of the enemy's forward defenses, they might wreak disproportionate havoc in the rear, represented an enormous gamble. Such bold offensive expedients are, again, the characteristic province of the weaker side in war, which must play high if it is to have a chance to win. The gamble paid off at first, but it was not the kind of thing that could last, being dependent on the most rudimentary kind of surprise. Isolated armored formations soon disappeared from the European battlefield, thanks to the development of effective human-portable antitank weapons, which made it impossible for tanks to operate for long periods except in mutual support of infantry. It was, ironically, the Germans who developed the best of these, the so-called Panzerfaust, a lightweight missile projector that struck fear into the hearts of Allied tankers.[23] Had French infantry possessed such weapons in 1940, the blitzkrieg would have been strangled at birth.

As it was, it died the following year on the steppes of Russia, where armored thrusts sufficient to punch through French defenses were simply absorbed by the vast body of the Red Army. The cost in human terms seems in retrospect to have been beyond endurance, yet the infliction of mass suffering is rarely sufficient to decide the outcome in war. In Russia the reflexive aggressiveness that had served the Germans so well since 1939 played them falsely—above all the habit of committing available reserves to exploit early breakthroughs—so that insufficient forces remained in the event the enemy managed to regain his balance and mount an attack of his own. Among the many risks of revolutionary innovation, one of the least appreciated is that it makes it hard to change your mind again later on.

At the tactical level, the feature of the blitzkrieg that points most firmly toward the future is the prominence of ground-attack aircraft, which were more numerous and of higher quality in the German air force than in those of its opponents.[24] British air planners in particular had placed greater emphasis on the development of air-superiority fighters, to counter the threat that "strategic" airpower posed to the British homeland. Their choice would be vindicated in the Battle of Britain, where the virtues of the Hurricane and Spitfire were fully displayed. In France, however, such fighters could do little to protect forces on the ground from low-level attack by German bombers, which stood in for the heavy artillery that the blitzkrieg left behind. Here, too, the tide of war would crash over the Germans, placing their achievement in less glamorous perspective. World War II, like World War I, was ultimately dominated by the crushing effects of indirect fire, against which the high-velocity maneuver warfare of 1939–1941 could do little. In 1944, German officers calculated that 60 to 80 percent of the combat power of their own army lay with the gunners,[25] by which point their Russian opponents had ninety divisions, plus an additional 140 brigades, comprising artillery alone.[26] But the Germans still deserve credit for being the first to embrace aircraft as instruments for the delivery of long-range fire support, and for integrating them effectively into modern combined-arms warfare, a role in which their significance has continued to grow long after other elements of the blitzkrieg have been reduced to romantic curiosities.

Did the blitzkrieg incorporate an element of revolutionary strategic reversal, then, of the kind that Roberts identified in the new-model armies of the seventeenth century? It certainly would have done had it succeeded, and not just because a German victory would have delivered Europe into the hands of the Nazis. In strategic terms, the triumph of a continental army, operating on principles that took no account of its own economic base but sought victory through tactical proficiency alone, would have represented a profound challenge to the logic of industrialized warfare as it was then (and still is) understood, the more so had that triumph been achieved—as it would have to have been in the long run—against a maritime coalition that commanded the world's oceans and the resources that moved across them. Such a victory, even if it had been won by a regime less terrible than Hitler's Germany, would have left the world a much different place than it is as of this writing.

But of course there was no such victory. Viewed in the unforgiving light of defeat, the revolutionary potential of the blitzkrieg appears much diminished, and rightly so; for in fact the reversal it promised was more in the nature of counterrevolution, a determined but doomed effort to hold out against the deepest tendencies of modern war. For all its reliance on mechanization, the blitzkrieg set its face in defiance of the mechanical battle that had emerged on the Western Front of World War I. By 1918 the modern battlefield was already dominated by the "predicted" fires of long-range weapons systems. These demanded the continuous, dispassionate integration of a wide range of data, obtained from remote sensors, aerial observation, technical range-finding, and a host of other complex techniques. Tactical decisionmaking had already devolved into forms of algorithmic reasoning—summarized in the twenty-first century under the rubric of "systems engineering"—that were utterly remote from the instinctive leadership of the professional warriors Roberts's revolution had produced.

The men who made the blitzkrieg were Roberts's men. They fought the direct-fire battle. They thought they could lead from the front, and they looked to personal initiative and "fingertip feel" to find the path to victory.

They may have imagined themselves to be revolutionaries. But they bet their lives on the warfare of the old regime.

Notes

1. Michael Roberts, "The Military Revolution, 1560–1660," reprinted in *The Military Revolution Debate: Readings on the Military Transformation of Early Modern Europe,* ed. Clifford J. Rogers (Boulder: Westview Press, 1995), 13.

2. Ibid.

3. Ibid., 15.

4. The volume edited by Clifford Rogers, cited above as a convenient source for Roberts's work, includes a representative selection of articles challenging, modifying, and defending Roberts's conclusions. A slightly older book by Jeremy Black, *A Military Revolution? Military Change and European Society, 1550–1800* (Atlantic Highland, New Jersey: Humanities Press, 1991), provides a fuller survey of the literature in English. The best comprehensive study is Geoffrey Parker, *The Military Revolution: Military Innovation and the Rise of the West, 1500–1800* (Cambridge: Cambridge University Press, 1988). In general, Black may be regarded as a critic of Roberts, Parker as a qualified supporter. Both regard the critical processes of military innovation in early modern Europe as extending over a span of time two or three times longer than the one Roberts addressed, a shared outlook that necessarily dilutes the claim of revolutionary impact, irrespective of how or when it occurred.

5. See, for instance, Marshall Berman, *All That Is Solid Melts into Air: The Experience of Modernity* (New York: Simon & Schuster, 1982).

6. Alexis de Tocqueville, *Democracy in America,* edited and translated by Harvey C. Mansfield and Delba Winthrop (Chicago: University of Chicago Press, 2000), 610.

7. See Williamson Murray and MacGregor Knox, "Thinking About Revolutions in Warfare," in *The Dynamics of Military Revolution, 1300–2050,* edited by Williamson Murray and MacGregor Knox (Cambridge: Cambridge University Press, 2001), 3n.

8. See, for instance, A. J. Bacevich, "Preserving the Well-Bred Horse," *The National Interest* (Fall 1994): 43–49.

9. The concept of sensitive dependence on initial conditions comes from chaos theory, and predicts that the behavior of a dynamic system will vary over the long term depending on small changes in its initial condition. The metaphor of the butterfly is owed to Edward Lorenz, who presented a paper at the 1972 meeting of the American Association for the Advancement of Science entitled "Predictability: Does the Flap of a Butterfly's Wing in Brazil Set Off a Tornado in Texas?"

10. An authoritative account of the Polish campaign is Klaus A. Maier et al.'s *Germany and the Second World War,* vol. 2: *Germany's Initial Conquests in Europe,* translated by Dean S. McMurry and Ewald Osers, and edited by P. S. Falla (Oxford: Oxford University Press, 1991), 101–150. German and Polish orders of

battle are on page 101; Polish casualties versus the Germans and Soviets are on page 124.

11. *Time* (25 September 1939), 25, available online at http://www.time.com/time/magazine/article/0,9171,761969-1,00.html.

12. The opposing forces are surveyed in Maier et al., *Initial Conquests,* 278–279. In 1940, Germany deployed 141 divisions in the west, against a combined total of 144 for its opponents.

13. The most telling of those accounts is undoubtedly that of Winston S. Churchill, *The Second World War,* vol. 2: *Their Finest Hour* (Boston: Houghton Mifflin, 1949), 25–46. Churchill's famous conversation with the French supreme commander, Maurice-Gustave Gamelin, in which he demanded, "Where is the strategic reserve?" and received in reply a shrug and the single word "Aucune [None]"—exemplifies the interaction between moral and military factors that ensured the French defeat. Julian Jackson's *The Fall of France: The Nazi Invasion of 1940* (New York: Oxford University Press, 2003) is an authoritative recent study of the French defeat and includes a good survey of the scholarly literature.

14. The final version of the plan to which Schlieffen's name is attached is in *Alfred von Schlieffen's Military Writings,* translated and edited by Robert T. Foley (London: Frank Cass, 2003), 163–174.

15. On 17 July 1870, Prussia and its allies mobilized against France, with first contact between significant forces on 6 August. The investment of Paris was complete on 2 September. The first day of mobilization for the Germans in 1914 was 1 August, with first contact the following day. The Battle of Marne, which represented the limit of the initial German advance, began on the outskirts of Paris on 5 September, thirty-five days after first contact. Mobilization is irrelevant in 1940, since the war was well under way. Initial contact between German and Allied forces occurs on the first day of the campaign, 10 May, and German forces reach Paris on 14 June, again, thirty-five days later.

16. For an account of the campaign of 1940 emphasizing the tactical deficiencies of the allies, see Ernest R. May, *Strange Victory: Hitler's Conquest of France* (London: I. B. Tauris, 2000).

17. Karl-Heinz Frieser, *Blitzkrieg-Legende: Der Westfeldzug 1940* (Munich: R. Oldenbourg, 1996), 72–73, 101; this work, which is now regarded to be the outstanding treatment of its subject, includes excellent maps comparing the evolution of Plan Yellow, as the initial offensive into France was called, with the earlier campaigns of 1914 and 1870.

18. J. B. A. Bailey, *Field Artillery and Firepower,* rev. ed. (Annapolis: Naval Institute Press, 2004), 207.

19. Trevor N. Dupuy, *Numbers, Prediction, and War* (London: MacDonald and Jane's, 1979), 113.

20. *Time* (25 September 1939), 25, available online at http://www.time.com/time/magazine/article/0,9171,761969-1,00.html.

21. The German army in 1940 comprised 157 divisions altogether, of which 10 were armored and 16 were motorized infantry. On the eve of Barbarossa (code word for the invasion of Russia), this ratio had scarcely improved. By then the army had expanded to 207 divisions, of which 21 were armored and 13 were motorized

infantry. For 1940, see Maier et al., *Initial Conquests,* 278–279; for Barbarossa, see Horst Boog et al., *Germany and the Second World War,* vol. 4: *The Attack on the Soviet Union* (Oxford: Oxford University Press, 1998), 317–318.

22. Frieser, *Blitzkrieg-Legende,* 409–412.

23. See, for instance, Max Hastings, *Armageddon: The Battle for Germany, 1944–1945* (New York: Vintage, 2004), 82–84.

24. In May 1940 the Germans possessed about 5,400 aircraft, against a combined total of just over 3,000 for their opponents. Bombers account for nearly all of this disparity; the Germans had 2,224, the Allies 708, of which 310 were based in Great Britain. See Maier et al., *Initial Conquests,* 279.

25. General Karl Thoholt, "A German Reflects upon Artillery," *Field Artillery Journal* 35, no. 2 (1945): 709, quoted in Bailey, *Field Artillery,* 340.

26. Ibid., 343n.

3

The Influence of the Information Age

Henrik Friman and Susan Higgins

> The two truly transforming things, conceivably, might be in networking and connecting things in ways that they function totally differently than they had previously. . . . Possibly the single-most transforming thing in our force will not be a weapon system, but a set of interconnections and a substantially enhanced capability.
>
> —*US secretary of defense Donald H. Rumsfeld*[1]

Our world is in transition. The information revolution is affecting all facets of our lives, including the realm of international security. The current transformation of defense capabilities is inextricably linked to the unfolding of the Information Age. Governments have continuous opportunities to improve the swiftness and efficiency of their military-related reactions to crises around the world, while international security organizations, such as the United Nations, have an unprecedented opportunity to develop global capacity for long-term crisis prevention.

This chapter discusses the influence of the Information Age on defense transformation. First, we provide some perspective by studying the transition from the Industrial Revolution to the Information Age, and the characteristics of the resultant electronically connected society. Then we explore the changing nature of security work done by the military in the Information Age. Finally, we discuss the emerging implications of these new roles and missions, with a focus on the new kinds of infrastructure, organization, and doctrine needed by people who are transforming defense organizations and working in those transformed organizations.

From the Industrial Age to the Information Age and Beyond

The recently christened Information Age is often viewed through the lens of technical advances in telecommunications, computer systems, and the spread of the Internet and World Wide Web. We are experiencing the confluence of several smaller streams that have been flowing for decades. In 1945 Vannevar Bush described the "Memex," a precursor to the World Wide Web.[2] In the same year, Arthur C. Clarke envisioned the geostationary satellite constellation needed to sustain global communications.[3] Marshall McLuhan used the phrase "the global village" when he described "the effect of radio in the 1920s in bringing us in faster and more intimate contact with each other than ever before."[4] These and other visionaries conceptualized what has come to be named the Information Age.

Industrial societies are organized around the production of goods and the resources needed to produce those goods. Production plants, the product market, and financial institutions all play key roles in the growth of industrial economies and the related well-being of a nation's citizenry. Recent demographic shifts are away from agricultural lands and into cities, as citizens relocate to be near factories and production plants. Emerging global markets for products, services, labor, and capital are replacing small-scale producers participating in local economies. Coupled with systematically higher rates of control and information density, commercial market forces are competing with old concepts and behaviors. These new societal conditions are leading many to conclude that the traditional models for military defense and global security also need to be reconsidered, if they are to adapt to the new realities of an Information Age society.

The effects of the Information Age began to take hold in the most socially and technologically developed societies in the late 1980s or early 1990s, as technological advances begun or prophesied earlier in the century were becoming reality. The world is "flattening"—to borrow a term used by Thomas Friedman to denote the sense of connectedness and immersion in a global marketplace. Friedman notes the convergence of three key technological innovations that have fostered the flat-world perspective: the personal computer, the combined emergence of the Internet and the World Wide Web, and the development of collaborative software such as wikis and blogs.[5] The transition to the Information Age is having ripple effects across a variety of realms: technical, sociological, political, economic, and cultural. One unintended consequence may be that unequal rates of entry into the "flatter" world economy contribute to global unrest and instability.[6] Thomas Barnett contends that it is in those geographic areas where people are most disconnected from the global economy that we should expect crises to erupt.[7]

Market interdependencies are increasing among nations at every level of development. While the United States, most European, and some Asian societies are now fully immersed in the Information Age, other parts of the world continue to develop their industrial and agricultural societies. Information-based societies depend on global industries and agriculture, just as industrializing societies have the potential to improve their productivity and profitability through the effective uses of information technologies. Even though the global Information Age transformation has a different meaning for different societies, two words stand out in every case: *digitization* and *globalization.*

Common Characteristics of the Information Age

In highly digitized and globalized societies, newly arising or changing Information Age characteristics are influencing thinking and behavior. The following categorization of relevant factors, the development of which was influenced by the work of Michael Lissack and Johan Roos, will help explain the common characteristics of the Information Age.[8]

Globalization means that international security problems cannot be solved by national means. At this writing, the world is even more complex than during the Industrial Age. Most parts of the global system are interconnected, so that actions in one part affect others in the system. The numbers of purely national crises, like civil wars, are decreasing. This means that leaders must think in terms of international, or global, security rather than national security, and look for solutions in international collaboration, not only between governments but also with international organizations.

Twenty-first-century international security systems, however, still often focus on local economies with an "Industrial Age" perspective. The national security systems in most countries primarily depend on military superiority within smaller, localized regions, intervening in new crises as they erupt. International and national laws still limit the abilities of individual nations to intervene in global problems. This familiar model, which follows long-standing patterns, should be reconsidered in the Information Age. National interconnectedness in global economies necessitates new structures, new processes, and new leadership competencies. Collaborations can be initiated, established, and fulfilled beyond national boundaries, and their effects dispersed across the world, while access to boundless knowledge via networks provides important advantages to future leaders of global security operations. Therefore, twenty-first-century military commanders need to be trained and educated to guide complex, multinational, and cross-sector interactions in addition to leading direct military actions. Globalization also suggests that it will no longer exclusively be military commanders who will lead future security-oriented operations; therefore, in the following text the term *leader* will apply to both civilian and military leaders.

Future leaders will increasingly need to cooperate with their counterparts on language and cultural issues. Many training and education programs as of this writing teach officers to deal with local situations, and to try to sort things out in a somewhat linear fashion, that is, one problem at a time; but the realities of the 2000s demand leaders who can adopt a global view and be open to new interactions and collaborative constellations. It is no longer possible to describe security crises as a game with fixed rules and borderlines; leaders must make a mental shift to think about the security environment as a complex ecosystem.

Complexity in the Information Age implies a massive flow of data in an increasingly dynamic environment. Complexity created by mass data can in many cases be handled by the automation, or digitization, of processes. But even as the level of sophistication in automated systems increases, expertise among users is catching up. Mastering complexity also implies understanding how to make sense of relationships among all parts of the global system.

One risk of attempts to minimize complexity in the early Information Age is that experts often limit access to information, using the equivalent of "no trespassing" signs such as network firewalls and password-protected areas. This tendency runs counter to the need for collaboration and dialogue in complex environments.[9] The value of collaboration must be seen as sufficient to overcome the risks associated with the complexity of open network systems.

From this perspective, if we simply digitize processes to solve the equation of complexity, then we have failed. Future leaders must, rather, develop a new mind-set, whereby open collaboration is a natural part of success in complex operations. It is important to approach new situations by asking how parts can be combined into new and better "wholes," instead of segregating parts to be treated as independent, self-sufficient "wholes."

Uncertainty is a normal attribute in the global security system. Increased uncertainty demands greater cognitive agility based on instant, or just-in-time, learning. Uncertainty means that future leaders must be able to function with minimal structure, to ensure maximum innovation, flexibility, and adaptability. The "leader's intent" (as opposed to "commander's intent") needs to be clear, and, within that, individuals should be given autonomy to adapt as local conditions demand. The tension between centralized control and greater autonomy among members of organizations, and across organizational boundaries, is a challenge inherent in the complexity of the twenty-first-century world.

To discuss Information Age characteristics without mentioning technology dependence would be unrealistic. The Information Age has produced a "high-tech" military environment with more sensors, increased communication ability, position-engagement precision, improved command and control, networked environments, and so on. But *high tech* is a relative term in social environments. In some parts of the world, a wired telephone in the village is considered to be high tech, while in other parts of the world, 3G mobile telephones are ordinary instruments for everyone in a family. The point here is that new technologies provide abilities to operate differently and to develop more effective processes. In response to crises, Information Age security organizations tend to arrive heavily technology dependent, without necessarily being cognizant of local environmental and infrastructure constraints. This might mean they bring complex technologies into a crisis zone that has limited support infrastructure, such as transportation, power systems, or cooling systems, which can limit the organizations' effectiveness.

Crisis intervention will often take the form of what are called distributed adaptive operations:[10] working in "hastily formed networks"[11] run on deployable, commercial, off-the-shelf systems. Future military personnel must be prepared to function globally in complex and uncertain situations. They must be ready to operate with nonmilitary personnel, such as local law enforcement, national-level institutions such as the US Department of State, and international nongovernmental and governmental organizations, such as Doctors Without Borders and the United Nations Office for the Coordination of Humanitarian Affairs. Successful leaders will need more advanced training and education in areas that include cross-sector leadership and management, language, and culture as a complement to traditional military tactics.

Shifting the Conduct of Security Operations

Most parts of the world are in the midst of transition, and gaining perspective on the changes can be daunting. This section provides a contextual framework that will illustrate and highlight how the conduct of security operations is changing.

It is hard to say when defense transformation began as a response to the Information Age. The US Navy pioneered developments in navigation and communication satellites in the 1960s. In the 1980s, US Navy vice admiral Jerry O. Tuttle recognized that effective war fighting would require consolidating the organizations that supported voice, video, and data technologies for the navy. These evolutionary technical and organizational precursors were necessary to establish the infrastructure for the Information Age military in the United States.

As the Information Age began to unfold, various observers tried to make sense of what they saw occurring in the realm of global security and defense. In 1991, Martin van Creveld described potentially disruptive new terrorist threats to the global security community.[12] By the late 1990s, US vice admiral Arthur K. Cebrowski had articulated the shift from "platform-centric" to "network-centric" warfare, an idea many consider to be the first real intellectual breakthrough in warfare concept development for the Information Age. The thinking behind networked forces grew out of the information business models used by stock markets and global enterprises like Wal-Mart and Amazon. Principles such as the "just-in-time" delivery of tailored products and services, as practiced by highly distributed, market-driven organizations, were adapted to military environments. In addition, two new military "markets" in which future "battle" could take place, information and space, emerged to complement the traditional areas of operations—land, sea, and air.[13]

As a result of Cebrowski's visionary thinking about how military forces would need to change, he was appointed inaugural director of the Office of Force Transformation, an organization within the Office of the Secretary of Defense (OSD), with the responsibility to lead the development of concepts for US force transformation. Cebrowski envisioned that network-centric approaches would revolutionize the way countries could conduct war, through the use of nearly real-time, high-precision weapons; the concept has in fact served as the model for many countries' security development.[14]

Robert Leonhard has proposed that war is a balance between absolute precision and absolute mass (the concentration of forces), and that Information Age technologies had shifted this balance and therefore changed the principles of war.[15] He notes that the Information Age has made it possible to dislocate and distribute operations, expand the search for opportunities, accelerate options, and speed up command. From an operational point of view, new technologies had instigated a shift from wars of attrition to true maneuver warfare. US admiral Bill Owens described this shift as "lifting the fog of war."[16] Owens based his deductions on new technologies that would reduce the level of uncertainty in security operations, such as high-quality, precise, real-time sensors that give the war fighter information superiority and improved situational awareness.

It has been argued that information has always been a critical factor in warfare. Some warn that new Information Age technologies have increased the vulnerability of those using them and have asked what happens when the technology fails. Information systems are no longer just a target, but can be used as weapons to damage the opponent and perhaps reduce the opponent's willingness to fight. The capability of technologically networked combatant forces was demonstrated for the first time in Afghanistan in 2001, and again in Iraq in 2003. Based on their superb performance, Cebrowski concluded that, despite concerns, networked forces outfight nonnetworked forces.[17]

Network-centric warfare, a key conceptual underpinning of force transformation, appears to have proved itself superior to traditional platform-based warfare. The technical improvements that the military had made during the late 1990s and early 2000s provided an information advantage that greatly contributed to the sense of victory the US-led troops carried with them into Baghdad after the 2003 invasion of Iraq. Few other operations in history have demonstrated such superior efficiency in combat as Operation Iraqi Freedom. Nevertheless, although the offensive combat part of the Iraq War was accomplished within three weeks, the allied forces continue to fight to "maintain the peace" more than five years later.

New forms of hostile attacks are creating serious challenges for traditional military organizations. As Marine Corps general Charles C. Krulak presciently noted, "The inescapable lesson of Somalia and of other recent operations, whether humanitarian assistance, peace-keeping, or traditional warfighting, is that their outcome may hinge on decisions made by small unit leaders, and by actions taken at the lowest level."[18] The skills of "strategic corporals" are increasingly critical to the success of operations against nontraditional enemies who use asymmetrical or guerrilla-style tactics. This implies that organizational structures will need to change, as well as leadership education and training at all levels.

In many countries, network-centric warfare has been considered the US way of fighting future wars. In Scandinavian countries, the concept, first developed by the Norwegian Armed Forces and later adapted by Sweden and Finland, became known as network-based defense. The British concept, called network-enabled capabilities,[19] has been further developed within the North Atlantic Treaty Organization (NATO) Network-Enabled Capabilities program. This program gives NATO and allied nations an Information Age framework for technical connectivity that will allow them to adopt similar technical concepts and principles, a prerequisite for technical collaboration in global environments.

Initial writings describing the influence of the Information Age on defense transformation strongly emphasized the technology domain. We know, however, that sustaining change requires close attention to people, processes, and organizational issues.[20] These nontechnical areas as they relate to defense transformation are being explored by a growing number of authors. David S. Alberts and Richard E. Hayes, in *Power to the Edge* (2003), describe agile organizational structures and behaviors that provide military enterprises with additional options for command and control.[21] When combined with technologies that foster a common operational picture and group collaboration, the military organization can feel "flattened," in a way not dissimilar to Friedman's flattened world.

Information Age technologies have not just altered the way military personnel carry out operations, they have also increased the public's involvement in crisis situations. Media coverage is a serious consideration for those planning crisis interventions and other forms of security work in the Information Age. This phenomenon, by which media are able to focus public and political attention directly on military actions in real time, has been described as the "CNN effect." The CNN effect allows the public to receive and demand information that directly influences political agendas. Leaders and soldiers must be prepared to face a news camera at the same time they are risking their lives in crisis situations. To handle the CNN effect, twenty-first-century military leaders work very hard to develop an open relationship with the media. During Operation Iraqi Freedom, news media reporters were even invited to be "embedded" with fighting units.

Different organizational structures are emerging. Hierarchically organized bureaucracies such as the military have limited effectiveness in producing successful outcomes when their roles and missions reach across organizations and sectors (e.g., public, private, nonprofit). Consortia offer a different organizational model. Comprising several organizations, consortia work together as partners on projects where cooperation, consensus, and resource sharing add value. The World Wide Web Consortium, for example, is an international group that establishes interoperability standards for use on the World Wide Web.[22] The rapid rate of the Web's growth in the last ten years can be attributed directly to the organizational structure created by this remarkably effective consensus-building consortium.

In addition to choosing new organizing structures, success in the complex military environments of the 2000s, such as the asymmetric operations of the "Global War on Terror," demands new kinds of leadership and other people skills. Nancy Roberts concludes that in highly complex situations such as peacekeeping operations (known as wicked problems), collaborative, collective approaches tend to be more effective than authoritative leadership.[23] Frank Barrett likens a successful leadership model in highly complex situations to that found in professional jazz ensembles. These ensembles, whose musicians are noted for improvisation skills, hand off leadership among members, and organize around a set of "minimal structures." Barrett emphasizes listening as a key skill in improvisation, as well as the willingness to create openings for someone else to take the lead.[24] Military leaders who practice cooperative, consensus-building leadership styles may seem at odds with traditional military models of success based on strict hierarchy and reflexive obedience. In increasingly nontraditional, complex military operations, however, the most successful leaders may be those who encourage the creativity of their juniors in solving complex challenges.

Transforming Roles and Missions in Security Work

This section explores how the roles and missions of military forces in the Information Age are changing, and provides a conceptual model for describing those changes. We offer a model that covers four phases: crisis intervention and war fighting, rebuilding peace, maintaining stability, and building resilience for crisis prevention. We do not intend to imply that this conceptual model is linear in nature, nor do we intend to minimize the inherent complexity in each phase. Rather, we wish to frame one way to address nontraditional missions and the organizational, cultural, training, and education issues and possibilities associated with them.

The traditional focus of the Department of Defense (DoD) on crisis intervention and war fighting reflects military roles that originated in the aftermath of World War II, while its organizational structures grew over the next several decades to confront Cold War challenges. The "military-industrial complex," which coalesced during these same years, and against whose political influence an alarmed Dwight D. Eisenhower warned in his departing presidential speech in 1960, is an American economic cornerstone on which our military posture and national security policy have come to depend. DoD's rigid structures, developed to operate in a more predictable world, are in many ways ill suited to the demands for institutional agility prevalent in the post–Cold War, post-9/11 world. The significant changes in US (and, hence, global) security triggered by the end of the Cold War demand different "tools," different organizing principles, and different approaches from those developed by the US military in the twentieth century. Fortunately, these calcified structures are showing signs of evolving. The transformation of DoD to enable this evolution will be essential to global security in the twenty-first century.

Since the end of the Cold War, DoD leaders have shifted their focus beyond war fighting to postconflict peace-building operations, as recent engagements in the Balkans, Afghanistan, and Iraq demonstrate. This shift was outlined in DoD Directive 3000.05, "Military Support for Stability, Security, Transition, and Reconstruction (SSTR) Operations" (November 2005), which states, "Future DoD policy will . . . provide guidance on the security, transition, and reconstruction operations components of Stability, Security, Transition and Reconstruction SSTR operations and DoD's role in each."[25] Stability operations combine the work of military and civilian organizations to maintain order in states and regions, across the security spectrum from conflict to peace.

The directive articulates the emerging roles of DoD. To use the current Iraq War as an example, the United States was prepared to invade Iraq and defeat conventional forces, a role that fits the traditional work of the military. As of this writing, however, the postconflict rebuilding and peace work has been going on for over five years with no end in sight. During this same time, the US military has also been a key player in humanitarian relief efforts following the 2004 Indonesian tsunami, Hurricanes Katrina and Rita in 2005, and the 2005 Pakistan earthquake. These latter efforts are examples of "emerging work" that the military must undertake to ensure security in the twenty-first century. Emerging missions include stability and peacekeeping operations and humanitarian assistance and disaster response. The US military is also demonstrating an understanding of the importance of working with other agencies to prevent terrorist attacks and crisis escalation in fragile states.

The phenomenon of hastily formed networks (HFNs), which has been seen to arise in complex crises, is one area of great interest. An HFN denotes a rapidly created social or technical network, or both, that emerges to solve a specific overwhelming problem or situation. "The effectiveness of [an] HFN depends as much on the participating people and organizations, as it does on the communication system through which they interact."[26] These networks consist of five elements: (1) a rapidly established network of people, (2) who come from different communities, (3) to work together in a shared conversation space, (4) in which they plan, commit to, and execute actions, (5) that fulfill a large urgent mission.[27]

Information Age influences create opportunities that never before existed. It is conceptually possible, for example, to create high-performing social or technical networks, or both, that are focused on building resilience for crisis prevention. The Internet, World Wide Web, and a variety of Information Age modeling and synthesizing tools make it possible for disparate organizations to share information about emerging trends and to establish monitoring indicators from individual nodes. Knowledge fused from disparate sources around the globe could lead to new insights and, it is hoped, better crisis prevention. As militaries increase cooperation with civilian security forces such as local and national police, they will collectively be better able to detect early warning signs of crisis and preempt or mitigate the next 9/11, rather than just prepare to react to it.

Conflicts today attract global attention, even when they are between local people in a distant location. This means that a greater number of people and organizations will be directly or indirectly involved in stability strategies around the globe, and they will need reliable communications networks for effective collaboration. The globalization and digitization of the Information Age have reshaped and transformed the great powers' security agendas, from a doctrine of containment, whereby security was equal with defense, toward a map where connectedness creates security. The meaning of national borders is altering, and the relations created by connectedness are increasingly important to security. But it is not just the ability to connect that will shift the competitive landscape; it is the information-sharing flow that facilitates those relations, and the effect of new collaborations between individuals and organizations, that are causing the real changes.

Military and civilian security operations are finding common ground. The chief obstacles are technical (e.g., networks still in use that were not designed to be interoperable) as well as social (e.g., extending beyond organizational boundaries is natural for some and seemingly impossible for others). It is more and more difficult to find the border between military and civilian activities in crises and security operations. Given that military forces have a legitimate concern for information security, progress toward creating a lasting, broad-based security environment slows when people cling to the closed Cold War mind-set of "need to know" instead of embracing a more open "need to share" frame of mind.

It is obvious that we will need to build capacity for collaboration between military and civilian players in the Information Age. Collaboration is more about mind-sets than technological solutions. Many forms of system integration and technical information sharing are possible in the twenty-first century. The increasing complexity of Information Age security work can lead to "disconnects" and breakdowns among organizations and people, ranging from an individual's inability to create meaningful connections with other individuals to organizational rules that prevent information from being shared outside the system. Building trust, opening to others' points of view, and listening are skills that will serve military members well, whatever their actual work.

In this section we have discussed the changing focus of military work in the Information Age, with commensurate changes in roles and missions. Military roles have moved beyond war fighting to peace building, stability operations, and complex emergency operations including humanitarian assistance and disaster response. In this new work, we are creating the capacity to react swiftly to crises, rebuild peace, and maintain security. And, perhaps most important, we are building resilience for preventing crises. This security work is possible because we are in an age of widespread information access and expanding globalization. Such an evolution requires a coherent approach to combine the appropriate people skills, processes, organizational structures, and technologies to transform national and global security.

Conclusion: Building Resilience for Global Security in the Information Age

Determining the influence of the Information Age on international defense transformation is an extensive and ongoing task. The following summary will highlight some of the issues that are most important for leaders to consider as they work to transform defense forces and ensure global security in the Information Age.

1. Roles and missions are changing. Success in new security roles necessitates contributions by a diverse global group. A key lesson of 9/11 was that no single organization held the keys to preventing the attack. Out of the complexity of what the United States calls the Global War on Terror, security solutions are emerging that are multinational, multiorganizational, and multiagency. They include examples of work that is about connecting, sharing, and collaborating across the public, private, and not-for-profit sectors.

2. Managing change requires a coherent approach. For any large-scale effort at transformation to succeed, leaders will need to create institutions that integrate people, process, organization, and technology. Rapid developments in technologies can outpace the time it takes to alter organizational structures, modify processes, and teach new skills to the people who do the work, which can lead to disruptions and even breakdowns at critical moments.

3. Preparedness and prevention go hand in hand. Firefighting approaches to problem solving may ensure short-term success but at potentially severe long-term cost. Sustainable solutions include the ability both to react swiftly to crises as they unfold and to sense smoldering problems before they erupt. Equally important, however, is the need to understand the underlying conditions that spark and fuel crises.

4. As roles expand, sharing and collaboration will be key. The Information Age provides new capacity to understand the early warning signals

of crises. The Internet, satellites, databases, and computer networks are tools that can be used for crisis prevention just as they have been perfected for war fighting. As the global war on terrorism is showing us, the problems are more complex than the military sector or a single country can solve alone. Resilience will grow as we learn to collaborate across agencies, sectors, and nations.

5. Leaders must learn new kinds of skills. Innovative education and training must be a priority for leaders if they are going to succeed in security work. Those skills include listening, collaborating, building and connecting social networks, sharing, and appreciating the cultural perspectives of others. There are many additional skills for leaders to consider: Learn to continuously learn, and embrace innovation in order to outlearn the competition. Learn to create a shared vision with others about the world we desire. Learn about networks and how to use them. Learn appropriate leadership styles for security work, including collaborative and consensus-building styles, in addition to authoritative styles.

6. Develop sustainable, long-term solutions. Sustainable solutions are systemic, and the skills associated with systemic thinking will enable leaders to develop these kinds of solutions. The ability to understand all the relevant factors of the global security system, including those political, economic, environmental, and social issues that can be underlying causes of instability, is critical for long-term success. Leaders must collectively learn to build resilient defense systems for both crisis prevention and crisis intervention.

Along with the ideas listed above, there are a few additional areas worthy of further exploration. First, the science of networks can provide critical insights. Just as military leaders are learning that "it takes a network to fight a network,"[28] they are also learning that it takes a network (of all the parts of a system) to "see" and understand a network (the whole system). Once they can see it, they can take actions appropriate to the whole system. Second, it is of fundamental importance that new organizations designed to meet the needs of the Information Age incorporate the appropriate structures. Highly centralized, hierarchical organizations may not achieve their intended results. Consortia can provide clues to emerging organizational structures that may be more appropriate for what is needed to grow and maintain Information Age security systems. Finally, reflection will reap new insights (the "observe and orient" parts of the OODA [observe, orient, decide, act] loop) that are key to success in this age.

The Information Age provides unique potential for ensuring security for the world's peoples. While the challenges are many, the opportunities are compelling. We can continue to operate as we have done for millennia—

perfecting our militaries' abilities to react to crisis after crisis as each erupts—or we can use the influences of the Information Age to transform militaries for both crisis prevention and crisis intervention. The latter choice is more complex than any one nation or group can do alone. Working together across nations, organizations, and sectors to build resilience for crisis prevention could be the most profound influence of the Information Age on defense transformation.

Notes

1. Donald H. Rumsfeld, speech at a town hall meeting on 9 August 2001, news transcript, Washington, DC, US Department of Defense, Office of the Assistant Secretary of Defense (Public Affairs), 1, http://www.defenselink.mil/transcripts/transcript.aspx?transcriptid=1570.

2. Vannevar Bush, "As We May Think," *Atlantic Monthly,* July 1945, http://www.theatlantic.com/doc/194507/bush.

3. Arthur C. Clarke, "The Space Station: Its Radio Applications," *Wireless World,* May 1945, reprinted in *Spaceflight* 10, no. 3 (March 1968): 85–86, http://lakdiva.org/clarke/1945ww/.

4. Marshall McLuhan, *Understanding Media: The Extensions of Man* (Cambridge: MIT Press, 1964), 5.

5. Thomas L. Friedman, *The World Is Flat: A Brief History of the Twenty-First Century* (New York: Farrar, Straus and Giroux, 2006), 5.

6. Ibid.

7. Thomas Barnett, *The Pentagon's New Map: War and Peace in the New Century* (New York: Putnam, 2004), 3.

8. See Michael Lissack and Johan Roos, *The Next Common Sense: Mastering Corporate Complexity Through Coherence* (London: Nicholas Brealey, 1999).

9. Nancy C. Roberts, *The Transformative Power of Dialogue,* vol. 12 (Oxford: Elsevier Science, 2002), 10.

10. Henrik Friman, "Network Based Effectiveness," paper for the Command and Control Research and Technology symposium The State of the Art and the State of the Practice, San Diego, 20–22 June 2006: 5, http://www.dodccrp.org/events/2006_CCRTS/html/papers/009.pdf.

11. Peter Denning, "Hastily Formed Networks," *Communications of the ACM* 49, no. 4 (April 2006): 15–20.

12. Martin van Creveld, *The Transformation of War: The Most Radical Reinterpretation of Armed Conflict Since Clausewitz* (New York: Free Press, 1991).

13. Arthur K. Cebrowski and John J. Garstka, "Network-Centric Warfare: Its Origin and Future," *Proceedings* (1998), http://all.net/books/iw/iwarstuff/www.usni.org/Proceedings/Articles98/PROcebrowski.htm.

14. David S. Alberts, John J. Garstka, and Fredrick P. Stein, "Network Centric Warfare: Developing and Leveraging Information Superiority," 2nd ed., CCRP Publication Series (Washington, DC: US Department of Defense, 1999).

15. Robert Leonhard, *The Principles of War for the Information Age* (Novato, California: Presidio Press, 1998).

16. Bill Owens, *Lifting the Fog of War* (Baltimore: Johns Hopkins University Press, 2001), 97–102.

17. Arthur K. Cebrowski, briefing to the Association for Enterprise Integration (AFEI), April 2003, www.afei.org/pdf/nco2003/apr16/Art_Cebrowski.pdf.

18. General Charles C. Krulak, US Marine Corps, "The Strategic Corporal: Leadership in the Three Block War," *Marines Magazine,* January 1999, 3, http://www.au.af.mil/au/awc/awcgate/usmc/strategic_corporal.htm.

19. Tony Skinner, "UK's Afghanistan Missions Shape NEC Programme," *Jane's Defence Weekly,* 23 April 2008: 14.

20. Henry Mintzberg, *Structure in Fives: Designing Effective Organizations* (London: Prentice-Hall International, 1983).

21. David S. Alberts and Richard E. Hayes, *Power to the Edge: Command . . . Control . . . in the Information Age,* CCRP Publication Series (Washington, DC: US Department of Defense, 2003), http://www.dodccrp.org/html4/books_main.html.

22. For more information, go to http://www.w3.org.

23. Roberts, "Transformative Power," 10.

24. Frank Barrett, "Radical Aesthetics and Change: Jazz Improv as a Self-Organizing System," in Stephen Linstead and Heather Hopft, eds., *The Aesthetics of Organizations* (London: Sage Press, 2000), 237–255.

25. "Military Support for Stability, Security, Transition, and Reconstruction (SSTR) Operations," DoD Directive 3000.05, 28 November 2005: 1, http://www.dtic.mil/whs/directives/corres/html/300005.htm.

26. Denning, "Hastily Formed Networks," 18.

27. Ibid.

28. John Arquilla, "9/11: Yesterday and Tomorrow," *San Francisco Chronicle,* 7 September 2003, http://www.sfgate.com/cgi-bin/article.cgi?f=/c/a/2003/09/07/IN186774.DTL&hw=John+Arquilla&sn=017&sc=365.

4

Patterns in Innovation

John J. Garstka

Organizations innovate to enhance their competitive position or organizational capabilities by introducing new ideas, methods, or devices. This innovation can be guided by the strategic objective of creating or sustaining an existing competitive advantage, or of re-addressing an advantage adopted by an existing or new competitor. Innovation is often undertaken in response to a significant organizational challenge, an emerging opportunity, or a combination of both factors.

Although the dynamics of competition differ between the public and private sectors, organizations in both sectors are often faced with the need to innovate in response to emerging challenges and opportunities. When the degree of innovation one realizes is so significant that the resulting new organizational capabilities have a large performance advantage over one's own existing capabilities or those of competitors, then the term *transformation* may be applicable to the resulting changes. Leaders in both the public and private sectors therefore need to be cognizant of the challenges associated with both innovation and transformation if they are to be effective in navigating their organizations through periods of significant change.

To the intellectually unprepared, opportunities to develop advantage or enhance organizational competencies may be squandered or not fully realized. The probability of success in an endeavor requiring innovation can be improved by recognizing established patterns in innovation. These patterns transcend sectors, and insights can be enhanced by casting a wide net to examine how innovation takes place in a variety of organizations.

Types of Innovation

There are six principal types of innovation: theory, material or technology, process, organization, people, and concept.

1. Theory innovation identifies or describes fundamental relationships among variables. This type of innovation often provides the underlying knowledge that enables further innovation. Examples include the theory of aerodynamics, Lanchester equations, operations research, energy-maneuverability theory, portfolio theory, and the Black-Scholes model.[1]

2. Technology innovation involves the development of new material or technological capabilities. Examples of commercial technology innovation include the internal combustion engine, the computer microprocessor, the Internet, and cellular communications. Examples of military technology innovation include firearms, the aircraft, the tank, the aircraft carrier, radar, and stealth technology.

3. Process innovation, which has to do with how organizations carry out their functions, is often closely linked with technology innovation, and the two must sometimes be pursued in a synergistic manner. For example, in the commercial sector, automated bond trading was enabled by a combination of technology and process innovation. In a military context, new processes translate to new doctrine or tactics, techniques, and procedures, or, in some cases, new methodologies for training. Examples of military process innovation include fighter-weapons school, tank engagement tactics, and tactics for air-to-air combat.

4. Organizational innovation consists of the development of new organizational constructs. Examples in the commercial sector include the rise of stock companies, labor unions, and employee stock ownership. Among historical military examples are the creation of the US Navy's Bureau of Aeronautics, the Army Air Corps and Army Air Force, the US Special Operations Command, and the US Space Command.

5. People innovation creates new means to develop, employ, and retain human capital, as well as establish organizational culture. Commercial examples include employee stock options, telecommuting, and 360-degree evaluations. Military examples include the levée en masse, professional armies, the aviation type commander, and the joint duty officer.

6. Concept innovation describes or articulates a new concept or proposed approach for combining technology, process, organization, and people. Examples include strategic bombing, blitzkrieg, air-land battle, and maneuver warfare.

The leader of successful innovation often must have an ability to synchronize changes in theory, concept, technology, process, people, and organizational structure. A new concept or way of doing things may be technologically feasible but difficult to implement because of impediments in the organizational and personnel sectors. For example, for an organization to successfully implement telecommuting, it must be able to combine needed innovations in technology (Internet, e-mail, video teleconferencing, collaboration software), process (performance tracking), organization (virtual meetings), and personnel (on-line training, supportive culture, trust).

Innovation in Commercial Organizations

Much has been written about the imperative for innovation in the commercial sector. Competition among businesses is continuous. A commercial organization's long-term competitive advantage is closely linked to its ability to develop new products and services. This would be analogous to a military force being constantly engaged in combat and needing to adapt continuously to a competitor's innovations. In some cases, key innovations involve how products or services are sold. Examples in retailing include mutual funds and Wal-Mart's and Amazon.com's business plans. New financial theories, such as portfolio theory and the Black-Scholes model, provided the intellectual underpinnings for twenty-first-century global financial markets.[2]

Technology innovation is key to many companies' ability to develop and produce new products. For consumer products, innovative design is critical to differentiate products with similar underlying functions. Examples of recent product development that has combined technology and retailing innovation are the iPod and iTunes. Many consumer electronic companies have developed similar products, but Apple brought together cutting-edge product design, consumer feedback, and the world-class software expertise from its computer division to develop these integrated products and services. As a result, the company has reaped a disproportionate share of the market for digital music players and music downloads, which now represent over 44 percent of Apple's revenues and an even larger share of profits.[3] Apple is a great example of a company that has mastered a core set of innovation skills and is currently having significant success in the marketplace. In the technology sector, however, new developments can occur rapidly, and decades of market leadership can erode quickly or disappear altogether.

Multiple factors can contribute to the erosion of a company's competitive position in the commercial sector. These can include changes in the regulatory structure, the behavior of a competitor, or the emergence of a new product or technology. To respond to an eroded competitive position, a chief executive officer (CEO) may need to significantly enhance his or her company's ability to innovate to develop new products or services.

Eastman Kodak provides an insightful case study in corporate transformation that highlights the importance of comprehending when fundamental shifts in key technologies have the potential for a dramatic impact on the market for a company's core products. Once the undisputed leader of traditional film-based imaging, Kodak was forced to reinvent itself as a digital imaging company when the market for film-based photography evaporated, owing to the spread of digital technology. Kodak's leadership predicted that the market for film products would eventually decrease, but not at the accelerated rate that it actually happened.[4]

To transform Kodak, CEO Antonio Perez had to change the organization and develop the competencies required to compete in the new digital imaging ecosystem. One of the most difficult challenges faced by Perez was to convince Kodak's senior executives that Kodak needed to change to survive. To succeed, he made significant changes at the senior leadership and lower levels of the company. He closed film factories and eliminated 27,000 jobs. He recruited new talent with the technical backgrounds in digital imaging, software development, chip design, and consumer electronic design needed to augment Kodak's deep-skill sets in film-based photography.[5] By embracing these new "digital competencies," Kodak was able to develop a range of digital imaging products that gained a significant market share. These products included digital cameras and small dedicated printers that easily docked with these cameras for printing photos. The extremely intense competition for the digital camera market, however, resulted in profit margins that were significantly lower than those for film products, creating a new challenge for Kodak.[6]

Sustaining and Disruptive Innovation

The concept of sustaining and disruptive innovation was initially posited by Clayton Christenson, based on his observations of innovation in the commercial sector.[7] Sustaining innovation enhances or improves existing products or services along the dimensions of performance that mainstream customers in major markets have traditionally preferred. In other words, they provide customers with something that has more or better attributes of the kind they already value. An example is the transition from Intel's 386 computer chip to its 486 chip. In contrast, disruptive innovation creates a new product or service with a value proposition that is different from the value proposition of products and services that already exist. These new products or services typically underperform established products when measured with mainstream market metrics. They often have other features, however, that are valued by some customers, including new customers, that enable the pioneers to gain a foothold in a market.

Christenson observed a close correlation between the incentive structure of successful companies and their strategies for pursuing growth. For example, a company with $10 billion in sales with a growth rate of 10 percent needs to add $1 billion in new sales to continue to grow at this same rate. As a result, company leaders tend to focus almost exclusively on products or services they believe will help meet this level of sales or provide the profit margins required to meet earning objectives. In addition, there is often a reluctance to pursue new, poorly defined markets with "unproven" technology. Two examples, steel minimills and hydraulic actuators, illustrate certain characteristics of competition involving sustaining and disruptive innovation.

Steel Minimills vs. Integrated Steel Mills

Integrated steel mills use traditional blast furnace technology to melt iron ore to produce a full range of steel products. Steel minimills melt down scrap steel to produce new steel products. Initially, minimills could produce only low-end steel for use in reinforcing bars (rebar) for concrete construction. Since rebar is a relatively low-quality, low-margin product, integrated steel companies initially ceded this entry-level market. Minimills then improved their capabilities and were able to produce seamless pipe. Integrated steel mills again ceded the market, because the margins were not there. Eventually, through sustaining innovation, minimills were able to extend their product line to include structural steel, and finally sheet steel that could compete in terms of quality and price with the products of integrated steel mills. At this writing, minimills virtually dominate the North American market for rods, bars, and structural beams.[8]

Hydraulic vs. Cable-Operated Construction Equipment

A different pattern was seen in the development of hydraulic construction equipment. Initially, heavy construction equipment, such as excavators, was actuated by steel cables. Companies that produced this equipment relied on sustaining innovation to improve the performance of cable-operated equipment.

When the technology associated with hydraulic actuators, a disruptive innovation, was first introduced in the mid-1950s, it was suitable for use only in low-end equipment, such as backhoes used to dig trenches for sewage and water lines. Digging these trenches was a task traditionally done by hand because the task did not merit the cost of using a large, relatively imprecise, cable-operated shovel. Construction companies could clearly see the value proposition offered by the hydraulically actuated backhoe. As a consequence, the hydraulic backhoe established a firm foothold in a previously unserved market. Over time, the performance of hydraulic actuator technology improved and construction equipment employing hydraulic actuators replaced cable-operated construction equipment in almost every market.[9]

Each of these patterns of innovation observed in the commercial sector—types of innovation, high rates of change, and sustaining and disruptive innovation—plays out in similar ways in the military realm.

Innovation in Military Organizations

Military organizations must be able to innovate to effectively respond to emerging opportunities and challenges. Opportunities are often created by new or rapidly maturing technologies; challenges can be presented by an existing or emerging competitor, a constrained fiscal environment, or persistent recruiting shortfalls. History shows that militaries that failed to innovate suffered disproportionately at the hands of competitors who were more successful at pursuing war-fighting innovations. Successful military innovation, however, does not necessarily correlate with winning wars. It may provide initial advantages for winning battles but will not guarantee military victory if strategy is flawed, operational proficiency is lacking, or a competitor is superior at creative military thinking.

An analysis of past military innovation demonstrates that realizing militarily significant capabilities requires creativity in all the areas of theory, concepts, technology, process, organization, and people. The record also shows that the trajectory of innovation in military organizations can be influenced by multiple factors. These factors include

1. The absence or presence of a clearly defined military challenge;
2. The existence of militarily exploitable technologies;
3. The degree to which the innovation is sustaining or disruptive;
4. The rate at which technology innovation is occurring;
5. The magnitude of technology change eventually realized;
6. Organizational culture;
7. An organization's capability for learning or experimenting or both;
8. The ability of innovators to marshal evidence for the military utility of a proposed concept or innovation;

9. The ability of innovators to leverage evidence in order to secure funding for a proposed concept or innovation;
10. The impact of external factors, such as treaties or the size of defense budgets, which limit force development in some way.[10]

The relationships among these factors and the degree to which they contributed to the success or failure of known military innovations will be clarified by an examination of the role innovation played in the development of armored warfare and carrier aviation.

Sustaining Innovation, Disruptive Innovation, and Order of Magnitude Change

The history of military innovation has shown that some types of technologies are more difficult than others to exploit and translate into a war-fighting advantage. Innovation that sustains or enhances an existing way of operating is demonstrably easier to introduce and exploit than innovation that disrupts existing organizational values, attitudes, and beliefs. Furthermore, disruptive innovation can be much more difficult to accomplish in military institutions than in commercial ones, owing to the lag times of the military budget and procurement processes, and the bureaucratic oversight imposed by a democratic leadership structure.[11] The benefits of succeeding, however, can be significant, while the costs of failure will be measured in terms of disaster and defeat.

In the past, successful disruptive innovation was central to a number of what are sometimes referred to as revolutions in military affairs (RMAs). A common characteristic of almost all RMAs is a significant change in a key dimension of warfare.[12] In some cases, the degree of change in an underlying factor eventually corresponds to an "order of magnitude" improvement in the conduct of warfare as a whole. This order(s) of magnitude, or "10X," improvements has the potential to change the rules of the game in a significant way, making it almost impossible for an organization that has not made similar 10X adjustments to compete effectively. The net result is that an existing war-fighting core competency is rendered obsolete. Some historical RMA examples are:

1. Fires: machine gun, aviation, precision-guided weapons;
2. Maneuver: chariot, cavalry, mechanization, helicopter;
3. Protection: armor for knights, armor for tanks, stealth;

4. Sense or information: radar, computer-enabled cryptography and code-breaking, satellite reconnaissance, night vision goggles;
5. Support: replenishment at sea, aerial refueling.

Some of these innovations created an order of magnitude improvement: machine guns multiplied the potential rate of fire for a small group of individuals; aviation increased the range at which sensing, and eventually engagement, could take place. For carrier aviation, this translated into a change from 1.8×10^1 (engagement range for battleship) to 1.8×10^2 (engagement range for carrier-based aviation). Mechanized warfare increased the speed of sustained maneuver.

There are multiple factors that make it more likely disruptive innovation will significantly complicate force development. In the majority of historical cases, the realization of a 10X change took from ten to a hundred years.[13] Furthermore, at the outset, there was often significant uncertainty regarding the degree to which a particular technology or collection of technologies would mature with time. In other words, the rate of change for the underlying technologies was not predictable. This uncertainty translated into operational risk. For example, it was possible to have three-year-old aircraft that were technologically obsolete because of the rate of change in the underlying technology, which made large investments for capital-intensive equipment, such as aircraft, something of a gamble. This was the case in the mid-1930s, when steep improvements in aircraft engines enabled the design of high-performance monoplanes with increased speeds.[14] This high rate of change in aircraft performance translated into a 120 percent increase in aircraft speed over twelve years, and a 37 to 54 percent increase in aircraft ceiling over the same period for carrier aircraft in the Imperial Japanese Navy, British Royal Navy, and US Navy.[15] Consequently, operating within the financial constraints of the interwar years, senior decisionmakers often had to make trade-offs between current operational risk and future operational gain.

Armored Warfare

The development of armored warfare involved disruptive innovation that was either amplified or attenuated based on each competitor's perspective on existing or emerging military challenges, prevailing organizational culture, and openness to experimentation and learning. Key concept, technology, process, organization, and people innovations associated with the development of armored warfare are portrayed in Figure 4.1.

Figure 4.1 Innovation in the Development of Armored Warfare

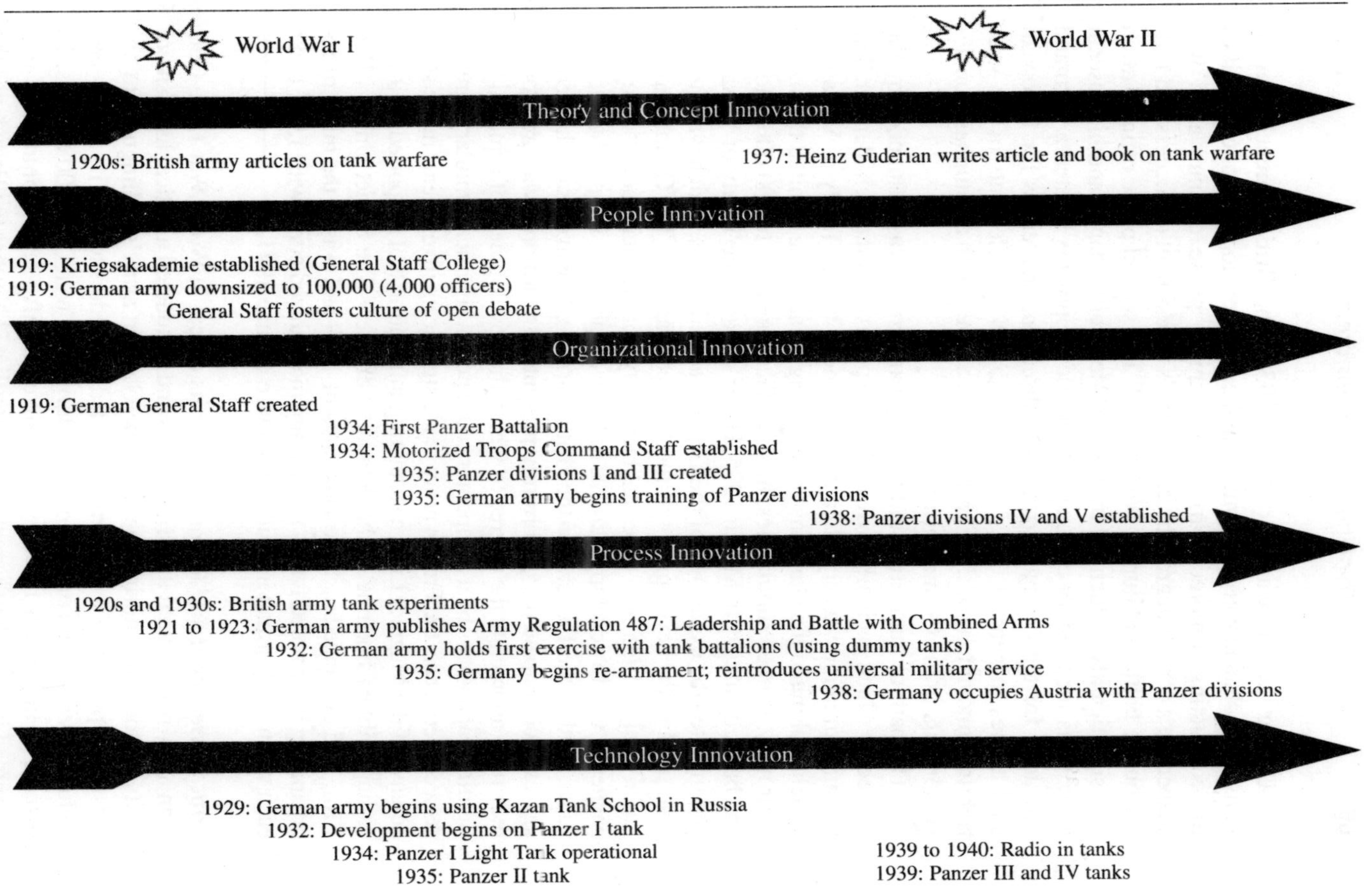

During the interwar years (1919–1938), the British, French, Soviet, Polish, Czech, and German armies pursued the development of capabilities for conducting armored warfare. The initial phase of innovation was shaped, to a certain degree, by each army's assessment of success and failure on the battlefield during World War I. The second phase of innovation was significantly influenced by Adolf Hitler's ascendancy and his nascent aspirations for military conquest. These developments created a "demand function" for the German army and subsequent challenges for European land armies in general. This section describes key elements of the war-fighting innovations of the European land armies, with an emphasis on developments in the German army.

The path of innovation in the European armies was influenced by the degree to which each army viewed its respective military challenges. The German situation was significantly influenced by the Treaty of Versailles, which prohibited the Germans from having an air force, limited the size of their navy, banned submarines, held the German army to 100,000 soldiers, and banned tanks.[16] In March 1935, Hitler violated the Treaty of Versailles and initiated the expansion of the German armed forces, which was the tipping point in the development of mechanized warfare.[17] The German army's initial goal in 1935 was to reestablish parity with its neighbors.[18] The next challenge was to develop offensive military capabilities. During the interwar years, neither the French nor the British armies, however, saw the need to aggressively pursue the opportunity presented by armored warfare, nor did they fully appreciate the degree to which the development of armored war-fighting capabilities by a competitor could pose a significant military threat.[19] As a consequence, the French army made significant investments in the static defense of the Maginot Line, a sustaining innovation that supported their prevailing military doctrine of the delaying defense.[20] The Soviet Union's Red Army had disbanded its large tank units in 1939 and was in the midst of reorganizing its armored forces into twenty mechanized corps with 1,031 tanks each when the German invasion took place in June 1941.[21]

Critical assessment and learning. After its defeat in World War I, the German army restructured its officer corps and conducted a critical assessment of its performance during the war. The German army's willingness to aggressively pursue lessons learned enabled its leaders to identify tactics and technologies that did or did not work during the war. Over 400 officers, 10 percent of the officer force, were involved in fifty-seven committees that examined in depth key aspects of the conflict.[22] Neither the British nor the French armies, by contrast, had the cultural disposition to assess their respective operational performance in such an open and critical fashion.

British army leaders finally did initiate an assessment in 1932, but a subsequent change in leadership resulted in the findings not being widely distributed.[23]

The German army synthesized the insights from its analysis to develop Army Regulation 487 ("Leadership and Battle with Combined Arms"), released in 1921 (Part 1) and 1923 (Part 2), which laid the doctrinal foundation for much of the war-fighting innovation that was to follow.[24] This combined-arms doctrine emphasized speed, surprise, mobility, decentralization, and exploitation.

The writings of two British army officers, Basil H. Liddell Hart and John F. C. Fuller, articulated the potential of armored warfare and emphasized the value of surprise, maneuver, and an indirect approach. When the British War Office decided to rewrite its infantry tactical manual, it assigned Liddell Hart, then a twenty-four-year-old officer with limited military experience, to the task. His innovative maneuver warfare concepts, however, were deleted from the completed 1920 manual.[25] Fuller, a tank corps officer in World War I, wrote plans for an integrated ground attack using tanks and aircraft that became known as "Plan 1919." Although the Armistice prevented Plan 1919 from being tried, Fuller's innovative ideas are generally considered to be the precursor to the German blitzkrieg.[26] Liddell Hart's and Fuller's works in fact had a greater influence on the Germans than on the British (contemporary French contributions to theories of armored warfare were inconsequential).[27] Two of the more insightful treatments of armored warfare were authored by General Heinz Guderian, who led the development and application of German tank warfare in World War II and was himself influenced by Liddell Hart and Fuller. His work consisted of an initial article, "Tank Attack by Fire and Maneuver," which appeared in 1937, and the book *Achtung Panzer! The Development of Armored Forces, Their Tactics and Operational Potential,* which was published in the same year.[28]

Early experimentation. The British army conducted a series of experiments between 1926 and 1934 that explored the operational utility of mechanized forces. The very success of some of the experiments and exercises, however, meant that they would be extremely disruptive. In 1926, for example, an exercise was ended early by a very successful 25-mile tank maneuver carried out by an enterprising lieutenant colonel. When he saw similar results two years later, the general in charge of the exercises bemoaned how the success of the new technology negatively affected the traditional branches of the army. He argued that it was wrong to equip only a part of the ground force with new armament, but maintained that mechanization and motorization should take place throughout the whole army.[29]

Key German leaders followed these developments closely and were able to learn from the results of the British experimentation.[30] In addition, the German army was able to develop some hands-on experience with tanks at the Kazan tank school in Russia between 1929 and 1933.[31]

The British, French, Soviet, Czech, Polish, and German armies all pursued technology innovation during the interwar period to varying degrees of success. In developing capabilities for armored warfare, the principal areas of innovation for tanks included speed, armor, armament, and radio communications. At the onset of World War II, most of the major European land armies had tanks in their inventory. The French and Soviet armies both possessed tank forces larger than the Germans', and each contained tanks that were qualitatively superior to the best German tanks.

Tank and armor innovations in World War II. The order of battle for the German invasion of France is portrayed in Table 4.1. The performance characteristics of the German, British, and French tanks—those characteristics deemed most important by their designers—are shown in Tables 4.2 through 4.4. The French Char B1 and the Char Somua 35 were viewed as superior to the best German tanks, while the British A-12 Matilda II, with eighty millimeters (roughly 3 inches) of armor, was virtually impenetrable by all German weapons except the 88-mm antitank gun.[32] Few allied tanks, however, were equipped with radios.[33]

The order of battle for Operation Barbarossa, the German invasion of the Soviet Union, is shown in Table 4.5. The Soviet forces in the west consisted of 190 divisions, which fielded approximately 15,000 tanks, as shown in Table 4.5.[34] The vast majority of the Red Army's tanks were T-26 and BT series tanks, both of which were designed for infantry support. Of the two higher-quality Soviet tank models, the T-34 and the KV-1, the T-34 was superior to all existing German tanks, but made up only 4 percent of the Red Army's tank force at the beginning of the war.[35]

The Germans had a distinct qualitative advantage in two areas: antitank weapons, with the 88-mm, dual-use, antiaircraft-antitank gun; and the radio, which significantly enhanced command and control. In both invasions the Germans were able to destroy the adversary's air forces on the ground, and to integrate their own airpower to a significant degree. Nevertheless, the greatest source of Germany's initial war-fighting advantage was to be found in its military doctrine, organization, training, and quality of leadership.[36] The German army successfully combined technological and organizational innovations with superior processes to create a significant change in a key dimension of warfare that rendered obsolete the core competency of static defense.

Table 4.1 Order of Battle: German Invasion of France and the Low Countries

Force	Axis	Allied
Divisions	136	135
Armored Divisions	10	7
Mechanized Divisions	4	10
Tanks	2,600	4,450
Aircraft	5,500	3,100

Source: Peter McCarthy and Mike Syron, *Panzerkrieg: The Rise and Fall of Hitler's Tank Divisions* (New York: Carroll and Graf, 2003), 71–74.

Table 4.2 Overview of German Tank Characteristics and Force Composition

Type	Armament (mm)	Armor (mm)	Weight (pounds)	Speed on Road (mph)	Crew	Invasions of France	Invasions of Russia
Panzer I	7.92	7–13	11,907	31.1	2	523	410
Panzer II	20	5–14.5	20,948	24.9	3	955	750
Panzer 35(t)	37	25		21.1	4	106	150
Panzer 38(t)	37	8–30	21,389	26.1	4	228	625
Panzer III	37	5–70	42,777	24.9	5	349	965
Panzer IV	75	10–80	43,439	24.9	5	278	440

Sources: Data from Peter McCarthy and Mike Syron, *Panzerkrieg: The Rise and Fall of Hitler's Tank Divisions* (New York: Carroll & Graf, 2003), 71, 99; David Miller, *The Great Book of Tanks* (St. Paul, MN: MBI, 2002), 108, 136–137, 144–145, 156–157, 168–169.

Table 4.3 Overview of French Tank Characteristics and Force Composition

Type	Armament (mm)	Armor (mm)	Weight (pounds)	Speed on Road (mph)	Crew	Numbers
Renault FT	37	22	13,010	4.5	2	2,500
Renault R35	37	43	22,050	12.4	2	1,000
Hotchkiss H35	37	34–40	26,460	17.4	2	800
Char B1	47 and 75	40	70,560	17.4	4	250
Char Somua S35	47	55	44,206	24.9	3	300

Sources: Data from Peter McCarthy and Mike Syron, *Panzerkrieg: The Rise and Fall of Hitler's Tank Divisions* (New York: Carroll and Graf, 2003), 71–72; David Miller, *The Great Book of Tanks* (St. Paul, MN: MBI, 2002), 118–119, 128–129, 122–123, 130–131; and Kenneth Macksey, *Tank: Facts and Feats—A Record of Armored Fighting Vehicle Achievement* (New York: Two Continents, 1974), 220.

Table 4.4 Overview of British Tank Characteristics and Force Composition

Type	Armament (mm)	Armor (mm)	Weight (pounds)	Speed on Road (mph)	Crew	Numbers
A-11 Matilda I	Machine Guns	1–60	24,610	8.0	2	200
A-12 Matilda II	40	78	22,050	15	4	75
A10 Mark I (Cruiser Mark II)	37	6–30	26,460	10	5	31
A13 Cruiser Mark IV	40	6–30	28,445	16.2	4	119

Sources: Peter McCarthy and Mike Syron, *Panzerkrieg: The Rise and Fall of Hitler's Tank Divisions* (New York: Carroll and Graf, 2003), 71–72; David Miller, *The Great Book of Tanks* (St. Paul, MN: MBI, 2002), 158-159, 182–183; and Kenneth Macksey, *Tank: Facts and Feats--A Record of Armored Fighting Vehicle Achievement* (New York: Two Continents, 1974), 220.

Table 4.5 Order of Battle: German Invasion of the USSR

Force	Axis	Russia
Divisions	150[a]	190
Armored divisions	17	34
Tanks	3,300	12,000–15,000
Aircraft	4,389	8,000

Sources: Peter McCarthy and Mike Syron, *Panzerkrieg: The Rise and Fall of Hitler's Tank Divisions* (New York: Carroll and Graf, 2003), 99; and David M. Glantz, *Stumbling Colossus: The Red Army on the Eve of World War* (Lawrence: University Press of Kansas, 1998), 154–159.

Note: a. Axis divisions included ten motorized divisions.

Table 4.6 Overview of Soviet Tank Characteristics

Type	Armament (mm)	Armor (mm)	Weight (pounds)	Speed on Road (mph)	Crew
BT 5/7	45	6–13	30,650	44.7 (tread removed)	3
T-26	45	7–16	20,948	17.4	3
T-34	76.2	90	70,560	32.9	4
KV-1	76.2	40	104,738	21.7	5

Source: David Miller, *The Great Book of Tanks* (St. Paul, MN: MBI, 2002), 88–89, 112–113, 202–203, 204–205.

In 1933 General Werner von Fritsch, the German army's future commander in chief, and General Ludwig Beck, then the army's chief of staff, built upon a 1921 "lessons learned" treatise, "Leadership and Combat of Combined Arms-Forces," to develop the tactical manual *Die Truppenführung*.[37] This manual provided the doctrinal foundations (processes and organizations) for the massed mechanized attack tactic that came to be known as blitzkrieg.

What, in retrospect, appear to be relatively "simple" process and organizational change issues were a significant point of contention within all armies and served as a major impediment to innovation in the French and British armies.[38] Even within the German army, there was significant discussion, debate, and disagreement regarding the proper role of armored forces. The major doctrinal argument revolved around whether tanks should support infantry or whether infantry should support the tank.[39] The human element was core to this argument, for its outcome would determine whether the status of the existing war-fighting elites—the infantry and the cavalry—would be sustained and reinforced or potentially diminished by the emergence of the new "armor elite." Guderian and fellow innovators in the German army were steadfast in their conviction that the effectiveness of armor could be fully realized only if the armored forces were used in a new way. They argued that tanks needed to be massed, and that the best way to accomplish this was through the creation of tank divisions.[40] In his memoirs, Guderian described organizational push-back as it manifested in his disagreements with General Beck, then chief of the German General Staff:

> I had to win a long-drawn out fight with General Beck before he would agree to setting up the Panzer Divisions and to the publication of training manuals for armored troops. Finally he went so far as to agree to the creation of two Panzer Divisions, while I was already insisting on three. I described the advantages of these new formations in the most glowing terms, and in particular, their operational significance. He replied "No, no, I don't want to have anything to do with you people. You move too fast for me."[41]

Despite the internal debates, the German army formed its first three Panzer divisions in 1935, epitomizing the accession of disruptive innovation. Guderian, then a colonel, was assigned command of the 2nd Panzer Division.[42]

Learning from operations. The path of innovation within these European armies was influenced by the degree to which each military organization's culture supported critical assessment, learning, and experimentation. One of the keys to the Germans' initial success with the development and execution of the blitzkrieg was the ability of a cadre of personnel to learn from operational successes and failures. Initial German experience in the Spanish Civil War in 1937 provided useful insight.[43] Although German tanks themselves were used in a piecemeal fashion in support of the infantry, German gunners determined that the 88-mm antiaircraft cannon was an equally effective antitank weapon. The deficiencies of the Panzer I and Panzer II nevertheless became readily apparent, particularly in operations against the more heavily armored and better-armed Soviet T-26 tank during the German invasion of the Soviet Union.[44]

Additional German experience was gained in the Anschluss (1938), when Germany incorporated Austria into the Reich. Lessons related to the maintenance and fueling of tanks were applied in the subsequent invasion of Poland.[45] These experiences revealed two shortcomings: that light divisions had limited operational effectiveness, which resulted in the creation of two more Panzer divisions; and that motorized infantry divisions were too large and unwieldy, which resulted in their being made smaller by the removal of their infantry regiments.[46]

Carrier Aviation

The development of carrier aviation involved sustaining innovation, disruptive innovation, and the eventual existence of a clearly defined military challenge. The US Navy's organizational culture, open to war gaming, tactical experimentation, and learning, contributed to the successful development of carrier aviation. The US Navy was also fortunate to possess leaders who were capable of spearheading large-scale disruptive innovation.

Ship-based aviation initially was developed and deployed as a sustaining innovation, and its introduction provided significant operational and tactical benefits. At the operational level, aircraft improved a fleet's scouting ability. At the tactical level, it extended the range of engagement for battleships. Innovations in gun design had progressed to the degree that a battleship's main guns could fire shells over the horizon, beyond the range of a battleship's organic sensing capabilities. Despite the increasing range of the guns, this sensing shortfall limited effective engagement to 20,000 yards. The introduction of sea-based aviation extended battleships' sensing range and enabled their main guns to engage targets over the horizon, out to 30,000 yards.[47] This was a significant increase, and clearly demonstrated the potential contributions of aviation to warfare at sea.

The development of carrier aviation in the US Navy, the British Royal Navy, and the Imperial Japanese Navy during the interwar years was influenced to varying degrees by military challenges. The Royal Navy was faced with the potential need to protect British interests in the Far East, as well as the possibility of being involved in a conflict in Europe or minor warfare on the borders of the Empire.[48] Both the US Navy and the Imperial Japanese Navy realized there was a distinct probability that they would need to project power across the vast reaches of the Pacific Ocean, and that well-developed and mature carrier aviation would provide significant operational benefits should hostilities break out. In response to the emerging military competition in the Pacific, the US Navy pursued a full range of technology, process, organization, and people innovations. Figure 4.2 provides an overview of these innovations and their relative sequencing.

One of the key obstacles that innovators in military organizations face is the need to secure resources to pursue a promising technology or concept. During the development of carrier aviation in the US Navy, one of the lead innovators, Rear Admiral William A. Moffett, worked closely with members of Congress to help them understand the potential of carrier aviation and to secure initial and then continued funding.[49] Moffett also played a key role in ensuring that naval aviation could be developed as a stand-alone entity and not be absorbed into a broader "air force," as was proposed by such early airpower advocates as General William L. "Billy" Mitchell.[50]

Consistent investments in research and development over time resulted in the development of carrier-based aircraft that had the speed, range, payload, and survivability to engage enemy combatants successfully beyond the range of a battleship's main guns. These advances in aircraft performance, combined with concurrent innovations in carrier design and the parallel development of tactics, techniques, and procedures for employing carrier-based aircraft, ensured that aircraft carriers would become the decisive asset in warfare at sea.

One of the key insights that emerged from war gaming and exercises was that airpower was most effective when delivered in a single pulse.[51] This finding provided the impetus to maximize the number of aircraft that could be launched from a carrier in a short period of time. Gradually, evidence gathered from the war games and tactical exercises conducted in support of the Fleet Problem series provided the information needed to influence investment decisions.[52] The body of empirical data, combined with an organizational willingness to follow the data, enabled the US Navy to allocate limited resources and make difficult but informed resource allocation

Figure 4.2 Innovation in the Development of Carrier Aviation

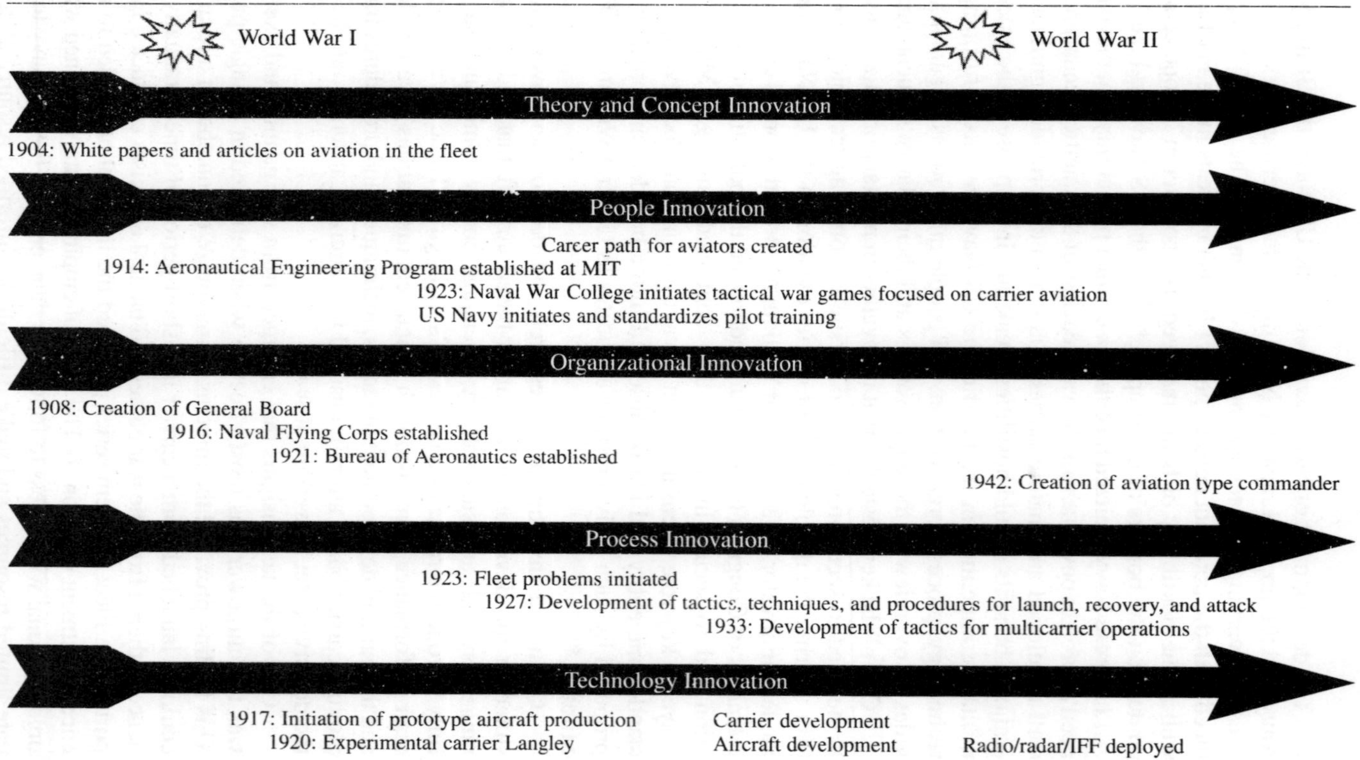

trade-offs among carriers, battleships, and aviation and other major platforms in the interwar years.[53]

Realizing the full potential of carrier aviation required people innovations that also were challenging. These innovations involved increasing the number and quality of US Naval Academy graduates entering naval aviation and establishing viable career paths for naval aviators, which eventually culminated in the creation of the "aviation type commander."[54] A key step was to establish policy ensuring that only naval aviators could command aircraft carriers and air stations.[55]

The creation of the aviation type commander position removed one of the last remaining impediments to the emergence of carrier aviation as a mature war-fighting capability, by codifying a viable "warrior" career path for the new war-fighting elite. This innovation had been initially proposed to the Navy's General Board in 1934 and rejected. It was not until almost a year after the attack on Pearl Harbor, in the autumn of 1942, that the position of the Aviation Type Commander was established.[56] In this same year, Admiral Ernest J. King became the first naval aviator to be selected as chief of naval operations.[57]

Conclusion

Innovation is critical to an organization's ability to develop and maintain a competitive advantage. Specific problems or challenges can play a key role in focusing an organization's innovation efforts. Organizations, however, need to have the agility to explore technologies that do not address an immediate threat, but could themselves pose a threat in the future if they were aggressively pursued by a current or potential future competitor.

Theory innovation is an elusive construct. In military organizations it has seldom arisen in response to top-down guidance. Breakthroughs in theory can come from academic researchers or operational practitioners with uncommon insights. Emerging theory may first appear in a partially coherent or incomplete form, only to be finalized when a sufficient evidence base is established. Theory innovation nevertheless can have a profound impact in both the commercial and security sectors.

Technology innovation often leads to other types of innovation and is critical to success in the commercial sector. Most military organizations do not innovate in technology per se. In most cases, they establish requirements, fund research and development, and acquire material capabilities. The actual technology development is typically performed in the commercial sector. What military organizations need to excel at are (1) being able to identify areas where research and development investments need to be made and (2) defining the right requirements for capabilities and systems.

Technology and process innovation are often closely linked in both commercial and military organizations. Process innovation needs to be a core competency of military organizations, since doctrine and tactics, techniques, and procedures are the "operating system" for military organizations. Organizations in both sectors need to have robust capabilities for learning from operational success and failure if they are to avoid rigid adherence to approaches or doctrine that are not working.

Well-developed experimentation capabilities can help determine the efficacy of new combinations of technology, processes, organizations, and people. In addition, the organization needs to develop a method for gathering empirical evidence that can be used for the benefit of a new technology, marketing strategy, or an emerging war-fighting capability. To pursue process and organizational innovations effectively, both the commercial and military sectors need to be open to the development of new organizational constructs. In some cases, such new constructs may be required to facilitate organizational learning and experimentation.

People innovation is often the most difficult to accomplish, yet can be the most critical to success. An organization whose culture inhibits critical assessment, organizational learning, or rigorous experimentation is not likely to successfully pursue innovation. Similarly, leaders in military organizations must recognize when new career paths are needed to fully realize the potential of an emerging war-fighting capability. Organizations that ignore these patterns of innovation do so at their peril.

Notes

1. Lanchester equations provided a theoretical basis for computing the effectiveness of forces in combat; operations research can be used to determine optimal resource allocation and played a key role in antisubmarine warfare in the battle of the Atlantic; energy maneuverability theory established a deterministic relationship between energy and maneuverability for fighter aircraft; portfolio theory defined a methodology for quantifying the relationship between risk and return to establish a diversified portfolio of investments; the Black-Scholes model established a methodology for computing the price of a derivative of a financial equity—sometimes referred to as the "trillion dollar equation."

2. Peter L. Bernstein, *Against the Gods: The Remarkable Story of Risk* (New York: Wiley, 1996), 304–328.

3. Steve Hamm and William Symonds, "Mistakes Made on the Road to Innovation," *Business Week*, 27 November 2006.

4. Ibid.

5. Ibid.

6. Ibid.

7. Clayton M. Christenson, *The Innovator's Dilemma: When New Technologies Cause Great Firms to Fail* (Boston: Harvard Business School Press, 1997), xv–xvi.

8. Ibid., 101–106.

9. Ibid., 61–76.

10. Richard O. Hundley, *Past Revolutions, Future Transformations* (Santa Monica: National Defense Research Institute, 1999), xx–xxi.

11. Terry C. Pierce, *Warfighting and Disruptive Technologies: Disguising Innovation* (London: Frank Cass, 2004), 19–27.

12. Hundley, *Past Revolutions,* 10.

13. Ibid., 16.

14. Thomas C. Hone, Norman Freidman, and Mark D. Mandeles, *American and British Aircraft Carrier Development: 1919–1941* (Annapolis: Naval Institute Press, 1999), 129.

15. Norman Friedman, *Carrier Air Power* (New York: Rutledge Press, 1981), 172–191.

16. Treaty of Versailles, Part 5, http://www.yale.edu/lawweb/avalon/imt/partv.htm.

17. Heinz Guderian, *Panzer Leader* (London: Penguin, 2000), 34–35.

18. Ibid., 35.

19. Williamson Murray and Allan R. Millett, *Military Innovation in the Interwar Period* (Cambridge: Cambridge University Press, 1996), 9–15.

20. Pierce, *Warfighting,* 37.

21. Bryan I. Fugate, *Operation Barbarossa: Strategy and Tactics on the Eastern Front, 1941* (Novato, California: Presidio Press, 1984), 36.

22. Williamson Murray, "Armored Warfare," in Murray and Millett, *Military Innovation,* 37.

23. Ibid., 20–21.

24. Ibid., 37.

25. Ibid., 21.

26. See Ari Unikoski, "The War in the Air: Ground Attack," 9 August 2003, http://www.firstworldwar.com/airwar/groundattack.htm.

27. Murray, "Armored Warfare," 32.

28. Guderian, *Panzer Leader,* 38–39. For an analysis of British and French military doctrine in World War II see Elizabeth Kier, *Imagining War* (Princeton, New Jersey: Princeton University Press, 1997).

29. Pierce, *Warfighting,* 34.

30. Murray and Millett, *Military Innovation,* 39–41.

31. Peter McCarthy and Mike Syron, *Panzerkrieg: The Rise and Fall of Hitler's Tank Divisions* (New York: Carroll and Graf, 2003), 24.

32. Ibid., 71–72.

33. Ibid.

34. David M. Glantz, *Stumbling Colossus: The Red Army on the Eve of World War* (Lawrence: University Press of Kansas, 1998), 154–159.

35. McCarthy and Syron, *Panzerkrieg,* 104–106.

36. Ibid., 74.

37. MacGregor Knox, *Common Destiny: Dictatorship, Foreign Policy and War in Fascist Italy and Nazi Germany* (Cambridge: Cambridge University Press, 2000), 196.

38. Guderian, *Panzer Leader,* 26–29, 31–34.

39. Ibid., 26.

40. Ibid., 25.

41. Ibid., 32.

42. Ibid., 36.

43. McCarthy and Syron, *Panzerkrieg,* 33–34.

44. Ibid.

45. Guderian, *Panzer Leader,* 54.

46. Ibid., 88.

47. Hone et al., *American and British Aircraft,* 12–13, 18.

48. Ibid., 100.

49. Ibid., 166.

50. Ibid., 39.

51. Pierce, *Warfighting,* 124.

52. The Fleet Problem series was exercises carried out between 1919 and 1938, designed to explore the value of carrier aviation following World War I. See Scot MacDonald, "Last of the Fleet Problems," *Naval Aviation News* (September 1962), http://www.history.navy.mil/download/car-6.pdf.

53. Hone et al., *American and British Aircraft,* 136–137.

54. Ibid., 76–79.

55. Ibid., 130.

56. Ibid., 79.

57. Ibid., 131.

5

Pressing Contemporary Issues

Scott Moreland and James Mattox

The conduct of modern warfare is profoundly influenced by contemporary issues on the battlefield. Over the past few decades, an increasingly unstable global security environment and rapid technological advances have expanded battlefield dimensions. Space-based surveillance and tracking technologies, sophisticated information networks, and the proliferation of weapons capable of mass effects have wrought a radical transformation in defense personnel, technologies, organizations, and processes. A shift toward technologically sophisticated, professional, expeditionary, and streamlined forces is the essence of defense transformation in the twenty-first century.

Adversaries have chosen a different path with important historical precedent. Transnational actors and rogue states acknowledge the conventional primacy enjoyed by Western militaries and have responded with age-old equalizers: terrorism, asymmetric warfare, and strategic patience. The United States and its allies struggle to combat a dispersed enemy that is embedded among the civilian populace in complex terrain. Long after major combat operations concluded in Iraq, for example, conventional military forces remained entrenched and inadequately trained and equipped for transitional security and peace enforcement missions. Battlefield commanders must prepare to not only engage and overcome rogue state actors equipped with advanced capabilities, but also consider the subsequent roles and missions that emerge from the chaos of ungoverned spaces: low-intensity conflict, counterinsurgency, and nation building.

The pressing issues faced by US and coalition troops in Iraq and Afghanistan are shaping the transformation of tomorrow's military forces. The strategic challenges of the early twenty-first century are unique in many ways. Disruptive technologies; multilateral, preemptive intervention; and unstable regional power distribution represent unfamiliar dimensions in the current and future battle space that will define the conditions for military missions on the foreseeable horizon. Joint forces must possess capabilities that not only are overwhelmingly effective and lethal in major combat but also contribute to a holistic engagement strategy that includes political, economic, and civil elements.

The United States and the North Atlantic Treaty Organization (NATO) have dedicated significant time and resources to the collection and analysis of lessons learned in modern military campaigns and exercises. Joint, allied, and component centers for lessons learned play an important role in the identification and development of new capabilities and solutions to address contemporary issues. Not surprisingly, there are recurring themes that emerge upon examination of the key difficulties and capability shortfalls facing military forces in Iraq and Afghanistan. This chapter will consider the implications of the most pressing issues drawn from US and NATO experiences and examine the effectiveness of interim and long-term solutions.

Compatibility and Interoperability

> There is at least one thing worse than fighting with allies—and that is to fight without them.
>
> —*Sir Winston S. Churchill*[1]

The operational effectiveness of joint and allied military forces hinges on compatibility and interoperability.[2] NATO defines *compatibility* as "the suitability of products, processes, and services for use together," while *interoperability* reflects "the ability to operate in synergy in the execution of assigned tasks."[3] US joint armed forces and NATO allies contribute significantly to international coalitions across the spectrum of operations, from humanitarian assistance and peacekeeping operations in accommodating environments to major combat operations in theater-level campaigns. Coalition partners provide a broad variety of unique capabilities to multilateral operations. To ensure that partner contributions are effectively utilized, their communications, control, employment, and logistics mechanisms must be compatible and interoperable throughout the supported coalition. Systems compatibility and service interoperability are essential to both joint forces and coalitions of all sizes and compositions.

Interoperability is a key factor in establishing unity of command in coalition military operations. Command challenges span strategic, operational, and tactical battlefield dimensions. Interoperability problems have been encountered at all levels in coalition operations in Iraq and Afghanistan. Moreover, the effects of strategic interoperability shortfalls tend to permeate to the operational and tactical levels. Communication incompatibilities and unclear command relationships and responsibilities increase the risk of mission overlap, fratricide, and inadequate intelligence sharing.

At the strategic level, the key compatibility and interoperability challenges in Iraq and Afghanistan include multilateral deployment, consistent and dependable logistical support to restricted-mobility environments, sustaining national political will and ambition for coalition contributions, and meeting evolving force structure requirements during the transition from major combat to stability operations. At the operational level, rotational planning, unified command and control, and information sharing are the primary concerns. The United States and other lead coalition nations must balance information sharing and information security by determining appropriate levels of direct control of national and theater intelligence, surveillance, and reconnaissance (ISR) assets, as opposed to contributions to a larger, shared information repository under coalition control.

Tactically, the key problem is the conduct of combined missions with coalition forces of varying performance capabilities. In Operation Iraqi Freedom, insurmountable problems with coalition tactical command integration, communications, and combat identification led to the division of the battle space, in order to segregate and compartmentalize air and ground coalition forces, resulting in a less than optimal fratricide avoidance measure.[4]

The United States and NATO attempted to address this acute capabilities gap by rapidly fielding the Blue Force Tracking System (BFTS) for British forces in southern Iraq, while sequentially fielding the Interim Forces Tracking System (IFTS) for NATO and partner nations operating in Kosovo and the Balkans.[5] Blue Force Tracking and its compatible IFTS NATO counterpart are durable computer hardware and software systems that establish secure, wireless "tactical internets" to link satellites, air and ground sensors, communications devices, and weapons platforms into an integrated digital network.[6] The success of the interim NATO system in Iraq has prompted the evolution of a Friendly Force Tracking program that links compatible national force tracking capabilities into a NATO-wide network.[7] In fact, the Friendly Force Tracking system is considered so critical to allied interoperability that NATO Response Force concept leaders Jeffrey P. Bialos and Stuart L. Koehl warn, "Without [FFT] interoperability, not only is the risk of fratricide increased, but the entire situational awareness capability on which network-centric warfare rests will be undermined."[8]

National and component-level "plug and play" capabilities like BFTS and FFT can minimize disruptions in coalition command, control, and communications; accommodate seamless force rotations; and maximize the efficiency and effectiveness of national capability contributions. The plug-and-play concept has already been developed to overcome technological challenges in coalition air-to-ground missions, through initiatives such as the standardized coalition combat identification system.[9] Plug-and-play capabilities must now be expanded to provide broader interoperability solutions, including standardized organization, doctrine, procedures, and personnel management and training.[10]

Deployment Planning and Execution

Rapid and efficient deployment is critical to the success of expeditionary operations. Deployment planning and execution are a major challenge in both the joint and multinational communities. Shortfalls of acute strategic lift (transport aircraft and vessels) limit the speed and flexibility with which coalition forces can be deployed, resulting in reduced theater combat power at critical operational transitions. An ambitious global operations tempo further complicates coalition deployments and rotations, as concurrent operations compete for limited air- and sealift assets.

NATO, in particular, suffers from a strategic airlift dilemma. To overcome it, two complementary plans are being implemented. In the near term, the Strategic Airlift Interim Solution (SALIS)[11] is a multinational consortium that has chartered six Antonov An-124-100 transport aircraft to meet critical lift requirements for current operations in Afghanistan, for the October 2005 earthquake relief mission in Pakistan, and for airlift support to African Union peacekeepers in Darfur, Sudan. Civilian assets have historically played an important logistical role in military operations, but NATO has initiated revolutionary organizational and procedural adjustments to maximize incentives for national contributions to SALIS, which could serve as a template for future collaborative capabilities development and management.[12]

The longer-term solution is the development of an organic Strategic Airlift Capability (SAC). The SAC "will represent a quantum leap in [NATO's] strategic airlift capability," according to NATO's Secretary-General Jaap de Hoop Scheffer.[13] The intended fleet will consist of three C-17 Globemaster III transport aircraft, controlled, maintained, and operated by crews from fifteen contributing NATO and Partnership for Peace countries.[14] The C-17s will be configured to have the same capabilities as the US Air Force and UK

Royal Air Force fleets, notably night vision and air-to-air refueling. When planes are not assigned to NATO missions, the contributing nations may use them for national purposes, within their given flight hour allocations.[15]

The deployment planning and execution process must combine interdependent operational and logistical elements. The Joint Operation Planning and Execution System (JOPES) is a technologically enabled procedural solution that has been in incremental fielding for over fifteen years. Within JOPES, Time-Phased Force and Deployment Data (TPFDD) synchronization strives to link troop deployments with logistics support and intertheater movement. TPFDD provides inputs into the Global Command and Control System (GCCS). The GCCS offers commanders an integrated, nearly real-time picture of the battle space necessary to conduct joint and multinational operations.[16] The TPFDD data expand the GCCS capability by enhancing awareness of personnel and equipment accountability, tracking, and readiness status.[17]

Interestingly, the Operation Iraqi Freedom deployments largely ignored the potential of TPFDD in preference to a more ad hoc deployment mechanism, the Request for Forces (RFF) procedure. The RFF concept is intended to be more flexible and responsive to unfolding contingencies than TPFDD's deliberately planned deployments. Using the RFF, combatant commanders analyze needs and request force packages through the appropriate channels for allocation of specific units and military capabilities. Conversely, the TPFDD is one document with a preselected set of capabilities that initiate sequential deployment upon receipt of an execution order, regardless of the contingency's particulars.[18]

In the initial phases of Operation Iraqi Freedom, the RFF appeared to be a vastly superior deployment mechanism for contingency operations. The flexibility afforded by the RFF allowed the most effective active component combat forces to be rapidly amassed for a sweeping march on Baghdad. As major combat operations subsided, however, the transition to nation building and the deployment of ponderous and less-prepared reserve component combat support and service support forces were hampered by the lack of a thorough and deliberate long-term deployment plan and supporting infrastructure.[19] In fact, rapid RFF deployments eventually pushed combat forces beyond their logistical support networks, resulting in early fuel distribution problems, limited rations, medical supply issues, and ammunition shortages.[20]

Once the deployment of forces is under way, strategic planners of expeditionary campaigns must be able to respond quickly to fluid environmental conditions, especially during the transition from major combat operations to stability and reconstruction. The Joint Capabilities Requirements Tool

(JCRT)[21] is a promising joint-force projection prototype that potentially will enhance deployment decisionmaking by clarifying requests from the theater for capabilities. The JCRT integrated network allows operational planners to search a Web-based, automated inventory to rapidly identify available capabilities that will fulfill mission requirements, and thus accelerate joint deployment planning and execution.[22]

NATO is developing a complementary tool that will incorporate ally and partner capabilities options into the JCRT database. The Coalition Reception, Staging, and Onward Movement network is intended to work in concert with the JCRT to provide a standardized, integrated inventory of multinational capabilities. This inclusive approach promises a radical transformation away from largely unilateral power projection to incorporate significant coalition contributions into future expeditionary campaigns.[23]

Information Sharing

Before the advent of network technologies, information sharing and situational awareness were quickly compromised in the chaos of combat operations. Missions required constant active-voice communications and coordination to maintain awareness at all echelons and among commands in the field. Joint and coalition operations were generally compartmentalized and limited in scope due to problems with compatibility and interoperability. Network-enabled operations have exponentially improved the speed, accuracy, and efficiency of joint, multinational, and interagency information management and dissemination.[24]

The needs of the multinational campaign in Iraq have prompted the rapid fielding of innovative technologies to enhance coalition information management. In March 2005 the US Joint Forces Command Joint Experimentation Directorate (known as J-9) deployed an open-standards network portal to Multi-National Force–Iraq that allows coalition partners to access and share information throughout the theater, by facilitating the cross-domain communication of data between US and coalition networks. It is available through the Combined Enterprise Regional Information Exchange System, or CENTRIXS.[25] Because it is Web-based, access can be extended to soldiers operating throughout Iraq so they can work from a common operational and tactical picture.

Unfortunately, CENTRIXS's potential is largely limited to unclassified-information sharing with coalition partners, owing to both technological compatibility problems and complex security classification hierarchies. Nominally secure networks like CENTRIXS must be improved to filter multilevel classification systems in accordance with coalition information-sharing agreements, not default to unclassified correspondence as the lowest common communications medium. Multilevel network access could give individual users access to information available at their security level, regardless of the access limitations of other network users. Better CENTRIXS security filtering that leads to better classified information sharing will in turn significantly enhance coalition and interagency communications, trust, and cooperation.[26]

The international intelligence community will be effective only if it exploits the rapid changes taking place in the twenty-first-century information domain. The very real need for information security must be balanced with the opportunities that arise in an interconnected environment. We can assume that flexible and inclusive information-sharing networks will trump isolated information hierarchies to define information dominance in the years to come.

Common Operational and Tactical Picture

Computer technologies have enormously enhanced the capacity to manage, coordinate, and disseminate massive amounts of data, while the unprecedented availability of timely and accurate information has greatly affected the conduct of modern warfare. At this writing, information dominance on the battlefield requires nearly real-time common operational and tactical pictures that include friendly information (blue forces), enemy information (red forces), digitally communicated battlefield control measures, and maneuver, fires, and logistics monitoring.

The ability to broadcast information across the operational space and provide nearly real-time updates depends upon a network infrastructure that joint and coalition partners at all echelons must be able to access and understand. Networked situational awareness is prompting a paradigm shift from top-down leadership and platform-based warfare to more effective war-fighting methods characterized by "self-synchronization." Under this concept, joint combat forces can meet interdependent tactical and operational objectives by working from a common operating picture and clear understanding of the combatant commander's intent.[27] This capability allows diverse and possibly isolated units to support each other and achieve broad strategic goals without relying on centralized command and control.

Another benefit of a common operating picture is the opportunity to reorganize the military leadership structure into a functional "bottom-up" configuration. Bottom-up leadership supports the fundamental war-fighting principle of simplicity, since it allows leaders to break complex military operations into simple, interconnected tasks. A common tactical picture gives field commanders from platoon to brigade level the ability to control the tempo and seize ownership of the initiative. By expanding networks to the individual and platform level, systems such as Blue Force Tracking can instantaneously gather, organize, and disseminate tactical information across the battle space and among all echelons of command.

Systems like the BFTS can be further enhanced by synchronization with other systems, like the logistical Movement Tracking System and the Joint Surveillance Target and Attack Radar System, which use aerial radar, satellite tracking, and radio frequencies to track ground movement.[28] Future systems will include the Net-Enabled Command Capability being developed by the US Joint Forces Command; this is a Web-based system that will integrate multiple "families of systems" into one. Technologies like these, tailored to achieve a multinational common operational and tactical picture, will augment solutions to other problems, such as fratricide prevention, fires coordination, and unified command and control.[29]

Battlefield Synchronization

> The goal is to enable the soldiers to see first, understand first, act first and finish decisively.
>
> —*General Peter Schoomaker, US Army chief of staff*[30]

War is a lethal competition. The successful battlefield competitor is the one who is able to rapidly and decisively exploit opportunities while disrupting or eliminating the adversary's freedom of action. Traditionally, military leaders have applied "fires" to impose dominance, with the destruction of enemy fires capability as the primary measure of effectiveness. In this "attrition-based" methodology, maneuver was perceived as an enabling principle that supported fires to achieve initiative, surprise, and positional advantage.

The capabilities-based approach enhances the role of maneuver through the effective synchronization of intelligence, surveillance, and reconnaissance (ISR). Western "maneuver theory" measures military dominance in terms of control rather than destruction. Defense analyst William S. Lind visualized maneuver as a means "to break the spirit and will . . . by creating unexpected and unfavorable operational and strategic situations, not to kill enemy troops or destroy enemy equipment."[31] Success in Iraq and Afghanistan will ultimately be determined by long-term domestic and international perception as much as by military primacy. Using ISR, fires, and maneuver in an integrated fashion, commanders are able to control adversaries more efficiently, while minimizing the kinds of peripheral damage that are detrimental to such strategic aims as stability or nation building.

The transition to this new conduct of war depends on actionable operational awareness. Control is established across the dimensions of space and time. In Iraq, persistent ISR is critical to identify opportunities for decisive action. Persistent ISR is the "unblinking eye" that, combined with precise fires and agile maneuver, denies the enemy sanctuary and respite through continuous surveillance and engagement.

The goal of integrated ISR, fires, and maneuver is to enhance sensor-to-shooter efficiency. As of this writing, this goal has been met with only incremental success. A "grassroots" approach to integration currently prevails, which focuses on producing organic ISR capabilities at the tactical level. The US Army Stryker brigade model is an example of incremental integration, in which a greatly enhanced user-level intelligence collection capability is coupled with direct access to theater-level close-air support and precise indirect fires on a priority basis. Though more efficient than centrally located sensors, this interim approach has preferred increased sensor capability at the user level to true ISR interdependence. This solution requires refinement. The use of unmanned aerial vehicle (UAV) sensors is especially problematic. Commonly, both tactical and theater-level UAV assets redundantly cover the same areas, sharing airspace without mutual cognizance. Tactical commanders ideally should have direct network access to higher-echelon sensors in their battle space, rather than compensating with redundant systems of their own, but the existing hierarchical intelligence dissemination mechanisms are prohibitively stovepiped.[32] The long-term solution is to streamline ISR analysis and dissemination at the operational level with innovative network mechanisms. If tactical commanders are able directly and unobtrusively to access strategic and operational space- and air-based sensors, they can forego an inefficient and redundant sensor capability at the tactical level.

The next phase in integrated ISR, fires, and maneuver is to link battlefield commanders to the global information grid. One promising prototype for enhanced sensor-to-engagement nodal integration is the Virtual Mission Operations Center (VMOC). The VMOC is a Web-based, space-ground mission control network that allows tactical-level users to connect directly to intelligence sensors aboard space and airborne reconnaissance assets. The VMOC handles satellites and UAVs as individual Internet protocol addresses, allowing tactical engagement nodes in remote locations to conduct ISR vicariously via orbiting spacecraft directly through the Web, operating much like enhanced versions of commercially available software applications such as Google Earth. Systems like VMOC ideally will enable small-unit commanders to routinely observe and engage beyond-the-horizon targets, effectively rendering the tactical task of "movement to contact" obsolete.[33]

Military Operations in Urban Areas

> [The urban] environment is not only terrain. It's infrastructure, it's culture, it's governance, it's rule of law, it's legality, food, water, fire and safety and all of those things that make up a complex environment of a city.
>
> —*Dave Ozolek, Joint Futures Lab executive director, US Joint Forces Command*[34]

Operations in both Afghanistan and Iraq have exposed US and coalition forces to some of the fiercest urban fighting in recent history. Urban combat is likely to cause civilian casualties and destruction of civil infrastructure that can harm long-term strategic reconstruction and nation-building objectives. Western public information strategists struggle to manage public perceptions and sustain an aura of legitimacy while waging combat in civilian-dense urban areas. Meanwhile, coalition forces face an entrenched adversary who uses these civilians as shields and employs the global media effectively as a tool to proliferate its propaganda campaign.[35]

The transformation of urban combat revolves around two driving concepts. First is the understanding that the urban environment is a complex combination of restrictive and multidimensional terrain; cultural, political, and economic symbols; and critical infrastructure. This context leads to the second concept: a successful transition to stabilization and reconstruction missions depends on stable, intact population-dense nodes, from which local control will eventually be restored.[36]

Training for urban operations is an important risk mitigator in preparation for urban combat missions. The military success of coalition forces in the Baghdad and Fallujah offensives of 2003–2004 was due in large part to prior joint and service-specific urban operations training. The US Marines–sponsored annual exercise Joint Urban Warrior introduced concepts such as remote countersniper operations and precise indirect fire support that later proved their worth during the Fallujah offensives.[37]

Innovative technologies and techniques developed during urban warfare exercises led to improved command and control, tactical maneuver, security, and combined arms utilization in the Iraq urban offensives. For example, the use of UAVs enhanced situational awareness on the ground, while Interceptor body armor dramatically improved dismounted infantry survivability.[38] In order to reduce the destructive footprint of urban fighting, future technologies must continue to focus on less-than-lethal fires and precision engagement. Directed energy weapons, such as the Active Denial System,[39] and precise remote-engagement UAVs are finding increased applicability in dense urban environments.[40]

In Fallujah, advanced technology was combined with the innovative use of legacy capabilities, still remaining from past operations, to achieve devastating effects on the enemy. The effective use of M1 Abrams tanks and M2 Bradley Fighting Vehicles in city streets increased the survivability of troops, enhanced lethality, and heightened the shock effect. In the air, A-10 Warthogs and Apache helicopters provided precise, close-air support, limiting damage to the urban infrastructure. Last, units at the lower tactical level capitalized on their experiences in training to better move, shoot, and communicate in an enclosed environment. Dispersed dismounted formations were networked to fire systems that allowed remote engagement using multiple methods, and maneuvered alongside armored vehicles on the ground for improved survivability and direct firepower.[41] The future of military operations in built-up areas is likely to be shaped by the marriage of enabling technologies and innovative tactics, combined with a better understanding of the civil and economic dimensions of the urban battlefield.

Joint and Multinational Training

> My aunt thinks that "jointness" is an arthritic condition. I hope it will become known as just the opposite.
>
> —*Admiral E. P. Giambastiani, US Navy*[42]

Joint and multinational operations have become the norm for militaries that face complex twenty-first-century global security threats. Multilateral and integrated engagement offers its participants legitimacy, enhanced capabilities, and a unified strategy for overcoming common adversaries. Military and defense leaders around the world understand the need for improved jointness and interdependence to ensure collective security. These essential characteristics can be developed only through robust and realistic joint training, which in turn can contribute lessons learned in a simulated environment that does not put the most valuable joint asset—the war fighter—at risk.

The Joint National Training Capability (JNTC) is the primary mechanism in the US military for improving joint military training. Its purpose is to provide realistic combat training against an adaptive and credible opposing force in a plausible operating environment. The JNTC promotes joint networking with compatible real-time information that is made accessible to a wide range of participants and partners. Through the JNTC, service and joint training centers such as the National Training Center and Joint Multinational Readiness Center are now being linked to command headquarters, multinational training sites, and research facilities, in an effort to transform joint and multinational training from what has been a series of isolated events into a certified, program-driven model of continuous training. This eventually will include an array of standardized and accredited training programs and sites, with the goal of establishing a consistent and collaborative training network.[43]

JNTC uses the joint training and experimentation network (JTEN) for reliable, worldwide voice, video, and data transmissions. The JTEN, for example, was connected to the Australian Defense Training and Experimentation Network for Exercise Talisman Saber 2007; this allowed the tactical forces to take advantage of manned simulators and sophisticated computer models.[44] The ability to connect live, virtual, and constructive simulations to joint and multinational command exercises via the joint training and experimentation network can improve the efficiency of training programs, offer an impressive level of realism, and provide more opportunities for operational-level training.[45]

Joint training is fraught with difficulties that require deliberate planning and preparation to overcome. Effective training requires all participants to contribute significant amounts of personnel, time, and shared resources. Although increasing global commitments to the war on terrorism are making it more difficult for aspiring participants to conduct vigorous and complex joint training exercises, joint and multinational training is imperative for successful, ongoing transformation. Coalitions must collectively determine their essential training requirements, and cooperate to balance training with competing operational needs.

The success of joint training is measured by the development of effective, universally applicable solutions that share a common set of tasks, conditions, and standards. Integrated training exercises should (1) identify doctrinal shortcomings, (2) develop effective tactics and techniques, and (3) assist in determining joint capabilities requirements. The US Joint Staff's Universal Joint Task List (UJTL) is one mechanism for establishing a common language to standardize approaches to training.

The UJTL identifies those strategic/theater, operational, and tactical joint tasks needed for successful integrated operations.[46] It classifies the operational environment in terms of conditions—physical, military, and civil (i.e., politics, the economy, and culture). Finally, the UJTL offers measurable standards for proficiency and effectiveness. The combination of universal tasks, conditions, and standards gives commands better tools to assess unit proficiency, identify capabilities shortfalls, and focus future training and resource allocations where they are most needed and likely to be most effective.

Joint training allows war fighters to become familiar with the joint operational environment before they are assigned to joint missions. Through joint training, leaders are introduced to critical joint capabilities that they will be expected to use responsibly, effectively, and collaboratively with their intercomponent and coalition counterparts on the battlefield.

Civil-Military Cooperation and Interagency Integration

> History has shown us over and over again that when we wait until we get on the ground to try to develop a joined-up strategy it's a little too late for an optimum outcome.
>
> —*Barbara Stephenson, director for planning, Office of the Coordinator for Reconstruction and Stabilization, US Department of State*[47]

Strategic engagement over all the dimensions of human and national security includes a diverse array of stakeholders. Due to growing global instability, there is an ever greater need for developmental, civil assistance, and humanitarian relief organizations to alleviate human suffering. Cooperation among national and international agencies, indigenous organizations, nongovernmental organizations (NGOs), international and private voluntary organizations (IVOs/PVOs), and coalition forces lends legitimacy to the military's involvement in nation building at the same time that it provides essential security for humanitarian operations.[48]

Military victories do not of themselves lead to successful nation-building at the diplomatic, economic, and security levels. Military operations are conducted to achieve effects that support a comprehensive approach of diplomacy, economic assistance, and civic engagement. The immediate goal of stability operations is to provide the local populace with security, restore essential services, and meet humanitarian needs. The military relies on civilian support to help establish order that in turn advances military interests and objectives. Ideally, the establishment of a secure environment will allow operational control to be turned over to an autonomous, stable government capable of providing essential services, a viable market economy, rule of law, democratic institutions, and a robust civil society. Many nation-building tasks are most appropriately and efficiently accomplished by host nation, foreign, or civilian professionals. Military forces should be prepared to perform all tasks necessary to establish or maintain order in support of civilian agencies and organizations engaged in nation building.[49] This civil-military cooperation is an essential component in "hearts and minds" campaigns, where earning the trust and support of the local communities is as important as military dominance to the security of the operational space.

To facilitate successful interagency operations, the roles and relationships among various national agencies, military commands, regional and local governments, country teams, and engaged organizations must be clearly understood by all actors. Provincial Reconstruction Teams (PRTs) and their local-level counterparts, Embedded Provincial Reconstruction Teams, are the emerging organizational model for civil-military integration. PRTs serve as the meeting place for military forces, government agencies, civilian authorities, international and regional organizations, NGOs and PVOs, and the local population. Although the PRT commander is a military leader, it is in the interests of the military to coordinate a team approach to problem resolution in preference to authoritative command. Since PRT commanders cannot compel interagency cooperation, they may leverage military resources and capabilities such as protection, logistic support, information, and communications networks that are frequently sought by nonmilitary agencies, and may facilitate interagency collaboration.

The NATO-led International Security Assistance Force in Afghanistan is a proving ground for the PRT concept. British forces, for example, have taken an "Afghans first" approach in their attempts to secure Helmand Province: local Afghan police and army troops are the first line of civil security, while British forces serve in a supporting role to enhance local capabilities and create an environment where the civilian populace places more trust in local law enforcement and the military. Meanwhile, an Estonian government agency provides equipment to local hospitals, and Afghani national contractors repair long-neglected roads and bridges.[50]

The PRT model is certainly encouraging, but in the contentious and hostile arenas of Afghanistan's remote provinces, it can be effective only under the protective umbrella of potent military security. Taliban offensives continue to dilute the success of PRT operations in Helmand and highlight the importance of multinational military commitments to establish stable environmental conditions for effective reconstruction activities, while respecting host nation autonomy to the extent possible.[51]

Building Cultural Skills

> We need to be able to understand the non-military advantage, to read intentions, to build trust, to convert opinions, to manage perceptions—all

> tasks that demand an exceptional ability to understand people, their culture and their motivation.
>
> —*Major General (retired) Robert Scales, US Army*[52]

The British approach in Helmand has met with some success, but the PRT still struggles against entrenched insurgents to win over Afghan civilians. Part of the problem lies with a fundamental misunderstanding of Afghan culture. This is a frequent problem for military units involved in humanitarian or reconstruction operations. These "soft" missions require significant and unfamiliar interactions with the affected civilian populace. Simply put, soldiers and commanders routinely deploy to stability operations without the requisite cultural skill sets—understanding of language, history, taboos, and traditions.

Prior to deployment to Operation Iraqi Freedom, soldiers in the 4th Infantry Division received almost no focused cultural-awareness training. Unit commanders and staff attempted a rudimentary overview of the Iraqi culture. The most basic admonishments—"don't display the soles of your feet" and "don't make eye contact with Iraqi women"—too often served as the extent of the army's cultural-awareness training.[53] Not surprisingly, when the infantry soldiers applied their combat training to their interactions with Iraqi civilians, the effects were less than optimal. Forceful detainee-handling procedures, destructive building-clearing tactics, and aggressive combat patrols created an aura of hostile martial law in the eyes of noncombatant Iraqis, which in turn fed the recruiting and propaganda agendas of the insurgency.[54]

Based in large part on lessons learned in Iraq and Afghanistan, cultural-awareness education and training has emerged as a critical part of defense transformation for the twenty-first-century war fighter. In an era when skeptical domestic constituents have direct access to global media, the actions of junior soldiers and leaders can have strategic implications. Warriors of this century must be able rapidly to distinguish friend from foe, respect and understand unfamiliar social hierarchies and traditions, and make on-the-spot tactical decisions under the unforgiving scrutiny of a camera lens. Future cultural-awareness training must reflect these realities and equip soldiers with the tools of the "warrior-diplomat," whose individual actions shape local conditions and influence global perceptions.[55]

Logistics Support in Limited-Access Environments

Extended expeditionary operations are a tremendous logistical challenge and can profoundly stress an already fragile postcombat indigenous infrastructure. In Iraq and Afghanistan, military forces are dependent on regional resources for basic life-support needs such as clean water, sanitation services, food, and building materials. This level of reliance poses obvious tactical risks. The threat to locally provided logistical support is magnified in the sort of hostile security environment and complex terrain common to Afghanistan and Iraq. Successful expeditionary logistics depends on a robust security commitment and the development of a healthy interdependence between military forces and indigenous support.

Prior to the onset of extended expeditionary operations, campaign planners must carefully consider alternatives for the provision of critical force sustenance. Strategic planners must procure the use of potential local facilities for life support, seaports, airfields, and communications networks while being careful to minimize disruptions to critical local infrastructure. Otherwise, they risk compromising concurrent political, economic, and civil endeavors in the operational space. Establishing a cooperative relationship with indigenous providers allows the military to embrace a comprehensive strategy for engagement in the reconstruction and nation-building phases of operations. When it is able to, the host nation assumes increased responsibility for power production, air and ground transport, and logistics security. Local providers benefit from the economic influx, and often increase security cooperation with military units to create a safe and stable work environment. Furthermore, by taking advantage of the logistical assets internal to the host country, organic supplies can be re-allocated for use in austere operating areas or crisis response.

In hostile or complex terrain, forward-deployed units may not be able to rely on local logistical support. In limited-access environments, Sense and Respond Logistics is an important transformational component of the modular deployment concept. Sense and Respond Logistics enables joint operations in austere terrain by mobilizing support "on demand" via an interconnected logistics network. It is a dynamic approach intended to maximize speed of delivery, flexibility, and efficiency for the battlefield commander. Networked systems provide a common logistical awareness that identifies and exploits all potential logistical support nodes, which can include a variety of nontraditional sources. Existing supply chains, for instance, can be augmented by consumer-to-consumer exchanges, in-transit emergency re-allocations, locally available suppliers, and even captured enemy resources, to provide commanders with unprecedented logistical flexibility that can be directly incorporated into operational planning.[56]

The Sense and Respond methodology is under incremental improvement to provide more proactive and cooperative logistics support. Anticipatory capabilities that are networked across logistics, intelligence, and operational domains will be essential to the support of future military operations. The incorporation of logistics into networked collaborative planning will help make decisionmaking more fluid and will improve distributed operations.[57]

Conclusion

Transformation is a demand-driven enterprise. Promising concepts as well as capabilities requirements frequently derive from pressing issues in the field. Since military leaders are the primary conduits for collecting lessons learned, they must have a basic understanding of transformational principles.

Technology and the effects of globalization have changed the character of war, but not its fundamental nature. Many of the lessons of Iraq and Afghanistan reflect historical challenges that are hardly unique to twenty-first-century adversaries; enhanced battlefield awareness, interaction with local populations, and the sustained deployment of expeditionary troops were as applicable to the Roman legions and Mongol hordes as they are to this century's campaign planners. Just as war fighters must embrace the tenets of transformation, those who are planning and implementing transformation must address the capabilities shortfalls of the commanders in the field.

A comprehensive transformational approach incorporates battlefield experiences to identify capabilities requirements and validate transformation priorities. Many emerging prototypes may falter in the heat of battle or prove unresponsive to the fluid conditions of conflict in this century. Certainly, every solution posited in this chapter will undergo incremental improvement or fade to obsolescence, but the force attributes they enable—expeditionary, networked, interoperable, and knowledge empowered—are enduring, and will determine the preeminent players on tomorrow's geopolitical map.

Notes

1. John Martin Carroll and Colin F. Baxter, *The American Military Tradition: From Colonial Times to the Present* (Lanham, Maryland: Rowman and Littlefield, 2007), 301.

2. "Backgrounder: Interoperability for Joint Operations," NATO online library, July 2006, http://www.nato.int/docu/home.htm#theme.

3. NATO Glossary of Terms and Definitions, http://www.dtic.mil/doctrine/jel/other_pubs/aap_6_02.pdf.

4. David A. Griffith, "Coalition Airspace Management and De-Confliction," White Paper, available at http://www.dodccrp.org/events/11th_ICCRTS/html/papers/094.pdf.

5. "Blue Force Tracking (BFT) Battle Management System," *Defense Update: International Online Defense Magazine,* no. 3 (2005), http://www.defense-update.com/products/b/BFT.htm.

6. Lieutenant Colonel Joe Chacon et al., "Final Minutes and Report of Friendly Force Tracking Interoperability Workshop," Allied Command Transformation, Brunssum, Netherlands, 10–12 October 2007, http://transnet.act.nato.int/WISE/FriendlyFo/FFTCurrent/FFTInterop/file/_WFS/FFT%20Interoperability%20Workshop%20Report%20v1.0.doc.

7. Lieutenant Colonel Joe Chacon, Allied Command Transformation, "NATO Friendly Force Tracking (FFT) Capability Development Case Study," presentation to the International Defense Transformation course, Monterey, California, 4 November 2008: 18–24.

8. Jeffrey P. Bialos and Stuart L. Koehl, "The NATO Response Force: Facilitating Coalition Warfare Through Technology Transfer and Information Sharing" (Washington, DC: Center for Technology and National Security Policy, National Defense University, 2005), 60.

9. Andrew Orillion, "Bold Quest 07 Begins to Test Coalition Combat ID," US Joint Forces Command news release, Norfolk, Virginia, 6 September 2007, http://www.jfcom.mil/newslink/storyarchive/2007/pa090607.htm.

10. Eric Larson Gustav Lindstrom et al., "Interoperability of US and NATO Allied Air Forces: Supporting Data and Case Studies," case study prepared for the US Air Force (Santa Monica: RAND Corporation, 2003): v–ix.

11. David Pratt et al., "Strategic Airlift Interim Solution (SALIS) MOU" [short title], signed 28 June 2004 in Instanbul by the defense ministers of Canada, the Czech Republic, Denmark, France, Germany, Hungary, Luxembourg, the Netherlands, Norway, Poland, Portugal, Slovak Republic, Slovenia, Spain, and Turkey.

12. Zbyšek Korecki and Martin Rejzek, "Strategic and Operational Mobility for the Czech Armed Forces," *Rusi Defence Systems: Military Operations Today* (October 2007): 107–109, http://www.rusi.org/downloads/assets/Korecki_and_Rejzek_0207_RDS.pdf.

13. Jaap de Hoop Scheffer, secretary-general, NATO, welcoming remarks at the NATO Summit in Riga, Latvia, 27 November 2006, text and audio recordings available at http://www.nato.int/docu/comm/2006/0611-riga/index.htm.

14. Denise Hammick, "Finland Agrees to Join NATO SAC Globemaster Programme," *Jane's Defence Weekly,* 2 April 2008: 15, http://jdw.janes.com.

15. "SALIS' Sibling: NATO's C-17 Pool Inaugurates In-House Heavy Lift," *Defense Industry Daily* online, 8 April 2008, http://www.defenseindustrydaily.com/salis-sibling-natos-c17-pool-inaugurates-inhouse-heavy-lift-02630/.

16. Defense Information Systems Agency fact sheet, "Global Command and Control System—Joint," Defense Knowledge Online, http://www.disa.mil/news/pressresources/factsheets/gccsj3.htm.

17. Office of the Joint Chiefs of Staff, "Joint Deployment and Redeployment Operations," United States Armed Forces Joint Publication 3-35, 1999.

18. Major Brian M. Newberry, US Air Force, "To TPFDD or Not to TPFDD: Is the TPFDD Outdated for Expeditionary US Military Operations?" School of Advanced Military Studies, United States Army Command and General Staff College, Fort Leavenworth, Kansas, 26 May 2005: 15–35.

19. Mark F. Cancian and Paul V. Kane, "Marine Corps Reserve Forces in Operation IRAQI FREEDOM," *Marine Corps Gazette* 88, no. 7 (July 2004): 50–57.

20. Gregory Fontenot, E. J. Degen, and David Tohn, *On Point* (Fort Leavenworth, Kansas: Combat Studies Institute Press, 2004), 408–409.

21. Nate Allerheiligen, "Command Examines Advanced Technology Demonstration," press release from the US Joint Forces Command, US Department of Defense, Suffolk, Virginia, 13 January 2006, http://www.defenselink mil/transformation/articles/2006-01/ta011306a.html.

22. Rita Boland, "Keeping Track of the Troops," *Signal* 62, no. 3 (November 2007): 37–42.

23. Ibid.

24. T. Buckman, "NATO Network-Enabled Capability Feasibility Study," NATO Consultation, Command, and Control Agency, The Hague, October 2005.

25. Cheryl Lilie, "Iraqi Portal Breaks Coalition Information Barriers," *Signal* 60, no. 12 (August 2005): 53.

26. Richard Chait et al., "A Further Look at Technologies and Capabilities for Stabilization and Reconstruction Operations," Center for Technology and National Security Policy, National Defense University, September 2007: 36–37, http://www.ndu.edu/CTNSP/Def_Tech/DTP%2043%20SROII.pdf.

27. David S. Alberts, John J. Garstka, and Frederick P. Stein, *Network-Centric Warfare: Developing and Leveraging Information Superiority,* 2nd ed. (revised), DoD C4ISR Cooperative Research Program, Washington, DC, 1999: 71–75.

28. Timothy L. Rider, "Blue Force Tracking to Expand Across Force," *Army AL&T* (September–October 2004): 2–5.

29. Kris Osborn, "'Battle Command' Summits: US Army Brings Experts Together for IT Roadmap," *Defense News,* 4 February 2008, http://www.defensenews.com/story.php?i=3329623.

30. General Peter J. Schoomaker, US Army, speech to conference of the Association of the United States Army, Washington Convention Center, Washington, DC, 10 October 2006, http://www.ausa.org/am2006/schoomaker.pdf.

31. William S. Lind, *Maneuver Warfare Handbook* (Boulder: Westview, 1999), 18.

32. Defense Science Board, Office of the Under Secretary of Defense for Acquisition, Technology, and Logistics, "Report of the Defense Science Board Task Force on Integrated Fire Support in the Battlespace," October 2004: 41–46.

33. Eric Miller et al., "Virtual Mission Operations Center (VMOC) Development and Experimentation," 5th Responsive Space Conference white paper, Los Angeles, April 2007, http://www.responsivespace.com/papers/rs5%5csession%20papers%5csession%206%5c6001_miller%5c6001p.pdf.

34. Quoted in Jim Garamone, "Command's Experiment Bringing Focus to Urban Challenges," American Forces Press Service, 19 October 2006, http://www.jfcom.mil/newslink/storyarchive/2006/no101906a.html.

35. P. M. Taylor, "Perception Management and the 'War' Against Terrorism,"

Journal of Information Warfare 1, no. 3 (2002): 16–29, www.terrorismresearch.net/docs/taylor.pdf.

36. US Department of Defense, "Joint Urban Operations: Joint Integrating Concept, Version 1.0," 23 July 2007: iii–iv, 18–23, http://www.dtic.mil/future jointwarfare/concepts/juo_jic_v1.pdf.

37. Gary W. Anderson, "Fallujah and the Future of Urban Operations," *Marine Corps Gazette* (November 2004): 52–58.

38. Interceptor Multi-Threat Body Armor System. For more information, see http://www.globalsecurity.org/military/systems/ground/interceptor.htm.

39. Jason Sherman, "Pentagon Considering Sending Non-Lethal Ray Gun to Iraq," *Inside Defense,* 5 March 2007, www.insidedefense.com.

40. David Eshel, "Think Fast: Technology Closes the Gap Between Sensors and Shooters," *Aviation Week* 2, no. 2 (March 2008): 14–15, http://www.nxtbook.com/nxtbooks/aw/dti0308/.

41. Rebecca Grant, "The Fallujah Model," *Air Force Magazine* (online) 88, no. 2 (February 2005), http://www.afa.org/magazine/feb2005/0205fallujah.html.

42. Admiral E. P. Giambastiani, US Navy, former commander, US Joint Forces Command, "Born Joint?," remarks at the Armed Forces Communications and Electronics Association West conference, San Diego, 4 February 2004, http://www.jfcom.mil/newslink/storyarchive/2004/sp021004.htm.

43. Jennifer Colaizzi, "Training Transformation Overhaul Moving Ahead," US Joint Forces Command press release, 13 October 2005, http://www.jfcom.mil/newslink/storyarchive/2005/pa101305.htm.

44. Chris Hoffpauir, "USJFCOM Gets Approval to Connect U.S., Australian Networks," US Joint Forces Command press release, 21 December 2006, http://www.jfcom.mil/newslink/storyarchive/2006/pa122106.html.

45. Chris Hoffpauir, "USJFCOM Continues to Improve Joint National Training Capability," US Joint Force Command press release, 10 April 2007, http://www.jfcom.mil/newslink/storyarchive/2007/pa041007.html.

46. "Universal Joint Task List (UJTL)," Chairman of the Joint Chiefs of Staff Manual (CJCSM) 3500.04D, Change 1, 15 September 2006, http://www.dtic.mil/cjcs_directives/cdata/unlimit/m350004.pdf.

47. Barbara Stephenson, director for planning, Office of the Coordinator for Reconstruction and Stabilization, US Department of State, remarks at the Media Roundtable for Multinational Experiment Four, Norfolk, Virginia, 13 February 2006, http://www.jfcom.mil/.

48. Patrick N. Kelleher, "Crossing Boundaries: Interagency Cooperation and the Military," *Joint Forces Quarterly* 32 (Autumn 2002): 104–110, http://www.dtic.mil/doctrine/jel/jfq_pubs/1932.pdf.

49. Karen Guttieri, "The Civil Dimension of Strategy," in Obiora Chinedu Okafor and Obijiofor Aginam, eds., *Humanizing Our Global Order* (Toronto: University of Toronto Press, 2003), 89.

50. Declan Walsh, "NATO Faces Its Most Perilous Mission in Afghanistan," *Boston Globe,* 11 June 2006, http://www.boston.com.

51. Ahto Lobjakas, "NATO Struggles with Security, Rebuilding in Helmand," *Radio Free Europe/Radio Liberty,* 7 February 2007, http://www.rferl.org/features article/2007/02/c315df0b-a563-455e-b8be-c69b2ec43d82.html.

52. Quoted in Stephen Hedges, "Military Voices Say Blame Isn't All on Civilians," *Chicago Tribune,* 15 August 2004, Perspectives section: 2.

53. Center for Army Lessons Learned Initial Impressions Report No. 04-13, May 2004: 39–41, http://www.globalsecurity.org/military/library/report/call/.

54. Thomas E. Ricks, "It Looked Weird and Felt Wrong," *Washington Post,* 24 July 2006: A1.

55. Egdunas Racius, "The 'Cultural Awareness' Factor in the Activities of the Lithuanian PRT in Afghanistan," *Baltic Security and Defence Review* 9 (May 2007): 57–75.

56. US Office of Force Transformation, Department of Defense, "Operational Sense and Respond Logistics: Co-evolution of an Adaptive Enterprise Capability," concept document, 17 November 2003.

57. Keith Aliberti and Thomas L. Bruen, "Prediction and Cooperation," *Army Logistician* 39, no. 1 (January–February 2007).

Part 2

Implementing Transformation

6

Collective Solution Guidelines

Kelly L. Mayes and Scott Graham

The tremendous potential of defense transformation can be realized only through a collective approach to the execution of joint concept development and experimentation. This chapter will address the need for such an approach in support of transformation, describing the methods through which it should be implemented.

The chapter will first discuss the three key elements of a capabilities-based approach and their critical interactions: joint concepts, joint capabilities, and joint experimentation. After discussing the theory behind the particular role of joint experimentation in transformation, the chapter will describe the reality of joint experimentation in the United States Department of Defense (DoD) and highlight key issues with the current approach. These issues have led some to question the utility of joint experimentation as it relates to capability development.

The chapter will propose a solution that uses a collective approach to develop and execute a DoD-wide Joint Concept Development and Experimentation (JCD&E) Campaign plan. The advantages of this proposal are shared situational awareness, informed decisionmaking, and a deliberate planning process, which will enable leaders at all levels to make better-informed decisions. The chapter concludes by describing the processes and elements required to develop and execute the JCD&E Campaign plan that promotes a collective approach to transformation.

Joint Concept Development and Experimentation Environment

> Eleven years after the Cold War, we are in a time of transition and testing. . . . We're witnessing a revolution in the technology of war. . . . The best way to keep the peace is to redefine war on our terms.
>
> —*President George W. Bush, 13 February 2001*[1]

With these words the president of the United States launched the Department of Defense on the path toward transformation. Key to transformation was a move away from the prevailing threat-based model for the development of defense capabilities toward one that took advantage of the perceived "peace dividend" resulting from the end of the Cold War. This new model focuses on acquiring a broad array of capabilities that would position the United States to deal with any adversary. It is a deliberate means to develop a broad portfolio of defense capabilities that will better enable the United States to operate in an uncertain world of unipolarity, global connectivity, failed or failing states, and a host of technologically empowered groups and individuals with the means to cause tremendous destruction.

The Theory

Three essential and interdependent processes underpin capabilities-based transformation: joint concepts development, joint capabilities development, and joint experimentation. Joint concepts development, led by the Joint Staff J7, a subdivision of the Joint Chiefs of Staff, lays the informed intellectual foundation for how the joint forces will conduct operations eight to twenty years in the future, and identifies the capabilities required to execute these concepts.[2] Joint capabilities development, led by the Joint Staff J8, informs DoD investment decisions by identifying potential solutions to existing gaps in the capabilities required to execute the concepts.[3]

Joint experimentation, with the commander of the United States Joint Forces Command (USJFCOM) as the executive agent, enables both joint concepts and joint capabilities development by fostering the co-evolution of new concepts, processes, organizations, doctrine, and technologies for both current and future joint operations.[4] This experimentation is conducted in an open, transparent environment where lives are not placed at risk, competition among potential capability solutions is encouraged, and failure is an acceptable outcome. Joint experimentation and assessment is designed to evaluate concepts, compare alternative solutions, and provide observations, insights, and actionable recommendations to senior decisionmakers so that they can determine which concepts and proposals are feasible, and establish measures of effectiveness for the desired capabilities.

Joint concepts and joint capabilities developed through fully integrated joint experimentation have the potential to radically and rapidly enhance the Department of Defense's ability to deal with the uncertain security environment it faces in the early 2000s and for the foreseeable future. In theory, the interaction of joint concepts development, joint capabilities development, and joint experimentation enables informed transformational change. That is the theory, but what is the reality?

The Reality

As of this writing, some individuals both inside and outside the DoD are questioning how serious the Department is about transformation, and the utility of and necessity for joint experimentation in general. While there has been a tremendous amount of experimentation activity over nearly a decade, it is hard to measure directly the contribution joint experimentation has made to the development of a particular new joint concept or the procurement of improved joint capabilities to enable those concepts. Joint experimentation efforts to date may be best described as lots of activity with limited productivity.[5] This perceived lack of productivity and the uncertainty about the utility of experimentation are due to several factors. First, while in theory the three foundations for transformation—joint concepts development, joint capabilities development, and joint experimentation—are mutually supportive and interconnected, the reality is that they are independent activities, each with its own governance, planning horizons, communities of interests, and procedures.

Second, there is no joint experimentation program; that is, there is no collective approach to improving current and future capabilities through experimentation. There are instead numerous experimental programs across separate organizations, each of which identifies its own priorities for concepts development, capabilities development, and experimentation.[6] See, for instance, Chapter 11 in this volume, on experimentation within the US Pacific Command. This lack of a DoD-wide experimentation plan to support joint concepts and capabilities development creates inefficiencies by precluding collaboration, creating unintended competition for scarce experimentation resources, duplicating solutions, not sharing situational awareness of joint experimentation activities, and preventing senior leaders from making informed decisions and judging the risks of transformational efforts.

Third, joint experimentation is not fully integrated with other DoD systems and processes. To ensure joint experimentation is both useful and productive in leading transformation, it must, by policy and necessity, be guided and influenced by other formal DoD systems and processes, such as the Joint Operations Concepts Development Process, the Joint Capabilities Integration and Development System, and the Joint Strategic Planning System.[7] Only by informing and being informed by these other DoD systems and processes can the need, utility, and value of experimentation be articulated in the form of measurable productivity.

Last, joint experimentation has been seen as an end in itself. The focus has been on the conduct of the experiment rather than on how well the experiment addresses the advancement of a joint concept or the development of a joint capability. To the contrary, the logical path must be from joint concept to joint capability through joint experimentation. Only by ensuring that these three essential elements of transformation are fully integrated can the DoD create the analytical rigor required to inform and accomplish its transformation efforts. This focus on the conduct of the experiment and not the design is one of the main reasons the DoD has been unable to assess the utility of joint experimentation.[8]

How can joint experimentation move from lots of individual activity to synchronized, integrated productivity that will enable the rapid development of relevant concepts and their associated required capabilities? More important, how do senior leaders acquire the shared situational awareness of DoD-wide joint experimentation efforts that will allow them to make informed decisions concerning transformation?

The Solution

The answer to the above questions lies in the development and execution of a JCD&E Campaign plan that establishes a Department of Defense–wide set of prioritized problems to be solved through experimentation.[9] A well-designed JCD&E Campaign plan will establish a cohesive Joint Concept Development and Experimentation environment, and promote collective action on joint, service, multinational, and interagency problems; potential solutions; and experiments. A JCD&E Campaign plan that synchronizes all experimentation and is fully integrated with other DoD systems and processes will establish a continuous, repeatable template and form the basis for transformation efforts. This ensures transparency of joint experimentation activities and, for the first time, enables senior leaders to make informed decisions and assess risks associated with transformation.

The JCD&E Campaign plan must include all the various DoD and non-DoD organizations involved in joint concepts development, joint capabilities development, and joint experimentation. The plan establishes a set of prioritized problems to be solved through experimentation. It identifies the widest set of potential capability solutions (or the lack of solutions) for each, and it promotes shared situational awareness of all experimental activities across the DoD to ensure the conduct and results of joint experimentation will be integrated with other DoD systems.[10]

Only a JCD&E Campaign plan that is developed, executed, and assessed using a collective approach can make joint experimentation relevant to transformation, bring order to the present chaos, and move joint experimentation from individual activity to collective productivity.

Joint Concept Development and Experimentation Campaign Plan

JCD&E Campaign plan encompasses a broad concept of operations that sequences a series of related joint operations or events, provides strategic direction and focus or objectives, achieves unity of effort, provides an orderly schedule of decisions and events, designates command relationships, and defines what constitutes success.[11]

The JCD&E Campaign plan brings a collective approach to joint experimentation to better coordinate and sequence the vast amount of experimentation activities across the Department of Defense, more rapidly develop joint concepts and joint capabilities, and thus strengthen the effectiveness of the joint force commander in the field. The JCD&E Campaign plan utilizes transparency, collaboration, vigorous debate, continuous refinement, prototyping, and experimentation to develop actionable recommendations for senior leaders concerning current and future program, budget, experimentation, and joint force investment decisions. The primary goals of the JCD&E Campaign plan process are twofold: (1) to develop and update a three-year plan that guides and synchronizes joint experimentation efforts, and (2) to assess periodically the progress of joint experimentation and the value of its results and recommendations.[12] While JCD&E Campaign plan development follows an annual cycle, the plan is continually refined to ensure its outputs are useful to the joint force commander.

JCD&E Enterprise

> Potential key enablers for tomorrow's joint task force commanders are exposed to experimentation techniques that range from workshops, to limited objective experiments, to complex events conducted within a sophisticated virtual environment that spans the globe.
>
> —*Rear Admiral James A. Winnefeld Jr., US Navy director for Joint Forces Experimentation, US Joint Forces Command*[13]

Experimentation in support of joint concepts and joint capabilities development must address several levels of complexity. First, it must be able to encompass the temporal nature of current and future security challenges. Second, it must address the experimentation needs of multiple customers: the armed services with their force development mission, the combatant commanders with their geographic and functional operational missions, the Joint Staff with their budgetary and doctrinal requirements, and senior civilian leaders with their oversight responsibilities. Joint experimentation must also be able to examine capabilities as they relate not only to matériel but also to doctrine, organization, training, processes, authorities, and culture.

Managing this complexity requires a collective approach, hereafter described as the JCD&E Enterprise, to the design, assessment, and execution of a JCD&E Campaign plan that promotes transformation. The term *enterprise* has been adopted by the joint experimentation community because it conveys a sense of synergy that is achieved when the physical, information, financial, and knowledge networks supporting joint experimentation are purposely designed and maintained to work cooperatively on complex activities. The JCD&E Enterprise plays a pivotal role in the accomplishment of tasks detailed in applicable strategic guidance regarding joint experimentation.[14]

This enterprise model ensures that all participants will be equally aware of joint concepts development, capabilities development, and experimentation activities across the DoD and non-DoD, as well as multinational organizations. JCD&E is the forum in which the combatant commanders, services, Joint Staff, Office of the Secretary of Defense, DoD agencies, allies, and other partners determine joint experimentation priorities and form joint experimentation teams to explore, investigate, and test capability solutions. It also provides a medium through which to engage civilian academia, military war colleges, and federally funded research and development centers like the RAND Corporation.[15]

Additionally, an enterprise or collective structure enables developed capabilities to move rapidly into the hands of the users by soliciting early agreement among participants on what challenge is being addressed, what capability is proposed to solve that challenge, and which organization will own the program of record for that capability. This collective approach is critical to the exchange of experiment information and knowledge among JCD&E members, and underpins and enables the development and execution of the JCD&E Campaign plan. Without the JCD&E Enterprise model, there is no joint experimentation plan; there is only individual organizational experimentation with no synergy, no metrics, and no focus—in other words, lots of activity and no productivity.

JCD&E Campaign Plan Process

The JCD&E Enterprise uses a six-step process to design, execute, and assess the JCD&E Campaign plan (see Figure 6.1).[16] While they appear sequential, these steps in reality are being executed simultaneously, with a change to one affecting all of the others. Such a dynamic plan demands cooperation among participants, backed by an interactive automated decision support tool and a collective management model.

Early on in the development of the JCD&E Campaign plan, a transition manager should be appointed to serve with the experimentation designer. The transition manager is charged with assessing the maturity of the potential solution and determining the type of experimentation required, as well as what tools are needed to get the solution to the next step in its development. The transition manager must also be empowered to kill any further experimentation if it is determined the solution will never work.[17]

Step 1: Collect the challenges. Before any joint experiment is either scheduled or executed, we must first understand the problem we are trying to solve. The first step the JCD&E Enterprise undertakes in the development of the JCD&E Campaign Plan is to identify what are called war-fighter challenges (WFCs). A WFC is a specific statement of what the DoD does not know how to do or have the capability to do to accomplish currently assigned or projected missions. A virtually unlimited number of WFCs are collected from all the enterprise members, both DoD and non-DoD, and can be either current or futuristic. The JCD&E Enterprise uses the results of previous joint experimentation, lessons learned from ongoing experiments and operations, and the identified capability requirements from developing joint concepts as just a few of the inputs for identifying WFCs. The result of this collection process is an unconstrained list of near- and long-term potential goals on which to focus joint experimentation; realistically, of course, there will never be enough resources to experiment on each and every one. That is why the next step is to prioritize the unconstrained WFC list.

Step 2: Prioritize the challenges. Once the unconstrained list of potential subjects for joint experimentation has been developed, the JCD&E Enterprise prioritizes the list. This prioritization is done cooperatively, using an automated decision-support tool and an agreed-upon set of common criteria, so that the entire JCD&E Enterprise is fully aware of all recommendations and decisions being made concerning prioritization.

The first step in prioritization is to screen and consolidate the unconstrained WFC list. This step reviews all the WFCs and eliminates those

Figure 6.1 JCD&E Campaign Plan Development Process

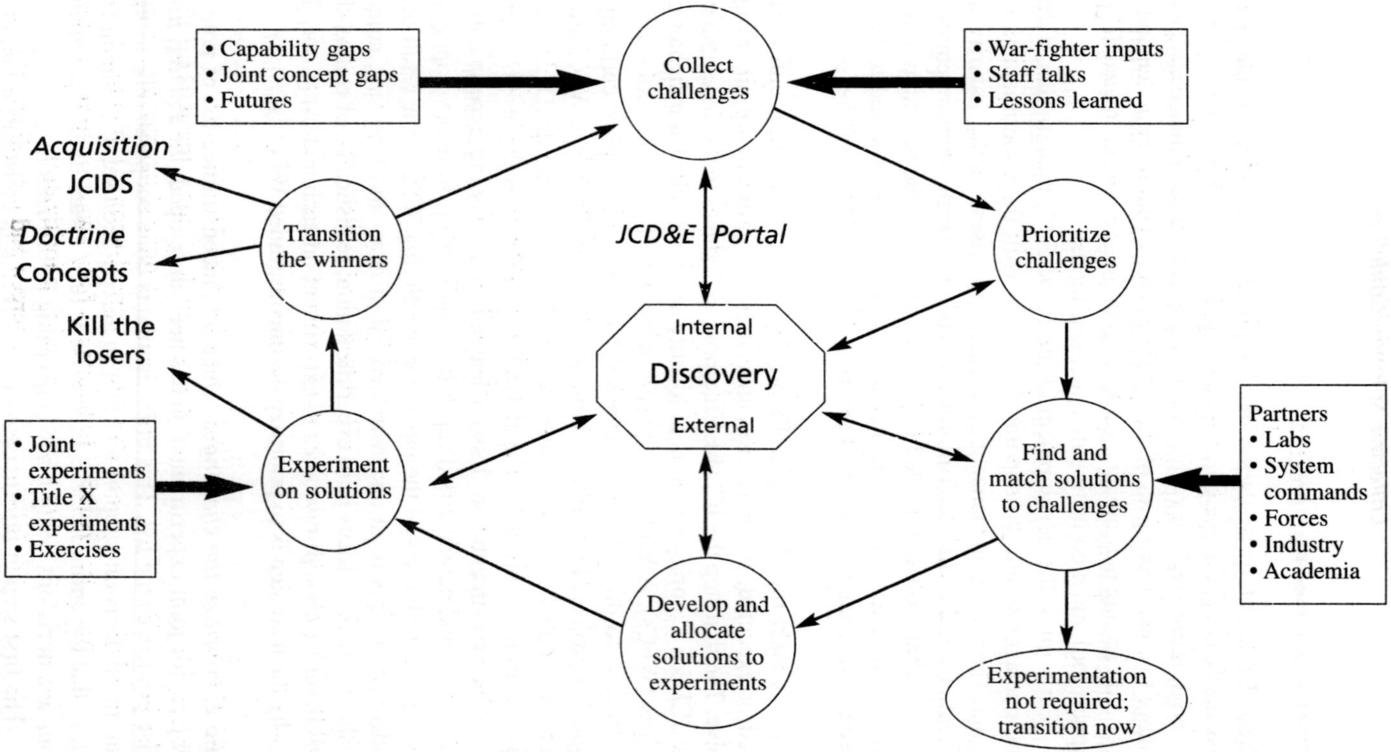

Source: Colonel Kelly Mayes, US Marine Corps, presentation to Joint Innovation and Experimentation Executive Council Meeting, hosted by David J. Ozolek, executive director, Joint Innovation and Experimentation, Suffolk, Virginia, 17 July 2007.

with limited joint value, those that are duplicative among several JCD&E Enterprise members, and those that are not challenges at all but, rather, are solutions looking for a problem. The result of this first step is a smaller list of WFCs that is now ready for prioritization.

Each WFC remaining on the screened and consolidated list is then weighed against established criteria to determine its relative priority for joint experimentation efforts over the next two years. These criteria include the criticality of the WFC and whether it is related to tasks stated in higher strategic guidance, the Joint Requirements Oversight Council approved list of Most Pressing Military Issues, or identified Joint Operations Concepts capability gaps. This "draft" prioritized list of WFCs is then staffed across the Department of Defense for concurrence and modification as required. At the end of this staffing, the JCD&E Enterprise has a one-through-n prioritized list of WFCs that forms the basis for designing and executing a department-wide JCD&E Campaign plan. (See Figure 6.2.)

Step 3: Find and match potential solutions to the prioritized WFCs. Once the final list of WFCs has been approved for joint experimentation, the JCD&E Enterprise finds and matches potential solutions to those challenges. In theory, a collective approach casts as wide a net as possible to find and match potential solutions to the WFCs. Academia, industry, and the science and technology community are critical to this step. Not all solutions for the WFCs are matériel, or new gear. Solutions can be doctrinal, organizational, procedural, or cultural, any of which requires a different form and type of experimentation (see Figure 6.3).

Another data point that may be as important as the potential solution is to identify where no likely solution exists. Currently, there is no way to communicate to academia, industry, and the science and technology communities what the solution needs are. Rather, the current practice is for individual organizations within the DoD to engage these outside resources individually or for the vendors to develop a solution to a perceived problem and then market it to the department.[18] This results in redundant capability development among different organizations or in the development of a solution that does not address one of the DoD's prioritized WFCs. By working collectively to identify the most important joint WFCs and any potential, or lack of potential, solutions, DoD can help direct these outside communities toward areas of interest that will better fulfill actual military requirements.

Once the potential solutions have been identified, they are assessed to determine their utility and maturity. If a prospective solution cannot be mapped to one of the prioritized WFCs, then it is not a candidate for joint

Figure 6.2 WFC Collection and Prioritization Efforts

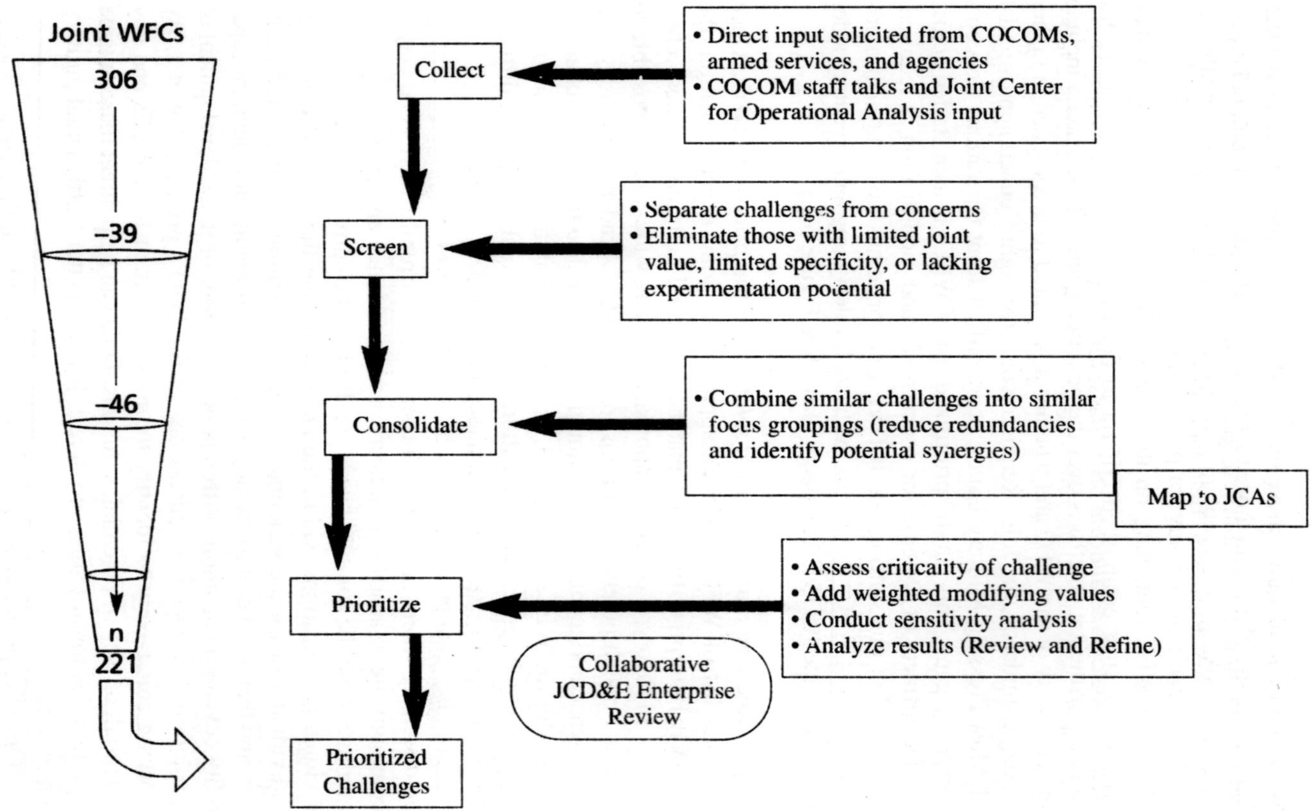

Source: Colonel Kelly Mayes, US Marine Corps, presentation to Joint Innovation and Experimentation Executive Council Meeting, hosted by Rear Admiral James Winnefeld, director, USJFCOM J9, Suffolk, Virginia, 30 January 2007.

experimentation. If there is a prioritized WFC with no identified potential solution, then the JCD&E Enterprise works with outside vendors to develop a solution. If an identified potential solution is assessed to be mature enough, it may go right to field validation without any joint experimentation.

Step 4: Develop and allocate potential solutions to joint experiments. Creating the nexus between the prioritized WFCs and potential solutions is the most critical step in developing the JCD&E Campaign plan. Once researchers understand the specifics of a particular security challenge and its potential solution, they can be ready to determine the type of joint experiment, the appropriate organization or organizations to conduct it, the product anticipated to come out of it, and the right scenarios, models, and simulations to support the experiment (see Figure 6.4).

The example in Figure 6.4 illustrates a war-fighter challenge submitted by USJFCOM, Marine Corps Combat Development Command, and Army

Figure 6.3 True Transformation

tT = *f*(organizations, processes, concepts, capabilities, authorities, and culture)

Source: USJFCOM J9 working equation.

Figure 6.4 Campaign Plan: WFC Example of Joint, Interagency, Multinational Interoperability

Tier 1 JCA Build Partnerships	Tier 2 JCA Communicate
Solutions	Leads
Cross Domain Collaborative Information Environment	USJFCOM
Irregular Warfare JOC	US NAVY
Joint Special Operations Logistics, Acquisition, and Responding Concept	USSOCOM
Events	Leads
Multinational Experiment 5 (MNE5)	USJFCOM & NATO
Unified Action	USJFCOM
Noble Resolve	USNORTHCOM

Source: Data compiled from Virtual Operations Center, USJFCOM, J9.

Note: The JFC requires interoperability among all conventional forces, special operations forces, other government agencies, law enforcement agencies, and multinational partners in order to conduct preventive, preemptive, or reactive counterterrorism operations and other security and forward presence operations.

Capabilities Integration Center during fiscal year 2007 (FY 07) for the FY 08/09 JCD&E Campaign plan. The submitting organizations developed a war-fighter statement that briefly described the capability not currently available. They also identified the appropriate Joint Staff–designated Tier 1 and Tier 2 Joint Capability Areas (JCAs).[19] The Enterprise community at large identified potential solutions that could solve the problem, at least in part. In addition, the Enterprise identified several experiments that would evaluate either the proposed solutions or the challenge directly through discovery experimentation.[20]

The JCD&E Campaign plan methodology of aligning WFCs with specific solutions, as a starting point from which to design and conduct joint experiments, ensures the analytical rigor for transformational activities required by senior leaders. This JCD&E Campaign plan approach enables joint experimentation to focus on the design of the experiment as opposed to its conduct, promotes productivity over mere activity, and allows a candid assessment of the utility of joint experimentation in transformation. A collective approach to the design and execution of a JCD&E Campaign plan creates critical visibility in joint experimentation activities across the Department of Defense, which makes it possible to reduce redundancies, remedy insufficiencies, and identify unproductive experimentation. Furthermore, visibility helps ensure that joint experimentation is fully resourced.

Step 5: Experiment on solutions. Joint experimentation takes place within some context or setting. "Joint context" is a flexible and scalable application of joint capabilities to experimentation, to better enable common transformational outcomes. Specific elements that contribute to joint context include

1. Scenarios: Realistic representations of real-world or projected future environments to provide participants with a common frame of reference for joint experimentation activities.
2. Force lists and capabilities: The mix of forces and capabilities needed to replicate required operations in a joint environment.
3. Command and control (C2) organizations: The C2 architecture and organization capabilities are often important elements of joint experiment objectives. They may span the strategic, operational, and tactical levels, and may interface with their interagency counterparts.
4. Facilities and tools: Scalable, based on the complexity and level of the experiment, these inputs can take many forms. For example, exercises and training activities provide a high degree of detail and opportunity to

support limited near-term experimentation; dedicated facilities and venues may, however, be more appropriate to complex joint experimentation activities that would be considered prohibitively disruptive in an exercise or operational environment. When overlaying joint experimentation on exercise and training events, great care should be taken to prevent the experiment from interfering with the required training and exercise objectives. Proposed solutions for experimentation (generally new concepts, systems or tactics, techniques, and procedures) should be mature and their application carefully scoped.

Joint context may not be necessary or desirable for independent experiments or for those focused on service interoperability and integration issues, but it is essential for joint experimentation.

In the JCD&E Campaign plan, the USJFCOM in its role as leader and coordinator offers unique support to combatant commanders, the armed services, defense agencies, and other experimentation partners through an array of capabilities, venues, and experts that can provide the level of joint context needed to examine a specific issue or problem. Generally, the USJFCOM should coordinate with the JCD&E Enterprise to prioritize joint experimentation resources at the operational level, since these types of experiments require a high degree of joint context due to the complexity of the environment.

Step 6: Transition the winners. The conduct of joint experimentation does not in itself lead to transformation. The products of focused joint experimentation must lead to the rapid introduction of improved operational capability to the field. Transition must also address the transfer of nonmatériel solutions, such as doctrinal, organizational, and conceptual products. This may be the most difficult step of the JCD&E Campaign plan process; without the successful transition of a solution into the hands of the user, the rest is just activity. This is the true measure of the value of joint experimentation.

Transition, above all, demands collective action to develop, field, and sustain a joint capability. The services must be full partners in joint experimentation. Currently, however, there are no joint acquisition monies. By Title 10 law, each service staffs, trains, and equips its force.[21] This includes the development of programs of record for matériel solutions. The United States cannot afford to spend millions of dollars to resolve a security challenge through joint experimentation, only to find there is no service to receive funding of that solution at the end of the process.

Conclusion

> How do you know you achieved what you were trying to achieve? I think we are successfully achieving the goal from a thought-process perspective. Now what we're trying to do is make sure our leaders and our civilians have the tools to be able to go and implement.
>
> —*General Lance L. Smith, US Air Force, Supreme Allied Commander, Transformation, and commander, US Joint Forces Command*[22]

The conduct of joint experimentation to support transformation must be a team effort. The complexity of the security environment the armed forces face in the early 2000s and for the foreseeable future dictates that no one organization can guarantee joint experimentation is productive and relevant. What is required is a collective approach to the design, execution, and assessment of joint experimentation. This approach provides all the various players in transformation with a common focus and goal, and fosters a collaborative environment that facilitates shared situational awareness, informed decisionmaking, and the ability to plan, coordinate, and execute joint experimentation.

Guiding this cooperative endeavor is the JCD&E Campaign plan, a six-step process that must be fully integrated into other DoD operations and systems. The JCD&E Enterprise uses the JCD&E Campaign plan to sequence and conduct joint experiments to ensure the rapid transition of joint concepts and joint capabilities to the force in the field. The JCD&E Campaign plan identifies and prioritizes the most important security challenges facing the Department of Defense today, matches potential solutions to those challenges, and then determines the joint experiments needed, along with the supporting requirements for those experiments. The cooperative structure of the JCD&E Campaign plan can be the true driver of transformation.

Notes

1. President George W. Bush, "Remarks by the President to the Troops and Personnel," Norfolk Naval Air Station, Norfolk, Virginia, 13 February 2001, http://www.whitehouse.gov/news/releases/20010213-1.html.

2. US Office of the Joint Chiefs of Staff, "Joint Operations Concepts Development Process (JOpsC-DP)," Chairman Joint Chiefs of Staff Instruction 3010.02B, 27 January 2006, directive current as of 4 December 2007: A1–A6, http://www.dtic.mil/cjcs_directives/cdata/unlimit/3010_02.pdf.

3. US Office of the Joint Chiefs of Staff, "Joint Capabilities Integration and Development System," Chairman Joint Chiefs of Staff Instruction (CJCSI) 3170.01F,

1 May 2007: A1–A10, http://www.dtic.mil/cjcs_directives/cdata/unlimit/3170_01.pdf.

4. Bud Hay, experimentation group director, USJFCOM J9, "Innovation and Experimentation Enterprise (IEE) Business Plan Vision," 7 May 2007: 2–3, http://www.msco.mil/files/DMSC/2007/Hay_ExperimentationCommunityOverview.ppt#382,1,J9.

5. Office of the Under Secretary of Defense for Acquisition, Technology, and Logistics, "Phase 1 Report on the Defense Science Board Task Force on Joint Experimentation," Washington, DC, September 2003.

6. National Research Council, "Strategy for an Army Center for Network Science, Technology, and Experimentation," report for the Division on Engineering and Physical Sciences (Washington, DC: National Academies Press, 2007), 15–38, http://sites.nationalacademies.org/DEPS/DataFiles/DEPS_037380.

7. See notes 2 and 3 above, and Vice Admiral V. E. Clark, US Navy, director, Joint Staff, "Joint Strategic Planning System," CJCSI 3100.01A, 12 September 2003: A1–E7.

8. Government Accountability Office, *Military Transformation: Clear Leadership, Accountability, and Management Tools Are Needed to Enhance DOD's Efforts to Transform Military Capabilities,* report to congressional committees, GAO-05-70 (Washington, DC: Government Printing Office, 2004).

9. Brigadier General Michael E. Rounds, US Army, acting director for Operational Plans and Joint Force Development, "The Joint Staff, Joint Operations Concept Development Process (JOpsC-DP) Pocket Guide," 9 January 2008: 25–30, http://www.dtic.mil/futurejointwarfare/strategic/jcsgjcde0108_3010pocketguide.doc.

10. General J. N. Mattis, US Marine Corps, director for Joint Forces Experimentation, US Joint Forces Command, "Department of Defense Joint Concept Development & Experimentation Campaign Plan 09/10," 15 October 2008: 1–2.

11. Ibid., 1.

12. Sharp, Memorandum for Service Chiefs, Commanders of the Combatant Commands, and Directors, Joint Staff Directorates, Enclosure entitled "Roles and Responsibilities for Joint Experimentation," 4 December 2006.

13. Rear Admiral James A. Winnefeld Jr., "Joint Experimentation: Shaping Doctrine and Capabilities," *Joint Forces Quarterly* 44, no. 1 (2007): 47, http://www.ndu.edu/inss/Press/jfq_pages/editions/i44/14.pdf.

14. Davenport, "Joint Concept Development and Experimentation Enterprise Process Guide 2008," 12 March 2008. Distribution limited; refer requests for document to Command and Operations Group, US Joint Forces Command, 115 Lake View Parkway, Suffolk, Virginia 23435-2697.

15. Winnefeld, "Joint Experimentation," 47–50.

16. Davenport, "Joint Concept Development."

17. Ibid.

18. Richard A. Kass, "The Logic of Warfighting Experiments," DoD Command and Control Research Program publication series, Washington, DC, 19 April 2008: 3–5, http://www.scribd.com/doc/2568991/The-Logic-of-Warfighting-Experiments.

19. Joint Capability Areas provide the foundation for capability management throughout the Department of Defense. Honorable Gordon England, deputy secretary

of defense, "Memorandum for Secretaries of the Military Departments, Joint Capability Areas (JCAs)," 14 February 2008, http://www.dtic.mil/futurejointwarfare/strategic/depsecdef_jca.pdf.

20. Robert Purcell, "Phase Two of Multinational Experiment 5 Kicks Off," Joint Forces Command press release, 9 April 2008, http://www.jfcom.mil/newslink/storyarchive/2008/pa040908.html.

21. US House of Representatives, US Code, Title 10—Armed Forces, http://uscode.house.gov/download/title_10.shtml.

22. Steven Donald Smith, "Commander Calls Multinational Experiment a Success," Armed Forces Press Services, Washington, DC, 19 May 2006, http://www.jfcom.mil/newslink/storyarchive/2006/no051906.htm.

7

The Role of Concept Development

Michael Hallett

The overall aim of defense transformation is to enable military organizations to maintain the initiative across the full spectrum of conflict, despite a continuously adapting, uncertain threat environment. A special effort to transform the military is necessary because all organizations are subject to inertia in activity and outlook. This inertia delays response to changes in not only the natural environment but also the political, economic, societal, cultural, and military domains that make up the human social environment. In the military domain this creates the tendency to develop equipment and procedures for fighting the type of enemy encountered as past, rather than emerging, threats.

Transformational concept development is a self-conscious effort to manage this bureaucratic tendency. The role of concept development in the military transformation process is to solve problems through the design of new capabilities *before* potentially dangerous elements in the environment impinge on us to such a degree that we are subject to effects we find unpalatable (or deadly). In order to explain the nature of concept development within the transformation process, this chapter will first discuss the nature of transformation as a response to what we term the tragedy of culture. This will be followed by a discussion of concept development as a design process. Once concept development has been clearly defined, the chapter will review the three-phase concept development process and the role of the concept developer in this process. The conclusion will discuss some of the major tensions, and the risks generated by those tensions, within the concept development process.

Concept Development and the Tragedy of Culture

The problem of preparing to engage those enemies to which the military is accustomed is an example of a more general difficulty, which sociologist

Georg Simmel referred to as the "tragedy of culture."[1] According to Simmel, all products of human ingenuity—conceptual, organizational, or physical—ossify and eventually hinder the achievement of their original purpose. The tragedy of culture is a way to describe this dynamic, through which cultural forms, created by individuals and groups to enhance life, after a time no longer meet the needs of the individuals and groups that created them, and eventually become a drag on the life processes they were originally developed to accelerate.

In the case of the military, the platforms and systems that were designed to respond to the problems posed by the last war are finally brought to a high degree of competence. As procedures and components become standardized and more efficient, the manufacturing and acquisition structures solidify. Both bureaucracies and individuals become vested in them and acquire a wide set of incentives to continue to support the capabilities proven effective in the last conflict. Yet the environment in which the military system was designed to generate certain effects continues to change. As a result, gaps emerge between the extant structure and the arena and subjects (or targets) of its attempted operations. These gaps are targeted for exploitation by enemies.[2]

Transformation is an effort to proactively manage this endemic process rather than simply to be reactive. We can define *transformation* as a means to manage the tragedy of culture, so that the impetus to change is not provided solely by the extremely effective stimulus of defeat.

Concept Development as a Design Process

The disjunction between the products of human creativity and the environmental conditions to which the products are intended to respond is, according to cognitive scientist Herbert Simon in his book *The Sciences of the Artificial*, a result of the nature of human rationality.[3] For Simon, all behavioral systems fail to adapt perfectly to environmental conditions owing to the epistemological limits of the human subject—we lack complete knowledge of the dynamic heterogeneous environment. Hence, we fail to build systems that are able to deal optimally with our environmental conditions. This does not mean that the structures and capabilities developed for the present and future threat environments are entirely without value; it means only that in light of the limits of human rationality and the tragedy of culture, continuous effort is required to develop capabilities appropriate to the extant situation.

According to Simon, this effort takes the form of a design process. People engage in design when they devise "courses of action aimed at changing existing situations into preferred ones."[4] Concept development is a design process that articulates potential solutions, in the form of enhanced or new capabilities, to respond to the problems that emerge from the gaps between present structures and shifting environments. Concept development is thus the fountainhead of transformation.

Definition of a Concept

Having situated concept development within the broader transformation process, we can now turn to a more precise definition of a concept followed by a description of the concept development process. A concept is an idea for solving a problem.[5] It is a specific product of artifice, an artificial output of organizational design. To do its job of guiding capability development, the concept must articulate three elements. The first element is a description of the existing gap between structure and environment, and the specific problem a new capability or set of capabilities is intended to manage. Understanding the specific problem is essential for proper capability development. This statement of the gap and problem bounds the concept development activity. The solution to the problem is the goal of the capability development process.

Second, the concept as interface must locate the potential set of capabilities that will serve as a solution in both current and possible future environments within the military domain. The nature of the environment and the means (the capabilities that generate desired effects) through which the military intends to interact with the environment are the key questions the concept must answer, rather than simply finding the raw numbers of existing military platforms that may be required.

Third, the concept must describe the interaction between the solution and the task, which is derived from the efforts by external or internal actors to generate desired effects, and the capabilities developed to perform the task. In other words, the method of employment or of actually solving the problem must be contained in the concept, so that it can serve to guide the development of specific components of the capabilities in terms of Doctrine, Organization, Training, Material, Leadership and Education, Personnel, and Facilities (DOTMLPF).[6] Thus, the concept describes the interface between the condition and the steps taken to respond to and deal with that condition. The steps will include the use of existing capabilities appropriately adapted, or capabilities developed specifically, to deal with the problem that stimulated formulation of the concept.

The ultimate utility of the concept depends on its ability to serve as a mental bridge or interface between current environments and current sets of capabilities and the anticipated future set of capabilities required for a wide variety of future environments. Thus, the concept serves as a visualization of future operations and describes how a commander, using military art and science, might employ capabilities. Ideally, the concept will produce a broad set of capabilities that render previous ways of war fighting obsolete.[7]

Role of the Concept Developer

The concept developer is a designer. As such, he or she is concerned with normative questions of how military capabilities ought to look and function so that they will attain the organization's goals in the anticipated environment. The concept developer need not begin as a subject matter expert, but will certainly become one as a result of leading the concept development process. Often the concept developer is a retired senior officer who possesses an array of experience drawn from operational command and joint staff positions, and knowledge earned through advanced academic degrees in national security and strategic studies.

Regarding role, the concept developer provides much of the conceptual content (even if ultimately derived from other sources during the preliminary phase). He or she must make sure that the concept is informed by consideration of the multiple environments, coordinate contributions to the concept, and ensure the coherence of the concept text itself. The primary task of the concept developer is to build the mental structure necessary to manage the multidimensional complexities of problem solving. The concept developer must take into account not only the existing capabilities and the extant environment but also the ways other actors will respond to the capabilities generated. The movement by nations and organizations away from the development of single-domain solutions like aircraft carriers or nuclear missiles toward comprehensive or whole-of-government approaches adds an additional layer of complexity to concept development.

The Concept Development Process

The three-phase concept development process described below is based on concept development practices at the North Atlantic Treaty Organization (NATO) Headquarters Supreme Allied Commander, Transformation.[8]

The Preparatory First Phase

The preparatory process moves through three steps, in which the concept developer succinctly defines the problem or gap in capabilities he or she will address, formulates and solicits from disparate sources some initial ideas for how to solve the problem, and then drafts an outline text that will serve to guide further development. It is in this preliminary phase that the dangers of habit and entrenchment are most likely to crop up, requiring the developer to be flexible, knowledgeable, and ready to think beyond familiar boundaries.

Gap discernment and problem articulation. The concept developer begins by examining the current condition and future needs, and then explores the problem or problems engendered by the gap between the two. This process is explicitly or implicitly informed by the use of scenarios about the future that have been prescribed by higher authorities.[9] Ideally, the concept should propose capabilities that can deal with a wide range of alternative futures as articulated in a full range of scenarios.[10] In a nonresource-constrained environment, this examination process would take place constantly, like scanning the horizon from the bridge of a ship. In practice however, owing to limited resources and the difficulty of resolving disagreement about the plausibility of various scenarios, the political leadership often provides the fundamental assumptions upon which the concept development will take place. This workload relief entails certain risks, however, which will be discussed below.

Often, the development of a concept is initiated by specific tasking. According to Allied Command Transformation, this direction can range "from a formal statement of operational need, lessons learned, a relevant discovery in an experiment, availability of new technologies or simply adapting a national initiative to the broader NATO [or any command's] environment."[11] This direction serves to further narrow the focus of the concept developer by providing the problem or cluster of problems the organization is willing to spend resources on to manage.

Potential solution development. Once the scenarios and problems are clearly defined (which can in itself be a contentious process), a set of potential solutions is developed. The concept developer moves through six sets of activities: a background survey; a state of the art review; examination of other concept development work, by both nations and organizations; interviews with subject matter experts; examination of visions of the future; and finally, an analysis of lessons identified. Lesson identification is the most uniquely military aspect of this process, since it is often the operational gaps and problems that first emerge here, at all levels of military activity, that provide the impetus for concept development.

In this phase, the primary task of the concept developer is to reach beyond the boundaries of the particular command, service, or national or international organization to which he or she belongs, and incorporate the intellectual resources and capital that have already been brought to bear to solve similar problems. This is essential for two reasons: first, to avoid duplicating effort on a concept already developed by a friendly organization; second, to build links with future partners at this phase of the concept development process and give them a stake in the success of the concept. If partners feel included from project conception, they are far more likely to work constructively through to the conclusion. Presenting desired partners with a concept (or description of an interface) in which their role is completely defined and with which their compliance is expected will seldom encourage cooperation. When stakeholders and potential partners participate in the design process early, they will be able to create their own interfaces, rather than being forced to fit in the remaining spaces; this can dramatically increase the operational effectiveness of both the concept development process and the capability itself.

The preliminary concept text. Having thoroughly studied the environment, problems, and potential solutions in the preliminary phase, the concept developer now generates a preliminary concept text.[12] In the next, "embryonic" phase of development, this concept text becomes the source from which further steps will unfold.

The development of the concept as a solution to a problem requires the concept to be removed to some degree from the context of current events to avoid the tragedy of culture. Although this decontextualization is essential, because the analyst cannot wrestle with the full scope of the problem all the time, it does pose some risk that the concept will lose its connection to the actual problems it was intended to manage. The concept developer needs to remain aware of the risks posed by this deliberately myopic view, to ensure that the concept remains relevant to the outside world and that the solutions it proposes are not bypassed by external events. Since the concept development process can be extremely lengthy, this major risk must be mitigated primarily by the concept developer's ability to maintain broad situational awareness, along with refusal to succumb to the tunnel vision encouraged by a focus only on the concept text itself.

Because the initial text sets the boundaries for future concept development, the sponsoring organization must ratify the preliminary text.[13] Organizational approval reflects a commitment to provide at least the minimal resources necessary for further development. At this point, initial conception is complete and the concept embarks on the embryonic phase.

The Embryonic Second Phase

At this stage, the concept developer composes an outline concept development plan and begins to flesh out the preliminary concept text into an initial concept document. The outline plan will be used to manage the use of the organization's intellectual capital and resources in concept development. The parties included in the plan will vary by organization, but at a minimum will include the concept development staff, other military organizations (the end users of the capability), experimenters, modeling and simulation personnel, and war gamers. Increasingly, this list will include external organizations and actors such as think tanks and interagency partners, international organizations (e.g., the UN Office of the Coordinator for Humanitarian Affairs, the UN Department of Peacekeeping Operations, or the International Organization for Migration), and nongovernmental organizations.

The concept development plan allows the concept developer to manage the complex contributions of multiple parties and maintain coherence throughout the development process. This coherence need not come from the concept developer's personal vision; however, it is the task of the concept developer to ensure that the product has the consistency and clarity of a single author, despite inputs from a wide variety of contributors. The plan is essential to articulate the process of interaction among the concept developers, other elements of the command involved in the project (technical researchers, war gamers, subject matter experts), and any external actors (academics, other military commands, lessons-learned centers, and government, private sector, and nongovernmental representatives). For example, in the case of Allied Command Transformation, the plan includes the activities of the integrated capability teams, functional domain representatives, and experts from international organizations and other NATO organizations, such as Allied Command Operations and the Joint Lessons Learned Center. The list will vary for each concept.

Why is an integrated plan so important? The answer is economic: scarce financial and human resources must be thoughtfully allocated for concept development to go forward in the most efficient manner possible. Therefore, the concept development plan must organize two broad areas of interaction—concept content and resource allocation. The expansion of concept content takes place through the maturation process, discussed below. Resource planning is essential to the maturating process, and the concept development plan must be sufficiently rigorous to enable each of the participating elements to articulate, and if necessary fight for, the funding resources they need for their contribution to the concept development process. If the plan fails to show how each element contributes to the overall development of the concept, the concept can become hostage to the funding vagaries of each contributing element. In such a case, the concept developer could end up spending more energy on helping the various contributors with their internal budget arguments than on developing the concept itself.

Any resource shortfall within a single component, such as experimentation, can seriously degrade or even halt the entire concept development process. To deal with the inevitable funding constraints, the concept development plan should be sufficiently robust to allow for delay, acceleration, or reduction in the scope of the concept should funding become unavailable. This is especially important in the area of experimentation; experiments can be expensive, but are essential for developing the concept. If exploration in an experiment is cut, the concept development plan should have branches and sequels (at least in the mind of the concept developer) to maintain momentum and provide solutions to service members downstream.

With the outline plan in mind, the concept development team fleshes out the initial text into an "initial concept document." The aim of this document is to refine the problem statement (e.g., information sharing in complex environments is inadequate) and the principles informing the concept (e.g., the degree of information sharing between civil and military actors will vary with the mandates and will of the organizations and environmental conditions). The embryonic stage concludes with approval of the initial concept document by the same organization that approved the preliminary concept text.

At Allied Command Transformation, the Transformation Steering Board serves as the midwife of the initial concept document. Approval is a vital step, because merely identifying the problem and possible solution does not ensure that the organization will act to develop the recommended capabilities. Despite the pressing nature of the problem, the organization may elect not to engage for three reasons: (1) the organization may decide that the risk of not addressing the problem is manageable; (2) it may determine that it is not the responsibility of the organization to deal with the problem; or (3) it may decide that the problem is being tolerably dealt with by another actor. Thus, a clear articulation of the necessity for this concept is crucial to obtaining a place on the organization's agenda.

Once the concept has completed the embryonic phase, indicated by approval of the outline concept development plan and the initial concept document, the concept is viable and moves into the maturating phase.

The Maturation Third Phase

The maturation phase is guided by the robust concept-development plan, implemented by a spiral development process. Spiral development is the incremental fielding of immature solutions, whereby promising concepts can be partially implemented while under development, then continually refined and perfected in the field.[14] The concept development plan includes six spiraling activities: (1) brainstorming workshops, (2) subject-matter-expert working groups, (3) limited-objective experiments, (4) war games, (5) operational experiments, and (6) modeling and simulation.

The six activities form what Simon refers to as a "generator-test cycle."[15] Within the cycle, ideas are generated and then tested against the demands of the actual problem environment. The decontextualization process required for initial concept development reverses here, so that the concept is tested against the complex, friction-filled variables of the actual world and appropriate projections of possible future environments. Maturation is thus a process of "recontextualization." As discussed below, the first two steps involve groups of experts whose job is to define and describe the concept in a way that will be acceptable to its sponsors. The four remaining steps provide feedback on the utility of the codified concept.

Workshops and working groups. Workshop members and working group experts expand the initial concept document by incorporating relevant content, principles, and operational insights into the text. To do this, team members may share responsibility for composing the text, select an individual to write a complete draft and provide it to the group for review, or use some combination of the two methods. Composition meetings often take the form of working through the text line by line and word by word as the text is projected on a screen. The working group should include as many future potential users of the capability as possible, including other military organizations and nonmilitary partners, especially for concept development within the area of civil-military interaction, humanitarian activities, or stabilization and reconstruction.

Of special importance is the inclusion at this point of people with expertise in the political environment and the input of those actors with a say in the concept's final approval. Especially in a multinational context, a proposed solution may be entirely unacceptable to one or more members due to higher-level political considerations. The concept may have to be more limited than optimally desirable so it can gain the approval of political leaders who have to take into account issues beyond the specific problem with which the concept is concerned. Reference to a larger concept may add value to the coherence of a subsidiary concept, for example, but if that higher concept is not universally accepted by political leaders, it may be more prudent to avoid mention of it. The failure to avoid political "red lines" (the politically contentious policies that are crossed out during approval review) can scuttle any progress in getting problems solved. Although reducing the scope of the proposed solution by limiting the scope of the concept is not optimal, it may be necessary to ensure the end user gets those improved capabilities soon enough to be actually useful.

Limited objective experiments (LOEs). Experimentation is essential to determine the validity of the concept and should take place prior to concept approval. LOEs are small-scale, relatively low-cost experiments that test an immature concept. The experiments focus on the operational utility of a technology or experimental tactic, technique, or procedure rather than simply measuring technological performance.[16] The LOE may take several forms, including tabletop discussions, controlled laboratory evaluations, or limited field trials; whatever form they take, their findings should be submitted before the concept gains final approval. Experimentation is a key means to force transformation; demonstration of a capability within an LOE can provide the best argument for supporting further concept development.

War games. By providing feedback on the utility of the concept from potential operators, war games also play an important role in concept development. They furnish a valuable "reality check" on the concept and illuminate the other capability requirements engendered by the concept in the DOTMLPF areas. NATO defines *war game* as "a simulation of a military operation, by whatever means, using specific rules, data, methods, and procedures."[17] There are two types of war games for concept development. The first, the *exploratory* war game, examines a concept under limited operational conditions to identify shortfalls and consider it against existing solutions or competing concepts. The second, the *scrubbing* war game, is a more rigorous test of maturing concepts that provide quantitative analysis of outcomes to inform a continuing concept maturation strategy.[18] War games reflect real-world possibilities to the extent that operational scenarios are used and actual military units are players.

The input provided through the war game allows the concept to adjust and manage real-world interface challenges that come to light. For example, although the members of a multinational interagency coordination group may individually possess the will to share information and engage in concerted planning with the military, they may not have permission from their headquarters to do so. Thus, the war game may show that approval of an information-sharing concept must precede the concept that deals with thicker forms of interaction.

Operational experiments. These experiments provide a venue for increased bench testing of the concept. They allow researchers to focus exclusively on the concept under development, without the unrelated distractions occasionally present in war games and exercises. The lead operational researcher for the concept will be closely involved with the entire concept development process. Operational experimentation is discussed more fully in Chapter 8.

Modeling and simulation. By providing additional visualization and analytical capabilities, modeling and simulation can add value to each activity in the maturation process. The rapidly increasing sophistication of computer programs and graphics has led modeling and simulation to become an integral part of transformation concept development as well as training in recent years. The ability to visualize complicated relationships is especially useful in concept development. Equally important, modeling and simulation promote integration and collaboration between concept development teams and their supporting defense technology experts. This synthetic operational environment provides a cost-effective, virtual venue by replacing live forces on terra firma with computer-generated entities in a bona fide operational context that can easily be manipulated to test relevant contingencies without putting anyone in harm's way. A successful modeling and simulation iteration provides a means to identify, develop, and measure experimental outcomes in a timely, useful, and realistic format that will guide the maturation of the concept.[19]

Within the generator-test cycle of the maturation phase, concepts sometimes fail to generate the desired effects. Yet far from being a loss, this failure in itself can provide valuable information and should therefore be viewed as a positive contribution to the concept development process. The application of knowledge gained from the failure takes place across a wide range of subsequent activities. The concept may need radical reconfiguration, either because the assumptions upon which it was based were incorrect or owing to lacks in other prerequisite capabilities that themselves are being worked through a concept development process. This does not necessarily mean that the imperfect concept should be discarded, but it could mean that the scope of activity of the concept developers and capability development teams must be expanded if the concept is to provide the desired capability.

Concept maturation continues through the six-step generator-test spiral stage until the concept is deemed once again to be worthy of submission to the approval authorities. The spiraling may continue as changes are made to the concept in response to feedback from those approval authorities.

Conclusion

The attempt to respond to the tragedy of culture by actively developing new capabilities, in light of lessons learned and visions of the future, is not without risk. Simon describes this risk thus: "A system can generally be steered more accurately if it uses feedforward, based on prediction of the future, in combination with feedback, to correct the errors of the past. However, forming expectations to deal with uncertainty creates its own problems. Feedforward can have unfortunate destabilizing effects, for a system can overreact to its predictions and go into unstable oscillations."[20] In the military domain, transformational efforts designed to manage responses to an uncertain future can generate the unintended effect of destabilizing the set of current military capabilities. This destabilization can potentially render the military organizations unfit to perform their established functions and thus degrade, instead of enhance, military readiness.

The political leadership is very aware of this risk and responds by enforcing a concept hierarchy.[21] High-level guidance from the political domain is appropriate and in full accordance with the centrality of civilian control of military activities to democratic political systems. Yet this system generates two challenges for concept development. First, the edifice of strategic, operational, and tactical concepts remains incomplete for military planners. In the absence of a structure wholly owned by the military, in which to fit new concepts, concept developers must work to fill gaps without cognizance of the intended whole. The "fog of war," by definition, also affects concept development.

Second, the rigidity of the concept hierarchy, and the need for political approval, can hinder innovative approaches to problem solving. The resulting tension between approved conceptual guidance and the need for innovative approaches to emerging threats is heightened by the need to find a balance between the competing demands of capability gaps in both the near and long term. While working on those problems that are generating strong demand signals in the near term, it remains important to pay attention to the weaker signals that may have long-term implications. Thus, near-term capability development should, whenever possible, result in a positive capability development for the long term. In other words, it is necessary and proper to direct significant attention to any near-term operational gap; at the same time, however, the concept developer should try to understand how the immediate problem set may indicate a longer-term gap, from which may issue more significant problems in the future.

The need to focus attention on immediate problems should not entirely subsume the long-term capability development required to preserve the initiative within the tragedy-of-culture dynamic. Such a dual-track approach to concept development is, of course, expensive in terms of intellectual and financial resources, but is far less expensive than defeat. This tension and the demands it places on the emotions and intellectual energy of the concept development team are also stimulating, and thus provide a salutary influence on the concept development process as a whole.

Concept development serves as the engine of transformational change in the military domain. Not all the work of concept development involves consensus building and bureaucratic battling. Indeed, concept development provides continuous opportunities to exercise the art of strategic thinking in every arena of military endeavor.

Notes

1. Georg Simmel, *The Conflict in Modern Culture and Other Essays* (New York: Teacher's College Press, 1968), 45.

2. David S. Alberts with John J. Garstka, Richard E. Hayes, and David T. Signori, *Understanding Information Age Warfare,* CCRP Publication Series (Washington, DC: Department of Defense, 2001), 66–72.

3. Herbert Simon, *The Sciences of the Artificial* (Cambridge: MIT, 1996).

4. Ibid., 111.

5. See Commander Brian Palmer, "Concept Development Process," NATO Allied Command Transformation draft text, Norfolk, Virginia, 2006: 1.

6. US Office of the Joint Chiefs of Staff, "Joint Capabilities Integration and Development System," CJCSI 3170.01F, 1 May 2007: A1–A10, http://www.dtic.mil/cjcs_directives/cdata/unlimit/3170_01.pdf.

7. US Office of the Joint Chiefs of Staff, "Joint Operations Concepts Development Process (JOpsC-DP)," Chairman Joint Chiefs of Staff Instruction 3010.02B, 27 January 2006, directive current as of 4 December 2007: A1–A6, http://www.dtic.mil/cjcs_directives/cdata/unlimit/3010_02.pdf.

8. "Managing Transformation," ACT Directive 80-7, Headquarters, Supreme Allied Commander, Transformation, Norfolk, Virginia, 20 April 2005; and Palmer, "Concept Development Process," 1.

9. Stephan De Spiegeleire and Rem Korteweg, "Future NATOs," *NATO Review* online (Summer 2006), http://www.nato.int/docu/review/2006/issue2/english/military.html.

10. See Peter Schwartz, *The Art of the Long View* (New York: Doubleday, 1996), for more information on the development of scenarios and their potential utility.

11. Palmer, "Concept Development Process," 3.

12. At NATO's Allied Command Transformation, it is called a High Level Summary; ibid., 2.

13. Within Allied Command Transformation, this is done by the Transformation Steering Board, which allocates capability development resources.

14. General Lance L. Smith, *Understanding NATO Military Transformation,* Allied Command Transformation Public Information Office, Norfolk, Virginia, ACT Multimedia Library, 2006: 14.

15. Simon, *Sciences of the Artificial,* 128.

16. "MCWL Analysis Reports," Marine Corps Warfighting Laboratory (MCWL) Fact Sheet, 1 March 2007, http://www.mcwl.quantico.usmc.mil/analysis.cfm.

17. North Atlantic Treaty Organization, "AAP-6 (2008)--NATO Glossary of Terms and Definitions," NATO Standardization Agency, 1 April 2008: 2-W-1.

18. Joint Chiefs of Staff, "JOpsC-DP," D-2, D-3.

19. Nathalie Harrison and Richard Lestage, "Science and Technology Support to Concept Development and Experimentation," paper presented at the NATO Research and Technology Organization symposium "Modeling and Simulations to Address NATO's New and Existing Military Requirements" (RTO-MP-MSG-028, 2004), Koblenz, Germany, 7–8 October 2004; the document can be downloaded from the NATO RTO website: http://www.rta.nato.int/search.asp#RTO-MP-MSG-028.

20. Simon, *Sciences of the Artificial,* 36.

21. The propensity to deal with uncertainty through management explains the hierarchical nature of concept development. Simon claims, "Uncertainty often persuades social systems to use hierarchy rather than markets in making decisions" (Simon, *Sciences of the Artificial,* 42). The military is an excellent example of the use of hierarchy to manage uncertainty. Western militaries, however, do allow for a certain amount of conceptual market competition between the services. The tension between joint approaches and service-concept market competition is beyond the scope of this chapter.

8

Scientific Rigor in Defense Experimentation

George T. Hodermarsky

The use of experimentation to support defense transformation generates a wide range of opinions. Some believe experimentation to be an essential tool that validates future-oriented concept development by applying canons and techniques that have proven to be effective in other disciplines. Proponents see experimentation as the logical extrapolation of scientific principles to military problems and a vital part of any transformation effort. Others contend that defense experimentation is no more than pseudoscience, an expensive and fruitless attempt to apply methodologies that are inappropriate for the task and the environment, which could lead to suboptimal and even dangerous decisionmaking. As is the case with most controversies, the truth is somewhere in between these extremes. The ability of experimentation to support defense transformation is, logically, a factor of the degree of scientific rigor in the experimentation process.

An objective of this volume is to examine and provide an overview of the key components of defense transformation in a multinational context. Earlier chapters addressed the justification for defense transformation and various approaches to it. The innovative ideas (or concepts) described previously in this text are among the essential elements of transformation. They are rarely mature at inception, however, and require some means of development and evaluation. One of these methods is experimentation, which is the focus of this chapter.

The attempt to develop and refine concepts gives rise to several problems: (1) the number of concepts can be large and unmanageable; (2) resource constraints preclude adoption of all proposed ideas; and (3) the adoption of a concept carries the risk that it may prove to be impractical or unachievable when put into practice. Experimentation is a practical means of testing, assessing, and validating concepts prior to implementation.

Concept development begins with the identification of a problem and its proposed solution. Further evolution and refinement of the concept require assessment of its key elements through some type of an evaluation process. The scientific method is a proven way to study and gather evidence that could support the value of new ideas. Therefore, most transformation efforts regularly link experimentation to concept development. In the United States, "concept development and experimentation go hand-in-hand."[1] Together they make up one of the four pillars of defense transformation. The North Atlantic Treaty Organization (NATO) postulates that "a targeted programme of experimentation, will test the most promising transformational concepts."[2]

Before embarking on a process of concept development and refinement through experimentation, a few critical questions must first be dealt with:

1. Can the scientific rules developed in laboratories apply to war-fighting experiments?
2. Can war-fighting experiments meet the requirement of scientific rigor?
3. Can the results of the experiments have any impact on transformation?

The premise of this chapter is that the response to all three questions is yes, but only after certain inherent obstacles are overcome. While these challenges are not insignificant, defense experimenters nevertheless have successfully applied the essential elements of the scientific method with a degree of scientific rigor. Even so, meeting the conditions for experimentation soundness is a necessary, but not sufficient, requirement for success. The relevance of the proposed experiments to transformation must also be a key consideration before creating a program of defense experimentation.

The defense transformation community is fortunate that several well-written and exceptionally useful guides, as noted throughout the chapter, are available to steer its efforts. These sources provide an often-cited foundation for applying rigor to this work, and those directly engaged in experimentation programs should be intimately familiar with them. There is no intention here to replicate their excellent and detailed observations and recommendations. Rather, this chapter provides some diverse observations on experimentation from an international perspective, as well as an overview of the process for those who are not routinely engaged in experimentation activities but require familiarity with it.

The chapter is organized into three sections. First is a lexicon to familiarize readers with common terms and ideas used in scientific experimentation.

While differences in terminology exist, agreement on the meaning of the essential terms will help foster a common understanding for subsequent discussions. The second section describes the logic and methodology of experimentation. To properly answer the question of how to apply scientific rules of experimentation to military transformation, this section examines the essential logic of the scientific method in experimentation, followed by a description of a basic model for experimentation in this context. The third section gives several examples of proven effective methods that contain sufficient scientific rigor to ensure the validity of experiments supporting defense transformation. Drilling down from broad conceptual ideas, these illustrations in turn respond to the third question—that is, the impact of experimentation on transformation.

The Lexicon of Experimentation

Experimentation in its broad sense is widely understood. Most high schools introduce students to the essentials of experimentation and the scientific method in their chemistry, physics, and biology laboratories. Among the accepted definitions of experimentation is this: "A test under controlled conditions that is made to demonstrate a known truth, examine the validity of a hypothesis, or determine the efficacy of something previously untried."[3] In its simplest manifestation, "an experiment is intrinsically about establishing cause and effect relationships,"[4] which normally involves the manipulation of a factor (independent variable) to determine its effect on another factor (dependent variable). Stated differently, we are testing the proposition, "If we do this (independent variable), then this (dependent variable) will happen." This relating of cause to effect is a useful start for experimentation in any discipline, but since the needs of defense transformation are quite specific, practitioners must pursue more precise characterizations of experimentation.

In his definitive guide on the topic, Richard Kass of the United States Joint Forces Command (USJFCOM) Joint Innovation and Experimentation Directorate describes what he calls "warfighting experimentation" as "experiments conducted to support the development of operational military concepts and capabilities."[5] Canadian practitioners use the term *defense experimentation,* defined as "the application of scientific methods to the examination of concepts in order to solve complex problems faced by the military."[6] In Australia the more commonly used term is *military experimentation,* whose purpose is "to acquire knowledge for force development by exploring innovative concepts and identifying capabilities required."[7] Within NATO's Allied Command Transformation, *operational experimentation* is the organizational term.

A multinational consortium, the Technical Cooperation Program, within the experimentation community of interest, which also uses the term *defense experimentation,* defines it thus: "The application of the experimental method to the solution of complex defense capability, potentially across the full spectrum of conflict types, such as warfighting, peace enforcement, humanitarian relief, and peacekeeping."[8] For the sake of clarity and simplicity, despite some subtle differences in meaning between the terms, this chapter will use *defense experimentation* as synonymous with military, war-fighting, and operational experimentation, without implying that the experimentation must be limited to purely military issues. The NATO military leadership contends that an effects-based approach to operations mandates the use of all aspects of national and alliance power to achieve desired end states.[9] For that reason, the examination of concepts through experimentation that involve other than military assets still falls within the definition of defense experimentation.

Logic and Methodology

The introduction established the important linkage between concept development and experimentation. This section will describe the actual methodology of experimentation for defense concept development. The experimenter will need to work closely with the concept developer to (1) plainly identify the specific problem to be solved, (2) develop a hypothesis statement that clearly articulates a proposed solution, (3) design a process for testing the proposal, and (4) present evidence that the results will benefit the overall transformation effort. The optimum tool for this progression is an adaptation of the scientific method.

As mentioned earlier, manipulation of a variable and description of the effect are the basis of experimentation. Scientific experiments normally begin with a hypothesis statement: If we do this (independent variable), then this (dependent variable) will happen. In the physical sciences, this could be, If chemists add oxygen to a combination of heat and combustible material, the outcome is production of higher temperatures—or, If we change the shape of an aircraft wing, increased lift will result. Practitioners can apply the same basic formulation of the premise to defense experimentation. Normally, the independent variable is a new capability and the dependent variable the anticipated military effect, potentially an increase or decrease in some measure of war-fighting effectiveness. Examples could be, If we develop effective means to disseminate friendly force information in a timely way to everyone who needs it, then friendly fire engagements that result in fratricide will be reduced; or, If we provide multinational forces with a more compatible command and control capability, then their interoperability will increase; or, If we employ more robust and persistent intelligence, surveillance, and reconnaissance capabilities, then enemy sanctuary will be denied.

At the conclusion of any experiment, the first task is to determine whether there has been cause and effect. All experiments consist of the possible cause (A), the independent variable, and the possible effect (B), the dependent variable. That is, if we took action A, was there any change to effect B? It is important, however, to avoid the error of *post hoc, ergo propter hoc* ("after this, therefore because of this"). Correlation is not causation. The essential tasks of the experimenter are first to prove that change in B actually occurred, and second, that B changed as a result of A. Detection of change is usually a less demanding task than isolation of the cause.

In a scientific laboratory the experimenters institute controls. In microbiology, for example, scientists establish a sterile environment to ensure that the changes detected in bacteria growth in a petri dish are the result of the intentional manipulation, and not other factors in the environment. The challenge is much greater in the defense experimentation realm. By its very nature, the battlefield is chaotic. To illustrate, a commander may have found measurable success with a new tactic or piece of equipment; when the new variable was used, the desired effect—for example, the adversary is no longer able to threaten one's force—occurred. We may know that effect B followed action A; there may even be evidence to support the hypothesis that B was in fact the result of A. When we consider other factors, such as enemy training, supply, morale, location, environmental factors, or leadership, however, we cannot be certain that A was the only cause of B. Further complicating the problem, even if we can contend with some assurance that action A caused effect B, how do we know whether it was a significant, much less the principal, cause of the effect? Hence, isolation of the independent variable, which a researcher may readily accomplish in a microbiology laboratory, becomes the defense experimenter's primary dilemma.

The challenge to those engaged in defense experimentation is to do everything possible to increase controls and mitigate the impact of the other independent variables. Finding a suitable laboratory in which to test the hypotheses is difficult. The Afghan countryside may provide a realistic test bed, but the demands and dangers of real-world operations might make it unsuitable. Additionally, since many of the components of military operations are in the cognitive domain, such as being dependent upon the imperfect perceptions of complex human beings, isolation of cause is exceptionally demanding. No two commanders will respond precisely the same way to a set of conditions and events. Furthermore, and as often observed, "the enemy gets a vote," and precise prediction of the response of an adversary to an action is elusive. Despite these challenges, the basic iterative process described herein is a useful guide to successful experimentation.

Step one, to *plainly identify the specific problem to be solved,* requires at minimum a close examination of the concept documentation. Since concepts are by definition ideas, their level of maturity will vary. For example, a concept for a new expeditionary headquarters structure might include a reduced forward-deployed staff. A proposed solution to the potential problem of fewer staff members not being able to accomplish all headquarters functions may be to provide "reach back," that is, electronic connectivity to expertise at other sites. This concept will likely have elements that need refinement. Taking numbers of staff personnel as an independent variable, experimenters could run multiple iterations of a task: for example, develop an operational plan, in response to a crisis, by using established reach back, and assign different numbers of personnel. Subsequent analysis would derive conclusions as to the effect of this particular manipulation. To try other variables, experimenters could keep the number of staff members constant and alter the sophistication of the communications equipment or the external resources available to the planners.

The second step, to *develop a hypothesis statement that clearly articulates a proposed solution,* appears at first glance to be simple. Yet this is the foundation for the experimentation process, so drafters must take great care with the creation of the statement. A well-constructed hypothesis is vital to provide clarity for subsequent experiment planning and execution. As introduced earlier, hypothesis statements are often in the form of "if-then" relationships. Continuing with the headquarters size example, one possible hypothesis is, If we provide a deployed headquarters staff with reach back to essential expertise, then all headquarters functions may be accomplished with fewer staff members forward-deployed. Stated more directly, The use of reach back will allow the number of forward-deployed staff to be reduced. The primary task, again, is to express the purpose of the experimentation as clearly as possible.

Similarly, experiment designers must take great care with the third part, which is to *design a process for testing the ideas.* This task will vary greatly according to the hypothesis itself. Detailed guides for experiment design are available; therefore, this limited discourse will present only a few fundamentals.[10] Experimentation cannot resolve all elements of complex issues and concepts, and requires making some assumptions that help limit the scope of possible variables. Following on from the reach-back hypothesis, assumptions could be that the size of the expeditionary headquarters staff is already optimum, it is populated with qualified personnel, the electronic conduits for reach back will be in place and function as needed, and sufficient numbers of experts will be available and responsive to the deployed staff.

Experimenters cannot eliminate all external factors; minimizing is the objective. While the experiment could support or refute the hypothesis, the experimenter must consider other factors. Was the experimentation cohort representative of an expeditionary headquarters staff? Was it created ad hoc from available assets? Was the operational planning crisis scenario realistic? Did the multiple iterations produce a "training effect" that could cloud the results?

Fulfillment of the last task, to *present evidence that the results of the analysis will benefit the overall transformation effort,* becomes more subjective. Defense experimentation does not exist in isolation; unlike much medical or academic research, it must serve the needs of transformation and not be designed for its own sake. Here the requirements for scientific rigor and the value of experimentation to defense transformation may run at counterpurposes. There may be an inverse relationship between rigid adherence to the scientific method and the overall relevance of the experimentation. The perfect experiment may not result in any meaningful impact on transformation. Unless the results of the experiment can further refine a concept under consideration, its value is questionable. The completion of this fourth objective depends heavily on the quality of the first three. If the experiment director identifies the wrong problem, provides a flawed hypothesis statement, or does not carefully design and execute the experiment, then the results could be of minimal value.

As an example, if the reach-back experiment proposed an unrealistic scenario, provided connectivity that would not plausibly be available to operational commanders, or chose a select team that was not representative of future headquarters staffs, then the relevance to actual operations could be insignificant. Even though the experiment itself is scientifically pure, its results may be of no discernable value to the refinement of the concept. Hence, the true measure of the effectiveness of an experiment is not entirely its conformity with scientific principles. Rather, it lies in its ability to contribute to the concept under consideration. This condition supports the argument for direct involvement of operators in the experimentation process, rather than assigning the work entirely to scientists. A partnership between the concept developer and the experimenter is critical to the successful completion of this task.

Applications

Defense transformation and its related experimentation are not creations of the early twenty-first century. The Greek phalanx, the English longbow, armored columns, and sea-based aviation are but a few historical examples of transformative concepts that were successfully adapted to military use. At some point, someone proposed an idea that revolutionized warfare. Rarely were these ideas complete and fully developed at inception. All required some type of refinement through experimentation before they realized their potential. The new model proposed here is to codify and structure the experimentation that supports transformation.

While the previous discussion focused on the hypothesis-supporting type of experiment, there are other subcategories within defense experimentation that also are worth addressing. The US Department of Defense's "Code of Best Practices for Experimentation" provides some useful definitions. "Discovery" experiments introduce novel systems, concepts, organizational structures, technologies, or other elements into a setting where analysts can observe and catalog their use. The objectives are to find out how the innovation applies and whether it appears to have military utility.[11] Workshops, working groups, limited objective experiments, and war games provide suitable venues. The United States, for instance, has conducted a series of Joint Urban Warrior discovery experiments that explore methods to alleviate challenges in the irregular warfare environment, such as strategic compression or population influence.[12] Within NATO the annual Crisis Management Exercises and Allied Reach events provide an opportunity to embed discovery experiments into recurring exercises.[13] Additionally, "discovery experiments often weed out unworkable ideas and lay the foundation for more rigorous testing, assessment, and refinement."[14]

"Demonstration" experiments re-create known truth. Military "equivalent activities are technology demonstrations used to show that some innovation could, under carefully orchestrated conditions, improve the efficiency, effectiveness, or speed of a military activity."[15] Operational experiments and modeling and simulation provide suitable venues. The objective of demonstrations is to examine technologies or methodologies for their potential to furnish desired capabilities. To take one example, for many years since this writing, businesses have used networks to coordinate activities, once developers had proved that basic enabling technology works. The US military experiments Millennium Challenge 2002 and Multinational Experiment (MNE) 3 demonstrated the utility of a collaborative information environment that links together a military command structure and supporting interagency staffs, separated by geography and organizational boundaries, using high-speed information connectivity and electronic collaborative tools.[16]

The boundaries between types of experiments are not rigid and impermeable. Linkages exist among all three, and a concept will normally go through multiple phases of experimentation. To illustrate, consider the evolution of the concept of coalition and interagency coordination. Earlier discovery experiments conducted by the United States and NATO recognized that a means of coordinating activities with organizations outside of the military structure would be an essential capability for anticipated future operations. They also made clear that extant processes and policies were woefully inadequate to complete this task. This engendered an embryonic idea for how to deal with this problem.

Moving on from mere recognition of a needed capability, the designers of MNE 3 experimented in 2004 with a prototype organization that would connect civilian and military government stakeholders, in order to improve interagency planning and coordination.[17] To demonstrate the potential value of such a structure, a Combined Interagency Coordination Group (CIACG) was established in the command headquarters for MNE 3. A CIACG is a multifunctional, advisory element that fosters regular, timely, collaborative, day-to-day working relationships between civilian and military planners.[18]

The 2006 follow-on program, MNE 4, continued to examine the key elements of operating in an international crisis environment, primarily through testing of the Multinational Interagency Group (MNIG) concept, which uses a new organizational element to bring cross-government expertise, perspective, and understanding to the planning and execution process.[19] In this event, some manipulation of variables occurred, as in a hypothesis-testing experiment. "Controllers inject events into the experiment—which explores new processes for averting military confrontation in an insurgency-based scenario—to create destabilizing effects to which experiment role players respond—either to avoid crisis or create a more stable environment."[20] The findings from the MNIG concept examined in MNE 4,[21] and associated prototypes like the collaborative information environment—which provides ready access to real-time audio, to text chat capabilities, and to shared "white boards" for users around the world—are already being applied to coalition operations in Iraq and Afghanistan.[22]

This brings up fundamental questions. At what point is experimentation complete? How much experimentation is enough? The response is, "It depends." Defense experimentation is not an endeavor without end. Its purpose is to solve problems related to concepts, yet knowing everything about a concept is not possible. At some point, concept developers and experimenters must determine that adequate information is available to turn the concept over to those who are charged with its implementation.

It is important to note that experimentation is relevant across all elements of doctrine, organization, training, material, leadership, personnel, and facilities.[23] Some experiments include more than one capability domain. In NATO, experimentation embedded within Crisis Management Exercise 2006 "investigated how the experimental Crisis Management Fusion Centre could contribute to shared situational awareness and understanding at the political/military strategic level."[24] Experiment directors used simulations to "develop information such as measurements of average cycle time (from entering the fusion centre until actions are taken), waiting times, predictions of bottlenecks, and recommendations for improvement."[25] The solution ultimately required technical tools, including a collaborative network, and organizational changes in the form of a new crisis-management structure.

Conclusion

This chapter presented the basic terminology for an introduction to defense experimentation and an overview of the methodology for the planning and execution of effective defense experimentation. Most important, the chapter emphasized the need to ensure the linkage between experimentation and operational concepts that will enhance transformation. The objective was to provide a basic understanding of defense experimentation so that those in decisionmaking positions regarding transformation may make informed choices. At this point, it is imperative to return to the three questions posed in the introduction.

1. Can the scientific rules developed in laboratories apply to war-fighting experiments? Here, the answer is an unequivocal yes. *Scientific* implies methodical, structured, and organized. Defense experiments can, and must be, all three. Even in discovery and demonstration experiments, careful pre-event planning that identifies the objectives and constructs the research questions that are the focus of the experiment is mandatory to optimize the experiment's results. *Scientific* also connotes analytical. Bring the analysts into the process early so that the event can produce the data necessary for useful results. The *Guide for Understanding and Implementing Defense Experimentation* (known as GUIDEx) and the Department of Defense (DoD) Command and Control Research Program's *Code of Best Practices* provide the experimenter with clear direction on how to apply the scientific method to solving the problems of defense transformation.[26] Ensure that your experimentation conforms to the principles contained in those guides.

2. Can war-fighting experiments meet the requirement of scientific rigor? Here the affirmative response is less explicit. Described simply, "Rigor requires discipline in the method of inquiry."[27] If the processes used in experimentation adhere to the basic principles provided in the guidelines, then the requisite discipline will be attained. To be intellectually honest, however, the complications inherent in defense experimentation challenge rigor. The first problem is the laboratory. While some isolation may be possible, military operations take place in complex and dynamic environments. The establishment of precise controls becomes problematic. Second, much of the military art is in the cognitive domain, and the selection of a representative subject group is difficult due to the variations in subject experience, knowledge, and motivation.

Nevertheless, the modeling and simulation (M&S) method offers some promise. It provides a controlled (and manipulation-capable) environment; may be programmed to meet specific experiment goals and objectives; and also important, allows multiple iterations to run, which deepens the statistical evidence analysts have to work with. The USJFCOM has used M&S extensively in experimentation programs. NATO is increasing its focus on networked battle labs and greater use of M&S to support experimentation.

3. Can the results of the experiments have any impact on transformation? Clearly, the response is yes. Both the United States and NATO have incorporated concepts, refined through experimentation, into their current operations. The concepts that were the foundation of the US Standing Joint Force Headquarters, collaborative information environment, and system-of-systems analysis capabilities were objects of experimentation. Adoption of the Crisis Management Fusion Center/NATO Strategic Overview concepts, introduced and refined through experimentation, may enhance NATO headquarters crisis-response capability. NATO experimentation with Friendly Force Tracking concepts led to the deployment of an operational system with the International Security and Assistance Force in Afghanistan.

This leads us to the question of what the future holds for defense experimentation. As stated earlier, a specialized field of defense experimentation, with an organization, structure, and dedicated practitioners, is still relatively new. In many ways, we are still experimenting with experimentation. Some envision an increased partnership among the military, academia, and industry, by which each provides its specialized capabilities to produce more efficient and worthwhile experiments.[28] Continuous experimentation environments with this full range of partners would be more responsive to transformation needs and could reduce the need for large and expensive events. As more nations create experimentation laboratories, multinational participation can be increased, at a reduced cost, through distributed events, in which nations may participate from their home facilities via networked communications and displays. The nature of future conflict, and the perceived need to involve all elements of national and alliance power in the resolution strategy, suggest that purely military concepts and related experimentation may come to have less weight. This transformation of experimentation, while promising, nevertheless does not reduce the need to adhere to the scientific principles described earlier.

To conclude, scientific rigor is not only possible but necessary, so that defense experimentation can effectively contribute to the overall transformation effort. A major challenge is that no single experiment can meet all scientific rigor requirements; the solution is to build a body of knowledge through a series of experiments with internal and external participants and processes. The methodology of choice is a comprehensive experimentation campaign that can provide the requisite breadth and depth of data needed for concept refinement. While defense experimentation cannot provide the scientific purity of chemistry or physics laboratories, the intelligent use of the scientific method establishes validity and enhances its overall contribution to transformation.

Notes

1. Arthur K. Cebrowski, *Military Transformation: A Strategic Approach,* Office of Force Transformation (OFT), Office of the Secretary of Defense, 2003: 3; available at the OFT website: http://www.oft.osd.mil/library/library_files/document_297_MT_StrategyDoc1.pdf.

2. North Atlantic Treaty Organization Headquarters, Supreme Allied Command Transformation, *Strategic Vision: The Military Challenge,* 2004: 17, http://transnet.act.nato.int/WISE/StrategicV/StrategicV/file/_WFS/stratvis0804.pdf.

3. *American Heritage College Dictionary,* 3rd ed. (Boston: Houghton Mifflin, 2001), under the word "experimentation."

4. Chris Morris, "Experimentation: What's It All About Then?" *NITEworks* 1 (Spring 2004): 6, http://www.niteworks.net/publications/docindex.asp?title=NITEworks%20Magazine&ID=2&section=36. NITEworks is an innovative concept of a partnership between the UK Ministry of Defense and industry to carry out defense experimentation.

5. Richard A. Kass, *The Logic of Warfighting Experiments* (Washington, DC: DoD Command and Control Research Program, 2006), vi; available as a pdf file from http://www.dodccrp.org/html4/books_downloads.html.

6. "In Unison, Annual Report, 2005–2006," *Defence Research and Development Canada* 40, http://www.drdc-rddc.gc.ca.

7. Dean Browley, Michael Brennan, and Stephen Cook, "Military Experimentation: A Systems Engineering Approach to Force Development" (Salisbury: University of South Australia, 2001), 3, http://www.unisa.edu.au/seec/pubs/01papers/F234_116-cook,bowley,brennan.pdf.

8. *Guide for Understanding and Implementing Defense Experimentation* (GUIDEx), the Technical Cooperation Program (TTCP), Ottawa, Canada, 2006: 39. TTCP comprises experimenters from Australia, Canada, the United Kingdom, and the United States. The GUIDEx is the most authoritative and complete multinational treatise available on experimentation related to defense transformation.

9. North Atlantic Treaty Organization, *Strategic Vision: The Military Challenge,* 2004, http://transnet.act.nato.int/WISE/StrategicV/StrategicV/file/_WFS/stratvis0804.pdf. This report states that an effects-based approach to operations involves the comprehensive application of all instruments of alliance power, both military and nonmilitary, to create campaign effects that will achieve desired outcomes. NATO's Allied Command Transformation conducted operational experimentation related to an effects-based approach to operations during Multinational Experiment 4 in 2006.

10. Among these are the previously cited TTCP GUIDEx; Kass's *Warfighting Experiments;* and David S. Alberts and Richard E. Hayes, *Code of Best Practices for Experimentation,* Department of Defense Command and Control Research Program, Information Age Transformation Series, Washington, DC, 2002, http://www.dodccrp.org/files/Alberts_Experimentation.pdf.

11. Alberts and Hayes, *Code of Best Practices,* 19.

12. "Joint Urban Warrior 07," US Joint Forces Command Fact Sheet, http://www.jfcom.mil/about/experiments/fact_juw07.html.

13. North Atlantic Treaty Organization, "Crisis Management: A Fundamental Security Task," NATO-OTAN website, 7 December 2007, http://www.nato.int/issues/crisis_management/index.html; and "NATO Response Force Leaders Consider NRF Missions," NATO Allied Command Operations headquarters news release, 4 May 2007, http://www.nato.int/shape/news/2007/05/070504a.htm.

14. "Pinnacle Impact 2003," US Joint Forces Command Fact Sheet, http://www.jfcom.mil/about/experiments/pi03.htm.

15. Alberts and Hayes, *Code of Best Practices,* 23.

16. Grover E. Myers, "MILLENNIUM CHALLENGE 2002: Setting the Mark," *Joint Forces Quarterly* 33 (Winter 2002–2003): 26, http://www.dtic.mil/doctrine/jel/jfq_pubs/win02_03.htm; and "Multinational Experiment Kicks Off," News from US Joint Forces Command (USJFCOM), 2 February 2004, http://www.globalsecurity.org/military/library/news/2004/02/mil-040201-jfcom01.htm.

17. Michael Wahl, "U.S. Joint Forces Command Multinational Experiment 3—An Overview," white paper by Working Group 33 at the 72nd Military Operations Research symposium at the Naval Postgraduate School, Monterey, California, 18 October 2004: 12–19, http://handle.dtic.mil/100.2/ADA428147.

18. Ibid., 13–17.

19. Christopher Hoffpauir, "USJFCOM to Test Multinational Interagency Group Concept During MNE4," News from USJFCOM (press release), 8 February 2006, http://www.jfcom.mil/newslink/storyarchive/2006/pa022306.htm.

20. Jennifer Colaizzi, "MNE4 Experiment Controllers Make Life Interesting for Role Players," News from USJFCOM, 7 March 2006, http://www.jfcom.mil/newslink/storyarchive/2006/pa030706.htm.

21. Dr. Elizabeth Bowman, "Measuring Team Collaboration in a Distributed Coalition Network," presentation to the twelfth International Command and Control Research and Technology symposium in Newport, Rhode Island, 20 June 2007, www.dodccrp.org/events/12th_ICCRTS/CD/html/presentations/124.pdf.

22. Donna Miles, "Multinational Experiment Lessons Already Benefiting Coalition Ops," US Armed Forces Press Service, 7 March 2006, http://www.defenselink.mil/news/newsarticle.aspx?id=15246.

23. This is the US DoD's list of capability domains, commonly referred to by the acronym DOTMLPF. NATO normally adds *I* for interoperability.

24. Joel I. Huval, US Navy, "ACT Supports Crisis Management Exercise 2006, Command Tackles Improved Response to Threats Through Modeling and Simulation," Allied Command Transformation, Transformation Network, 7 March 2006: 1, http://www.act.nato.int/content.asp?pageid=897.

25. Ibid.

26. See notes 8 and 10.

27. Cebrowski, "Criteria for Successful Experimentation," Memorandum for the Secretaries of the Military Departments et al., Office of the Secretary of Defense, Office of Force Transformation, 7 July 2007, 2, http://www.oft.osd.mil/library/library_files/press_224._Criteria%20for%20Successful%20Experimentation.pdf.

28. Jon Cupp, US Army, "Wood Addresses Experimentation, Transformation at Industry Forum," News from USJFCOM, 6 April 2005, http://www.jfcom.mil/newslink/storyarchive/2005/pa040605.htm.

9

The US Shift Beyond Capital Assets

Rich Butler

Events subsequent to 9/11 have had a profound impact on defense transformation in the United States. The concept of transformation, which appeared regularly in military discourse by the late 1990s, quickly became mantra inside the US Department of Defense (DoD) following Donald Rumsfeld's confirmation as secretary of defense in 2001, a post he had previously held in the 1970s. His flair for analysis and his desire to instill continuous change and efficiency within the military establishment were the foundations for a clear and consistent ideology. Just as no one foresaw the devastation of 9/11, however, military leaders of the time could not foresee how the concept of transformation would itself change as a result of the current campaigns of the war against international terrorism.

This chapter will look at the shift in transformation priorities that have occurred since the US military became fully engaged in the global war on terrorism following the invasion of and subsequent operations in Iraq beginning in 2003. Given the breadth and depth of the subject, a general discussion of the nature of this shift within the DoD will be followed by a few examples drawn from each of the four American military services to demonstrate how the US military is using lower-cost technologies and adaptive concepts to meet the urgent challenges of the twenty-first century in a fiscally constrained political environment. The goal is that readers, particularly defense officials and military service members of other nations, will be able to appreciate the nature of this shift, and see ways in which their own militaries can use American experiences either to embark on their own transformational processes or to operate more effectively alongside US armed forces.

Initial Policy Steps: From Joint Vision to the Capstone Concept for Joint Operations

> There is no way that a big organization can be led from the top. It has to be led from throughout by people who have the same culture and the same orientation and the same desire to see those changes implemented.
>
> —*Donald H. Rumsfeld, US secretary of defense*[1]

Following the end of the Cold War, the defense community in the United States recognized that the time was right for change and modernization. Given the dominant military posture of the United States around the world and its lack of an apparent peer competitor, Washington could safely invest in new technology and innovative concepts designed to prepare its military for future operations against foes yet unnamed. These investments focused generally on preparing the United States and its allies for future conventional challenges, especially against the next foreseeable peer competitor. Forces were designed to achieve preeminence in major combat campaign–type missions, such as air superiority, sea supremacy, forcible entry, and air-land battle.

This outlook was articulated by the chairman of the Joint Chiefs of Staff in *Joint Vision 2010,* published in 1997, and its subsequent revision, *Joint Vision 2020,* published in 2000.[2] The crux of the Joint Chiefs' position was that the US military and its allies could win against any enemy provided the services achieved "full spectrum dominance," in which information superiority and technological innovation would create asymmetric effects in the battle space.[3]

Very little in these two documents addressed the actual source of the expected threat, indicating that the military was moving toward a capabilities-based, as opposed to a threat-based, approach to warfare. This would not be officially codified until the 2001 Quadrennial Defense Review (QDR), which was developed under the personal supervision of recently installed Secretary of Defense Rumsfeld.[4] Joint Vision 2010 referred to potential adversaries simply as "states or groups that oppose or threaten American interests and values or those of our friends and allies."[5] Joint Vision 2020 is even vaguer, giving no obvious definition of potential adversaries. Neither document describes the differences between state and nonstate actors, and both use the opaque term *adversary* in discussing the capability of a modern US military to defeat a state-directed force using the full-spectrum dominance concept.

Published a scant three weeks after September's terrorist attacks on the US homeland, QDR 2001 was modified to clearly highlight the significant dangers now posed by ideologically charged nonstate actors. First and foremost, however, the document articulated Secretary Rumsfeld's desire for a much more rapid pace of change than that originally intended by senior military leaders. Ultimately, a greater number of legacy systems, current acquisition programs not seen as transformational, and personnel end-strength would be sacrificed to permit greater investment in newer weapons systems designed to secure US military dominance far into the twenty-first century.

Over the next six years, the problem of addressing nonstate actors and rogue nations employing irregular, catastrophic, and disruptive methods became increasingly important to the national security strategy of the United States. The low-end threats emerging worldwide challenged the status quo reflected in the original transformation process. In some respects, transformation needed to be transformed. This shift in defense priorities was captured in the "Capstone Concept for Joint Operations" (CCJO), released in 2004 and modified in 2005.[6] This document essentially superseded the *Joint Vision* papers, although they were not officially canceled. The Capstone Concept espoused the need for a truly joint military, able to act in a nonstovepiped (that is, cooperative and seamless), nonlinear (that is, networked and distributed) way, and capable of integrated operations with other nations as well as with nonmilitary organizations. Unlike the *Joint Vision* papers, it defined a full range of possible enemies, labeling transnational security threats and nontraditional adversaries as the most important long-term threats to US security. The credibility of the CCJO was reinforced by the 2005 National Defense Strategy, the 2006 National Security Strategy, and the 2006 QDR, all of which champion the need to find new approaches to dealing with the threat of nontraditional and nonstate actors.

The Office of Force Transformation: Getting Outside the Box

> The role of good management, of the transformational leader, is to look at and identify perfectly predictable surprises and act in advance. The responsibilities of transformational leaders are to identify disparities before they take place and stop wasting time with optimizations and efficiencies that will be irrelevant in the face of policy changes.
>
> —*Vice Admiral Arthur K. Cebrowski, director, Office of Force Transformation*[7]

Besides providing guidance toward capability-based planning, the 2001 QDR also ushered in another significant change regarding how the military would transform to meet future threats, by announcing that the DoD "will establish a new office reporting directly to the Secretary and Deputy Secretary of Defense. The Director, Force Transformation will evaluate the transformation efforts of the Military Departments and promote synergy by recommending steps to integrate ongoing transformation activities."[8] The Office of Force Transformation (OFT) stood up in October 2001. The man chosen to be the director was retired US Navy vice admiral Arthur Cebrowski, an influential military futurist who possessed a keen conceptual awareness and strategic vision for implementing the information technology revolution in military affairs. OFT itself was transformational in nature, having a staff of fewer than twenty, a limited budget of $20 million, and the ability to conduct in-house assessments of the DoD bureaucracy and its large competing service staffs. OFT's most important role, however, was to act as a clearinghouse for transformational issues.

Transformation, as acknowledged in the 2001 QDR, was seen as a continuous process reaching into all aspects of the military, and Admiral Cebrowski's staff worked to help transformational ideas embed themselves in each service's acquisition strategies, warfare concepts, and integration with sister services. OFT also had the power to propose alternative strategies and concepts and was especially active in the broad realm of network-centric operations. In addition, the office conducted operational lessons-learned analyses and recommended solutions. In 2004 OFT published two cornerstone documents: *The Elements of Transformation* and *Military Transformation: A Strategic Approach.*[9] The former expanded and codified the nature and components of transformation, which had been originally framed in the *Transformation Planning Guidance* (TPG) published by the Office of the Secretary of Defense in 2003.[10] The latter explained how the transformation process would work at the macro level, describing the playing field and providing ground rules. The TPG appeared to centralize the power of OFT by providing the following direction: "The Director, Office of Force Transformation (OFT), will monitor and evaluate implementation of the Department's transformation strategy, advise the secretary, and manage the transformation roadmap process. He will help ensure that joint concepts are open to challenge by a wide range of innovative alternative concepts and ideas."[11]

The TPG's "transformation roadmap process" referred to the use of service-produced documents that enabled OFT, and the secretary, to better oversee the transformation process. The roadmaps gave the DoD leadership the ability to verify at the macro level, and well in advance of procurement, that the money, labor, and time devoted to a multitude of projects were indeed transformational. Roadmaps were to be updated yearly as well as reviewed to ensure that the services were building the capabilities necessary to execute joint concepts. In August 2006 the Defense Department decided to close the OFT, believing that transformational thinking had matured and was engrained throughout the department.[12]

Transformation in the Individual Services: Reevaluating Their Priorities

Prior to 9/11, the US military's advantage in technology and resources—the hallmark of America's modern way of war—had been focused, at least for the time being, on "the wolf closest to the sled." At that time, military strategists and planners had completed critical analysis and planning regarding the transformation that needed to occur to meet a conventional state competitor. Generally, this was defined as the modification or replacement of crucial capital assets by each service. The army had begun a study of what it initially called the Objective Force, which was predominantly a high-end, platform-centric construct modeled around platforms like the Crusader tracked artillery vehicle and the Comanche attack and reconnaissance helicopter. The navy had expanded its concept of network-centric warfare and was pursuing its next-generation carrier, destroyer, and cruiser to take advantage of advances in joint-strike warfare and missile defense. Naval planners also were working to integrate the US Navy–Marine Corps team for the kinds of coordination required by the conceptual documents "Forward from the Sea" and "Ship to Objective Maneuver."[13] The air force was aggressively pursuing major acquisitions such as the F-22A Raptor jet fighter and the Global Hawk unmanned aerial vehicle; was working toward a large-scale organizational change, as reflected in the Aerospace Expeditionary Force concept; and was investing heavily in high-end programs related to space and laser technology.

Army: From Heavy Conventional Warfare to a Lightweight, Modular Full-Spectrum Force

> We are ultimately working toward an agile, globally responsive army empowered by modern networks, surveillance sensors and weapons that are lighter and less manpower-intensive, and employed in modular units that are able to operate effectively, again, across the spectrum of conflict with joint and coalition partners.
>
> —*General George Casey, US Army chief of staff*[14]

Following the end of the Cold War, the army evaluated its organization and equipment and concluded that its force was far too heavy and cumbersome to meet the threats and budgetary restraints of the new millennium.

Two concepts emerged from this evaluation: the Brigade Combat Team (BCT) and the Future Combat System (FCS).

The BCT model was put forward in 2000 with the intention of increasing the army's flexibility, a reaction to the fact that operations such as Restore Hope (Somalia, 1993) and Allied Force (Kosovo, 1999) had suggested that the army would be unlikely to move entire divisions as the base unit of combat, and that force flow would need to be much more rapid and scalable. In the BCT force, the standard deployment unit would be a brigade of combined combat (maneuver companies) and combat support elements (intelligence, police, signal, engineer, artillery, and so on). The flexible modularity of the BCT has proved to be extremely responsive to the needs of Operation Iraqi Freedom, by providing a larger pool of deployable force packages for the combatant commander while giving greater stability to individual soldiers. In response to an increase of 65,000 soldiers, the army is working to create forty-eight modular BCTs in the active army and twenty-eight in the Army National Guard.[15]

The army's Future Combat System is considered to be the cornerstone of its full-spectrum modernization effort:

> FCS is not just a technology development program—it is the development of new Brigade Combat Teams. These new brigades, with more infantry, better equipment, improved communications, and unmatched situational awareness, will change the way the Army fights wars. These BCTs will prove invaluable during asymmetric and stability operations, allowing for precision targeted fires (keeps civilians out of harm's way) and more infantry on the ground (to patrol civilian populations). Through sensors connected to the Brigade Combat Team's network, they offer real-time situational updates allowing for the Army to kill the enemy before they [*sic*] strike military or civilian targets (see them first and take them out).[16]

Its component systems, all linked together by a robust information network, comprise

1. Unattended ground sensors
2. Non-Line-of-Sight Launch System
3. Two classes of unmanned aerial vehicles (platoon- and brigade-level)
4. Small Unmanned Ground Vehicle
5. Multifunctional Utility/Logistics and Equipment Vehicle
6. Eight variants of manned ground vehicles[17]

Army vice chief of staff General Peter W. Chiarelli states, "New Army fighting vehicles promise to transform the nature of war as dramatically as the tank did in the 20th Century," as they are "designed for the full-spectrum fight."[18] The lead prototype in the family of eight manned ground vehicles is the Non-Line-of-Sight-Cannon (NLOS-C), which successfully fired an artillery projectile in September 2008. The NLOS-C is much different from all the other combat vehicles produced thus far, with a fully automated ammunition loading system and a hybrid electric chassis.[19]

Notably absent from the platform production schedule are the most expensive army acquisitions proposed following the end of the Cold War, the Crusader helicopter and Comanche artillery vehicle, which were terminated in 2002 and 2004, respectively, along with the Objective Force concept.

In July 2004 the army announced plans to accelerate the delivery of select FCS (BCT) capabilities to the current force. Three FCS "spin-outs," designed to reduce operational risk during ongoing asymmetric operations, will mature over five years. They will first be field-tested by the Army Evaluation Task Force based at Fort Bliss, Texas.[20] For example, spin-out 1 technology includes

1. Network Capability Integration "B" Kit, containing the System of Systems Common Operating Environment for translating army, joint, and coalition message formats, which will be integrated into existing Abrams, Bradley, and Humvee combat platforms;
2. Unattended urban and tactical ground sensors for target detection, location, classification, and identification;
3. Non-line-of-Sight Launch System consisting of an unmanned platform-independent Container Launch Unit with fifteen precision attack missiles.[21]

The spin-out integration of FCS equipment into the current force will provide an intriguing look at how the newest technologies can be incorporated into traditionally equipped militaries; furthermore, the equipment should be attractive to Washington's allies as they seek greater capabilities of their own and enhanced compatibility in allied or coalition operations.

Navy: From Traditional Blue Water into a Maritime Security Force

> *The Cooperative Strategy for 21st Century Seapower* articulates an approach that integrates seapower with other elements of national power in cooperation with our friends and allies. Our desire is to move beyond episodic involvement and execute a strategy that ensures security and prosperity.
>
> —*Admiral Gary Roughead, chief of Naval Operations*[22]

The campaign in Afghanistan showcased the navy's ability to project striking power and logistics great distances as part of a joint force. As the land wars in Afghanistan and Iraq evolved, however, the navy found it increasingly difficult to justify larger expenditures in traditional blue water, navy-centric missions. Additionally, nontraditional naval missions such as coastal warfare and civil affairs actions have, as of this writing, risen to prominence for the first time since Vietnam. The development of the Littoral Combat Ship (LCS), the retention of the Cyclone-class Patrol Coastals, and the creation of the Navy Expeditionary Combat Command (NECC) are examples of how the navy has adapted to new challenges presented by transnational security and rogue-nation threats.

The LCS concept evolved from the unique anti-access needs of littoral warfare. Its technology platform is related to that of the "street fighter" concept first developed in 1999 by then-admiral Cebrowski and Wayne Hughes, a retired captain.[23] The LCS represents a significant departure from traditional ship design, technological experimentation, and acquisition. It is the first hull built from the keel up using off-the-shelf computer technology, to take advantage of the Information Age revolution in military affairs.

The LCS is a modular hull that is reconfigurable depending on mission area. Surface, antisubmarine, and mine-warfare-mission packages are under design or ready for delivery.[24] There has also been discussion of counterterrorism payloads (that would focus on maritime interdiction to capture terrorists and suppress the proliferation of weapons of mass destruction) as well as a humanitarian aid package.[25] The entire combat suite can be lifted out and replaced on short notice, making the LCS lethal in single mission areas; and, although far less robust than its Aegis-equipped cousins, the LCS is much more affordable. While it will be heavily dependent on unmanned vehicles to complete its missions, helicopter detachments will also embark. The navy's 313-ship fleet plan features fifty-five LCS seaframes, but owing to design problems, even a recent boost in the per-ship cost cap from $220 million to $460 million might not be enough for production.[26] Meanwhile, the number of mission packages and the number and location of LCS homeports and mission-package installation sites needed to optimize availability for operational plans are under study.[27]

The perceived advantages of this type of vessel extend well beyond its modularity. The vessel is corvette-sized and will use technology to minimize personnel and cut costs. Like the army's FCS, the plan for the LCS and its associated modules was to employ spiral development to help achieve project maturation approximately twice as fast as is required for a traditionally procured ship. Furthermore, the navy opened a competitive bid to both Lockheed Martin and General Dynamics for design and production of two types of experimental hulls—one a semiplaning steel monohull, the other an aluminum trimaran. Both have a relatively shallow draft, wide girth, and maximum speed in excess of 46 miles (40 knots) per hour—features that provide extra payload area and collective versatility.[28] The Lockheed Martin version in particular capitalizes on readily available foreign-designed or -built systems, like British gas turbines and water jets, Danish countermeasures, a Swedish 57-mm gun, German 3-D (three-dimensional) radar, and a Spanish fire-control system.[29]

While production of the modules has gone well, however, the transformation of a commercially designed hull into an entirely new type of naval warship has turned out to be more complicated than its planners anticipated. Despite a ceremonial launching for the Lockheed Martin prototype LCS *Freedom* in September 2006, both projects have run several years behind schedule and hundreds of millions of dollars over budget. Nevertheless, compared with the cost of most navy combat ships, navy officials still consider even a near–$500 million price tag for the LCS to be a bargain.[30] The *Freedom* (LCS 1) was finally commissioned by the navy in Milwaukee, Wisconsin, on 8 November 2008, officially placing the Lockheed Martin–constructed vessel into active service four years after contract award.[31]

Retention of the Cyclone-class Patrol Coastals, following their deployment to Iraq in 2003, was another important step toward ensuring that the navy has the right capabilities to help win the global war on terror. Originally, these assets were to decommission in 2003 for want of a perceived mission. The 179-foot gunboats, however, have proved to be a superb littoral asset, acting as a bridge between the open ocean strike groups and the coastal and riverine units. They have decent endurance, fair seakeeping capability, and superb speed and maneuverability, as well as a very shallow draft that allows them to go anywhere required. They are also much cheaper to own and operate than frigates, which makes them perfect for low-end missions like oil platform protection.[32] Similar in size and capability to most of the assets of foreign navies, these units are particularly useful for regional engagement and training.

As part of its larger organizational transformation, in 2006 the US Navy established the Navy Expeditionary Combat Command (NECC) to centrally manage the current and future readiness, resources, manning, training, and equipping of approximately 40,000 expeditionary sailors. The NECC provides a full spectrum of operations, including waterborne and ashore antiterrorism force protection, theater security cooperation and engagement, and humanitarian assistance and disaster relief.[33]

Following Vietnam and the inception of the Nixon Doctrine, which devolved the burden of defending US allies from the US military to the individual countries themselves, many of the NECC's functions were relegated to reserve units or abrogated as a core role of the navy. After 9/11, in response to the sharpened focus on force protection, the navy provided increased coastal and harbor defense, not only by activating reserve Coastal Warfare Squadrons but also by creating two new active-duty squadrons composed of Mobile Inshore Underwater Surveillance Units and Inshore Boat Units.[34] The navy also commissioned three Riverine Squadrons, relieving the Marine Corps of this mission area, starting with patrol of the Euphrates River in western Iraq in spring 2007.[35] By aligning these Naval Coastal Warfare (later called Maritime Expeditionary Security) and Riverine Squadrons under the NECC, along with other disparate elements, such as Explosive Ordinance Disposal Groups, Naval Construction (Seabees) Division, Expeditionary Logistics Support Group, Combat Camera, Maritime Civil Affairs Group, and Navy Individual Augmentees, one command headed by a flag officer can oversee the rapid deployment of adaptive detachments for maritime and land security missions.

The return of these mission areas to the active-duty navy is a watershed. The newly organized NECC units contribute maritime combat support forces to joint war-fighting commanders worldwide, and in many cases relieve stress on the joint force. Thus, the NECC, by providing navy expeditionary forces beyond big-deck capital assets, plays an important role in the maritime cooperative strategy to protect and sustain national security and world prosperity.[36]

Marine Corps: From Conventional to Counterinsurgency Operations

> As we meet the irregular challenges of Small Wars, "A Concept for Distributed Operations" is intended to promote discussion and to generate ideas for specific combat development initiatives . . . innovation that is squarely focused on our most important weapon—the Marine. "Distributed Operations" describes an operating approach that requires new ways to educate and train our Marines and that guides us in the use of emerging technologies.
>
> —*General Michael W. Hagee, 33rd commandant, Marine Corps*[37]

In 1989 an interesting and controversial article in the *Marine Corps Gazette,* entitled "The Changing Face of War: Into the Fourth Generation," put forward an argument that future ground combat operations would be conducted by smaller, more lethal and independent units of action, creating asymmetry in the decisionmaking process and outperforming the enemy through superior tactics, training, and equipment.[38] The article described the first generation of modern warfare as the evolution of smoothbore muskets and line tactics; the second as encompassing the development of the rifled musket through the machine gun, and the eventual failure of linear movement; and the third as maneuver warfare embodied in the German blitzkrieg. This article was republished in November 2001 in response to discussions of the asymmetric warfare methods employed by Al-Qaida.

Marine leadership in the 1980s reinvigorated the Corps with the philosophy of maneuver warfare, so it should not be surprising that marines are conceptually leading the way in reinvigorating interest in the counterinsurgency mission. They are also providing substantial tangible input into how to fight and win on this challenging battlefield. Years of experimentation at the Marine Corps Warfighting Laboratory (MCWL) led to the concept of Distributed Operations, which describes an approach that will create an advantage over an adversary through deliberate separation into small units that use coordinated, interdependent, tactical actions made possible by better access to functional support and enhanced combat capabilities at the small-unit level.[39]

In April 2005 General Michael Hagee, then commandant of the Marine Corps, signed "A Concept for Distributed Operations," which set the stage for a series of experiments intended to institutionalize better training, manning, and equipping of Marine Corps tactical units for operations on the distributed battlefield. The paper does not designate the concept as a fourth generation warfare function; instead, it describes the empowerment of small units, operating with a clear understanding of their commander's intent, as the highest form of maneuver warfare. The concept nevertheless bears the hallmarks of fourth generation warfare, and will allow Marine Air-Ground Task Forces to operate more effectively over battlefields of much greater dimensions than ever before.

The first experimental "DO (distributed operations) platoon" completed training and workups under the auspices of the MCWL and forward-deployed to Afghanistan in late 2005. Noncommissioned officers from the British Royal Marines and the Australian Army were key participants in the DO platoon's Small Unit Enhancement Training regimen. The DO platoon marines had an enhanced DO communications suite and were provided higher levels of instruction in, for example, close air support. On concluding its training, the DO platoon conducted a limited-objective experiment against a numerically superior opposing force; the outcome was impressive.[40] During the deployment, and during the course of a DO platoon long-range security patrol, a convoy from another unit was attacked by insurgents using improvised explosive devices, mortars, and small arms. The convoy commander was unable to maintain communications with higher headquarters or call in indirect fires.

The DO platoon relayed communications and took control of close air support and evacuation of the wounded.[41] Analysis of this first platoon's performance shaped subsequent DO experimentation in 2006 and continues to influence long-term experimentation within the MCWL.

In 2006 a second limited objective experiment took place, introducing specific training and equipment designed to assess the viability of the DO concept in different tactical scenarios. As an example, the Wasp micro–unmanned aerial vehicle (UAV) and its associated training package were added to the platoon headquarters for the event. Partly as a result, Wasp is now being fielded to Marine Corps tactical units at the company level.

Among the additional training provided to the marines were

1. Fires training, which includes qualifying the platoon's commander and platoon sergeant as Joint Tactical Air Controllers and the squad leaders as Joint Fire Observers, using a combination of classroom, simulation, and live terminal control.
2. A "Train-the-Trainer" (T3) mobile training team (MTT) from the Marine Corps Training and Education Command course instructed small-unit leaders within the platoon to better and more effectively train their marines.
3. In the wake of the T3 MTT, an experimental Tactical Small Unit Leaders Course for the fire team leader was incorporated. This course has now been standardized and is being implemented Marine Corps–wide.
4. Core Skills and Small Unit Enhancement Training, which focused on cross-training and teaching new tactics, techniques, and procedures.[42]

Unfortunately, experimentation has demonstrated that providing an additional tactical communications capability (given current [as of this writing] program-of-record equipment) comes with a literally heavy price, since the platoon carried an extra 100 pounds of communications gear. On top of this, each marine was equipped with rifle-mounted and handheld night vision scopes, a thermal sight, a personal GPS (Global Positioning System) monitor, and a small Personal Role Radio for intrateam communications. Additional platoon-level communications equipment included

- Three PRC-117 radios (multifrequency, satellite, and secure capable).
- Two PRC-150F radios (high frequency, voice, or data capable).
- Eleven Expeditionary Tactical Communication Systems consisting of modified iridium phones, to allow marines to receive and transmit voice and data while on the move.[43]

In aggregate, this first phase of DO experimentation (2005–2006) demonstrated that marines, if trained properly and provided with state-of-the-art equipment, could perform offensive missions (surveillance, ambush, and raid) at a level well beyond units not similarly trained and equipped. Perhaps most important, the two-year experimentation program spawned the Infantry Battalion Enhancement Period Program (IBEPP) developed by the DO Implementation Working Group.[44] The IBEPP has been accepted by the Marine Corps as its force generation model, designed to ensure that deploying units are manned, trained, and equipped to the standards identified and validated by DO experimentation.

MCWL experimentation continues. Its single focal point is to comply with the current (at this writing) commandant's simple but eloquent guidance: "Our Marines and Sailors in combat are our number one priority."[45] This translates into development of enhanced capabilities for Marine tactical units and their small-unit leaders. The MCWL recently concluded the Combat Hunter series of limited-objective experiments, designed to instill a "hunter's mindset" into offensive operations on the modern battlefield. It placed heavy emphasis on enhanced observation skills, battlefield anomaly detection, and improved training on all day and night observation devices. The results have already been incorporated into the formal training pipeline for all marines, not just the infantry.

Ongoing experimentation includes development of a standardized company-level intelligence cell; an Infantry Skills Simulation Working Group that is developing a simulation "system of systems" to virtually train small units and enable virtual mission rehearsal; use of simulation to train every infantry squad leader to be a Type II Close Air Support observer; development of a new Combat Functional Fitness program; and, finally, a Lighten the Load study of the effects of equipment weight on the physical and cognitive abilities of marines in combat operations. Marine Corps "transformation" is about supporting those marines where the rubber meets the road in the US global war on terrorism. The end result, however, will be "a multi-purpose Marine Corps that is capable of operating with greater autonomy across the spectrum of conflict."[46]

Air Force: Reinvigorated Support for the Ground Warrior

> We've learned we cannot repeat the mistakes of the past. We've learned we cannot rest on the [laurels] of our current dominance. We've learned to anticipate future security environments and to shape ourselves accordingly. And we've learned that transformations do not happen overnight—they take time, [expert] planning, patience, and sufficient funding. We are acting on these lessons. We anticipate a future security environment that is fundamentally different than we have anticipated before.
>
> —*General T. Michael Moseley, US Air Force chief of staff*[47]

Like the other services, the US Air Force (USAF) has modified its transformation flight plan as a result of the global war on terrorism. The perceived need for additional advanced air-superiority capability has waned to a certain extent as the struggle against international terrorism has evolved. While plans for the acquisition of high-end manned aviation assets like the F-22A Raptor have been curtailed (from 341 in 2000 to 187 in 2008), the UAV has risen in prominence. The air force has revolutionized UAV operations, using them not just for intelligence, surveillance, and reconnaissance missions but also as kinetic kill vehicles. In Yemen in 2002 a supersonic Hellfire missile launched from a USAF-flown CIA Predator UAV killed Al-Qaida terrorists traveling in a vehicle, categorically ushering in the era of the armed UAV.[48]

Focusing primarily on medium- and high-altitude overland UAV missions, the air force currently operates the medium-range MQ-1L Predator A, armed with Hellfire missiles; is flying and updating the long-range RQ-4 Global Hawk for carrying synthetic aperture radar, electro-optical, infrared, and signal intelligence payloads; and is deploying the hunter-killer MQ-9B Predator B armed with a laser-guided GBU-12 bomb, GBU-38 Joint Direct Attack Munition, and Hellfire.[49] The use of armed UAVs by the USAF and Central Intelligence Agency has expanded dramatically in Afghanistan and Iraq, where around-the-clock persistence and reactive striking power are advantageous in close air support, interdiction, and combat search and rescue missions.[50] The USAF is also using the tactical RQ-11 Raven UAV in Iraq to see events on the ground, like the placing of improvised explosive devices on the side of roads, from miles away.[51]

The air force investment in UAV development is important from a number of standpoints, and relevant to nearly every military around the globe. In terms of cost, the medium-altitude UAV, at $5–10 million per platform, is dramatically less expensive than manned aircraft, although as a system that includes the control suite, its initial cost is more comparable. If a UAV airframe does crash, however, the control suite survives; therefore, recurring costs decrease, as does the threat to the controller. UAV accident rates—at this writing, 100 times higher than manned aircraft—can be expected to decrease as reliance on human control decreases.[52] The greatest value of UAVs is in their on-station time and sensor package. They are useful in nearly any environment where manned aircraft dwell-time is limited, freeing up pilots to perform tasks for which they are better suited. Most important, the increase in loiter time for UAVs increases the likelihood of a mission kill against low-observable and mobile targets such as terrorists.

The USAF, like its sister services, has revised how it outfits and trains many of its men and women to meet new mission requirements. The concept of the Battlefield Airman grew directly out of lessons learned in Afghanistan, where command, control, and coordination among the army, air force, and Special Operations Forces broke down during combat operations (such as Operation Anaconda in March 2002), costing the lives of several troops.[53] The term *Battlefield Airman* refers to the organizing, training, and equipping of Pararescue, Combat Control, Tactical Air Control, and Battlefield Weather professionals, each of whom delivers distinctive air force expertise in a ground combat environment.[54]

Then–secretary of the air force James Roche formally announced the Battlefield Airman concept as a high priority in April 2005, stating, "Just as we have a family of airmen we call pilots with a variety of specialties—helicopter, fighter, tanker, airlift, bomber—we need to start thinking about these specialized warriors, these battlefield airmen, in similar terms."[55] The service invested about $34 million in fiscal years 2004–2005 to fund the Battlefield Airman concept—a relatively small amount of money that has had a significant impact. For example, when the army needed to increase the number of air force tactical air control parties in the distributed battle space of Afghanistan and Iraq, the air force responded by training additional airmen equipping them with better radios and modifying their personal equipment to be in line with USAF standards.[56]

Conclusion

This chapter has explored only a few of the low-end transformational initiatives that have begun or been accelerated since the US entry into the global war on terrorism and following the start of the protracted US presence in Iraq. Military planners are now placing greater emphasis on developing capabilities that create an asymmetric advantage to defeat counterinsurgency and terrorist threats, dangers that can be expected to persist well into the future. A strategic shift is clearly evident in the move from transforming to meet a future traditional, conventional threat to meeting irregular, catastrophic, and disruptive challenges posed by transnational and nontraditional adversaries. This shift in approach to transformation has produced significant changes in the missions, organization, and platforms of the US military.

The examples in this chapter were specifically chosen to illustrate how the US military is utilizing less-expensive and easy-to-use equipment, along with adaptive war-fighting concepts, to defeat a global enemy that challenges the safety and sovereignty of the international community. This approach—utilizing affordable, usable, and practical capabilities to counter asymmetric threats, demonstrates that transformation does not entirely rely on expensive, high-end platforms operating in futuristic concepts. The shift in American war-fighting capabilities beyond capital assets not only encourages greater integration and efficiency among the US military services, it also opens opportunities for other nations to become more capable and compatible.

Notes

1. Donna Miles, "Rumsfeld Shares Transformational Policy with Chinese Military," *Armed Forces Press Service,* http://www.defenselink.mil/news/newsarticle.aspx?id=18023.

2. US Department of Defense (DoD), Office of the Chairman of the Joint Chiefs of Staff, *Joint Vision 2010* (Washington, DC: Government Printing Office [GPO], 1997), www.dtic.mil/jv2010/jv2010.pdf; US Department of Defense, Office of the Chairman of the Joint Chiefs of Staff, *Joint Vision 2020* (Washington, DC: GPO, 2000), www.dtic.mil/jointvision/jvpub2.htm.

3. DoD, *Joint Vision 2010,* 14–27.

4. US Department of Defense, Office of the Secretary of Defense, *2001 Quadrennial Defense Review,* September 2001: 13–14, https://acc.dau.mil/CommunityBrowser.aspx?id=32489.

5. DoD, *Joint Vision 2010,* 10.

6. US Department of Defense, "Capstone Concept for Joint Operations, version 2.0" (Washington, DC: Joint Electronic Library, 2005), 20–23.

7. Quoted in K. L. Vantran, "Transformation Begins with Leadership," Armed Forces Press Service, http://www.defenselink.mil/news/newsarticle.aspx?id=27340.

8. DoD, *2001 Quadrennial,* 29.

9. Both reports are available at the OFT website: http://www.oft.osd.mil.

10. Office of the Secretary of Defense, US Department of Defense, *Transformation Planning Guidance* (Washington, DC: GPO, 2003), 12, http://www.oft.osd.mil/library/library_files/document_129_Transformation_Planning_Guidance_April_2003_1.pdf.

11. Ibid.

12. Josh Rogin, "Defense Transformation Searches for New Identity," *Federal Computer Week,* 16 April 2007, http://www.fcw.com/print/13_11/news/98234-1.html.

13. Both documents are available online at www.globalsecurity.org.

14. General George Casey, "Army Chief of Staff's Remarks at the National Press Club," 14 August 2007, http://www.army.mil/-speeches/2007/08/15/4436-army-chief-of-staffs-remarks-at-the-national-press-club/.

15. Andrew Feickert, "U.S. Army's Modular Redesign: Issues for Congress," Congressional Research Service (24 January), Order Code RL32476 (Washington, DC: US Library of Congress, 2007), 3–9.

16. Department of the Army, US Department of Defense, "Future Combat Systems (Brigade Combat Team [FCS BCT]): Systems Overview," 14 April 2008: 2–3, https://www.fcs.army.mil/news/pdf/FCS_White_Paper_APR08.pdf.

17. Nathan Hodge, "Avenues of Approach: The US Army Is Getting a Glimpse of How Future Combat Systems May Work on the Battefield," *Jane's Defence Weekly,* 20 February 2008: 23–30.

18. Department of the Army, US Department of Defense, quoted in John R. Guardiano, "Vice Chief: FCS Vehicles Will Transform Warfighting," 8 October 2008: 1, http://www.army.mil/-news/2008/10/08/13149-vice-chief-fcs-vehicles-will-transform-warfighting.

19. Department of the Army, US Department of Defense, "The U.S. Army's FCS Program Fires First Round from a Fully Automated Cannon," 18 November 2008: 1, https://www.fcs.army.mil/index.html.

20. Scott Gourley, "US Army Set to Start User Testing on FCS Systems," *Jane's Defence Weekly,* 4 June 2008: 8.

21. US Department of Defense, Department of the Army, "Future Combat Systems Spin Out" (Washington, DC: GPO, 2007), 1–2, http://www.fcs.army.mil/mediaflyers.html.

22. "Statement by Admiral Gary Roughead, Chief of Naval Operations, Before the House Armed Services Committee on the Cooperative Strategy for 21st Century Seapower," House Armed Services Committee, 13 December 2007, http://armedservices.house.gov/pdfs/FC121307/Roughead_Testimony121307.pdf.

23. Greg Jaffe, "Risk Assessment: Plans for a Small Ship Pose Big Questions for the U.S. Navy," *Wall Street Journal,* 11 July 2001: A1.

24. Zachary M. Peterson, "No Ships Yet, but LCS Mine Module Delivered," *Navy Times,* 17 September 2007, www.navytimes.com.

25. Chris Johnson, "Littoral and Mine Warfare Office Outlines Key Needs for Industry," *Inside the Navy,* 27 November 2006; available with permission from the "Inside Defense" website: http://www.insidedefense.com.

26. Christopher J. Castelli, "General Dynamics' Littoral Warship Faces New Cost Growth," *Inside the Navy,* 24 March 2008; available with permission from the "Inside Defense" website: http://www.insidedefense.com.

27. Brien Alkire et al., "Getting the Most Out of Littoral Combat Ships," Research Brief RB-9301-NAVY, RAND Corporation, 2008.

28. Chief of Naval Operations Public Affairs, "First Littoral Combat Ship Christened," *Navy Newsstand,* 24 September 2006, http://www.news.mil/search/display.asp?story_id=25737.

29. Christopher P. Cavas, "Lockheed's LCS an International Product," *Navy Times,* 31 January 2005: 18.

30. Philip Taubman, "Lesson on How Not to Build a Navy Ship," *New York Times,* 25 April 2008, http://www.nytimes.com/2008/04/25/us/25ship.html?th&emc=th; "The USA's New Littoral Combat Ships (Updated)," *Defense Industry Daily,* 29 April 2008, http://www.defenseindustrydaily.com/the-usas-new-littoral-combat-ships-updated-01343/#controversies.

31. Diana K. Massing, Lockheed Martin, "First Littoral Combat Ship Commissioned by Navy," 8 November 2008: 1, http://www.lmlcsteam.com/news.html.

32. Andrew Scutro, "Navy Calls on Cyclone Class," *Navy Times,* 5 December 2005, www.navytimes.com.

33. US Department of Defense, Department of the Navy, NECC website: www.necc.navy.mil.

34. Andrew Scutro, "Coastal Warfare Unit Raring to Go," *Navy Times,* 22 May 2006: 20.

35. Andrew Scutro, "Third Riverine Combat Unit Stands Up," *Navy Times,* 12 July 2007, www.navytimes.com; Zachary M. Peterson, "Riverine Patrols Target Hadithah Dam Hotspot," *Navy Times,* 3 December 2007: 10.

36. General James T. Conway, US Marine Corps; Admiral Gary Roughead, US Navy; and Admiral Thad W. Allen, US Coast Guard, "A Cooperative Strategy for 21st Century Seapower," October 2007, http://www.navy.mil/maritime/.

37. US Department of Defense, Department of the Navy, "A Concept for Distributed Operations," cover letter, US Marine Corps, 25 April 2005.

38. William S. Lind et al., "The Changing Face of War: Into the Fourth Generation," *Marine Corps Gazette* (October 1989): 22–26, http://www.d-n-i.net/fcs/4th_gen_war_gazette.htm.

39. DoD, "A Concept."

40. Vincent J. Goulding Jr., US Naval Institute, "Just DO It," *Proceedings* 132, no. 11 (November 2006): 32–35.

41. Colonel Vincent J. Goulding Jr., US Marine Corps (retired), "DO Platoon," *Marine Corps Gazette* 90, no. 6 (June 2006): 57.

42. "Distributed Operations Limited Objective Experiment (LOE) 2, After Action Report (AAR) (Draft)," Marine Corps Warfighting Laboratory, Quantico, Virginia, 2006: 6–10.

43. Ibid., 11–14.

44. Colonel Vincent J. Goulding Jr., US Marine Corps (retired), "DO: More Than Two Words," *Marine Corps Gazette* (April 2008): 77–78.

45. General James T. Conway, US Marine Corps, "2006: Commandant's Planning Guidance," Introduction to "Marine Corps Operating Concepts for a Changing Security Environment," internal document, June 2007: v, http://www.mcwl.usmc.mil/index.cfm.

46. Lieutenant General James F. Amos, US Marine Corps, "Marine Corps Operating Concepts for a Changing Security Environment," Annex D: Distributed Operations for a Complex Environment, internal document, June 2007: 105, http://www.mcwl.usmc.mil/index.cfm.

47. General T. Michael Moseley, remarks made to the Air Force Association Air Warfare Symposium, Orlando, Florida, 8 February 2007, http://www.af.mil/library/speeches/speech.asp?id=302.

48. Air Force Technology commercial website: http://www.airforce-technology.com/projects/predator.

49. Office of the Secretary of Defense, "UAS Roadmap 2005," 4 August 2005: 3; www.fas.org/irp/program/collect/uav_roadmap2005.pdf.

50. Bill Sweetman, "Predators Ditch TESAR, Move into Strike Role," *Jane's Defence Weekly,* 11 January 2006: 7; and Thom Shanker, "Air Force Yields Some Glamour: Increasing Use of Unmanned Craft Is a Contentious Issue," *International Herald Tribune,* 5 June 2008: 2.

51. Senior Airman Eric Schloeffel, 506th Air Expeditionary Group Public Affairs, "UAVs Aid Force Protection Efforts," news release, 17 March 2008, http://www.af.mil/news/story.asp?id=123090441.

52. Harlan Geer and Christopher Bolkom, *Unmanned Aerial Vehicles: Background and Issues for Congress* (Washington, DC: Congressional Research Service, US Library of Congress, 2005), i; available from the University of North Texas CRS website: http://digital.library.unt.edu/govdocs/crs/searchform.tkl?PHPSESSID=b65d442b0ad325e1905365b48e2b1dff.

53. Elaine M. Grossman, "Air Force Unveils Fresh Commitment to Supporting Ground Troops," *Inside the Army,* 23 Februrary 2004, http://www.insidedefense.com.

54. US Department of Defense, Department of the Air Force, "Battlefield Airmen Factsheet," http://www.af.mil/factsheets/factsheet.asp?fsID=187.

55. Quoted in Hampton Stephens, "USAF Looks to Improve Equipment and Training for 'Battlefield Airmen,'" *Inside the Army,* 3 September 2004: 1, http://www.insidedefense.com.

56. Stephens, "USAF Looks to Improve."

10

The NATO Response Force Initiative

Paul Giarra

Reports of the demise of the North Atlantic Treaty Organization (NATO) are greatly exaggerated, to paraphrase Mark Twain. In the past decade, NATO has shifted radically from struggling to find twenty-first-century relevance to ambitiously embracing a host of twenty-first-century challenges. The evidence of this new course is the success, still incomplete but increasingly substantial, of the NATO Response Force as the alliance's engine for transformation. The history of the NATO Response Force (NRF) is the history of NATO's decision to transform itself, and its objectives and achievements largely are those of the alliance itself since the turn of the century. Likewise, the shortcomings of the NRF highlight where the alliance has more work to do.

After the attacks of 11 September 2001, in a very deliberate response to the escalating but not unprecedented imperative for change, NATO laid out a broad program of political revitalization founded on a strategy of membership enlargement, global deployment, and military transformation. NATO's European members explicitly rejected the "coalitions of the willing" approach promoted by the United States, in favor of more closely integrated NATO command relationships that would enhance the power of transatlantic cooperation.

NATO's plan for the future rested on a strategic military transformation encompassing alliance doctrine, culture, and operations. It would be based on the principles of enhanced transatlantic political and military cooperation, rapid operational response, military innovation, joint and networked forces, integrated logistics and superior information sharing, and out-of-area deployment. The instrument of this strategy was to be the NATO Response Force, which, as the harbinger of transformation, would both implement and facilitate new NATO missions and the greatly expanded geographic interests and responsibilities of the alliance. The deployment and operations of the NRF would force members to confront the issue of change and implement alliance transformation in the field rather than in the conference room. Once operational, the NRF, utilized not always but often, would be "the focal point for force transformation, serving as a testing ground for new technology, doctrine and procedures."[1]

NATO's commitments to transformation came at the nadir of post–Cold War transatlantic relations, impelled by pressure from a US secretary of defense in response to the attacks of 11 September 2001. US secretary of defense Donald Rumsfeld, a strong proponent of military transformation, was motivated by the new "Global War on Terrorism" and the conflicts in Afghanistan and Iraq to increase NATO burden sharing in international security.[2]

The evolution of NATO's internal decisionmaking, mission and force design, achievement of new military capabilities, and realignment of the alliance's strategic posture remain works in progress, but provide a roadmap and scorecard for alliance transformation. Furthermore, there are lessons in the story of the NRF for the nations of NATO, for NATO aspirants, and for any country that desires to develop its own transformational force. This review will describe the NRF, its origins and history, the transformational rationale behind the NRF, an accounting of progress to date, and implications of the NRF for alliance transformation.

Gap in Capabilities

Former US deputy secretary of defense John White was not alone when, in his introduction to the 1999 book *Mind the Gap,* he expressed concern over the decline of transatlantic relations:

> When American defense officials meet informally with their allies and friends from other North Atlantic Treaty Organization countries, the conversation often turns to the growing disparity in combat capability between European and U.S. forces. . . . If we allow this divergence to continue, it could marginalize the North Atlantic alliance that has served its members and the world so well for the last half century. The failure of NATO to close the gap has implications beyond the creation of incompatible forces. It would mean that the alliance will have failed to adapt its enormous capabilities (economic, political, and military) to the new challenges that we all face.[3]

By the end of the twentieth century, the opinions expressed by White and other influential thinkers had prompted serious discussion among key decisionmakers regarding the political and military foundations of the NATO alliance. The resulting decisions would determine whether the alliance's post–Cold War transatlantic divergence would continue or a new vision would restore what Hans Binnendijk and Richard Kugler refer to as "the principles of shared risk and responsibility that have been the alliance's foundation since its inception."[4] As it turned out, they would have to wait until the catalyzing events of 11 September 2001.

Early Proposals

David Gompert, Richard Kugler, and Martin Libicki laid out the theoretical basis for change in *Mind the Gap,* establishing the rationale for extending NATO innovations already in hand in 1999:

> The CJTF (Combined Joint Task Force) concept that NATO instituted a few years ago, mainly to plan and mount operations other than to defend allied territory, could be useful in presenting NATO authorities and, through them, national governments with shared views on key military tasks and the roles of various allies in accomplishing them. . . . At present, CJTFs are intended to plan and mount lesser operations, such as peacekeeping or crisis intervention in and on the perimeter of Europe. . . . However, if NATO is going to help rebuild a U.S.-European military coalition capable of common defense of common interests, CJTFs should be used for the entire spectrum of operations (other than border defense), including large-scale power projection and high-intensity conflict. The requirements identified and transmitted by CJTF planning can help immensely in guiding an Atlantic RMA.[5]

Framework for Change

Mind the Gap presented ideas whose time had not quite yet come, but less than three years later the Al-Qaida attacks on the United States changed everything, not least the transatlantic relationship. Washington was looking for partners in the global war on terror, in what was perceived to be a campaign that devolved upon tried and true principles of shared risk and responsibility, despite a growing US instinct for unilateralism. Washington's resort to NATO as a primary recourse was a natural and necessary development in response to the 9/11 attacks, and its practical outcomes would be the impetus for what became, inter alia, the NRF.

By the time US president George W. Bush spoke before the German Bundestag in May 2002, initial concepts for NATO transformation were taking shape. Referring to NATO's emerging challenges, the president outlined the change in approach:

> As it faces new threats, NATO needs a new strategy and new capabilities. Dangers originating far from Europe can now strike at Europe's heart—so NATO must be able and willing to act whenever threats emerge. This will require all the assets of modern defense—mobile and deployable forces, sophisticated special operations, the ability to fight under the threat of chemical and biological weapons. Each nation must focus on the military strengths it can bring to this alliance, with the hard choices and financial commitment that requires. We do not know where the next threat might come from[;] we really don't know what form it might take. But we must be ready, as full military partners, to confront threats to our common security.[6]

A few months later, at a meeting of the North Atlantic Council in Warsaw, Secretary Rumsfeld expanded upon the NATO transformation theme. He mentioned the NRF explicitly, in remarks presaging the official alliance decision to field the NRF that would come in Prague two months later:

> We have most assuredly entered a new security environment, one that is dramatically different from the one that this alliance was formed to deal with some 50 years ago. It's a world in which terrorist networks, terrorist states and weapons of mass destruction come together in a way that can cause unprecedented destruction to our cities, our people, and our way of life. . . . To be ready, NATO will need 21st Century capabilities. In that connection we did discuss the possible creation of a NATO response force that could give the alliance a capability to deploy and sustain a significant fighting force in a matter of days or weeks rather than in months or years.[7]

Prague Declaration

By the time of the Prague summit in November 2002, NATO had turned a corner. The alliance's summary of events, titled "NATO After Prague," recognized a fleeting opportunity to alter mind-sets decisively and spur momentum toward change. Alliance leaders asserted the importance of NATO as the "central institution for collective defence, security consultation and multinational military actions."[8] The leaders announced three major initiatives for improving NATO's defense capabilities: promulgating a new capabilities initiative, embodied in the Prague Capabilities Commitment; creating a NATO Response Force; and streamlining NATO's military command structure.[9]

The NRF was envisioned as a "technologically advanced, flexible, deployable, interoperable and sustainable force, including land, sea and air elements ready to move quickly to wherever needed."[10] It reestablished the importance of a high-readiness expeditionary capability for NATO. Perhaps more important, the NRF served as a symbol of the alliance's deliberate commitment to improve its collective military capabilities, as well as an endorsement of transformation in general.

In the end, American pressure had prevailed for a focused, deployable, useful force that could be the template for specific transformation programs that would be familiar in the United States, emphasizing deployability, jointness, and networks. In contrast, the Prague Capabilities Commitment, with its hundreds of initiatives, was anything but focused, and could never serve as a program for transformation.[11]

Brussels and Istanbul

> The NATO Response Force is at the centre of the Alliance's military transformation. It not only gives us a high readiness and deployable force in which all the Allies will engage together. It is also a hothouse in which advanced technologies and doctrines flourish. And because all Allies have the possibility of contributing forces to the NRF, the benefits will flow throughout the Alliance.
>
> —*NATO secretary-general Jaap de Hoop Scheffer*[12]

In Brussels in June 2003, the NATO defense ministers approved the NRF concept at a meeting of the North Atlantic Council, and tasked the NATO military authorities with establishing the NRF with initial operational capability (IOC) as soon as possible but no later than October 2004. Full operational capability (FOC) was to be achieved no later than October 2006. The defense ministers considered the NRF to be a vital outcome of NATO transformation that would extend the alliance's reach beyond the heartland. In addition to the NRF's applicability to Article 5 of the North Atlantic Treaty[13] and its expeditionary qualities, it would serve as the catalyst for alliance integration, interoperability, rigorous operational standards, and, most important, solidarity.[14]

NATO established specifications and developmental programs throughout the organization; in 2003, NATO Allied Command Transformation set forth the following requirements for NRF:

1. The NRF will be tailored to the needs of a specific operation, and be able to move quickly to wherever needed. It will not be a permanent or standing force. The NRF will be able to carry out certain

missions on its own, or serve as part of a larger force to contribute to the full range of alliance military operations.
2. The NRF will be composed of national force contributions, which will rotate through periods of training and certification as a joint force, followed by an operational "stand by" phase of six months.
3. The NRF will be a key catalyst for focusing on and promoting improvements of Alliance military capabilities, in very close relationship with the national and multinational elements of the Prague Capabilities Commitment and NATO force planning overall.[15]

By the time of the Istanbul summit in June 2004, the definition of the NRF had been refined and confidence in the Force's value was palpable. The press statement issued from the summit delineated NRF objectives and missions:

> The NRF is a rapidly deployable multinational unit made up of land, air, maritime and special forces components. Numbering some 24,000 troops when it reaches its full operating capability in October 2006, it will be able to start to deploy after five days' notice and sustain itself for operations lasting 30 days or longer if resupplied.
>
> The NRF will be able to deploy worldwide, as and when decided by the North Atlantic Council. At full operating capability, the NRF will consist of a brigade-size land component with a forced-entry capability, a naval task force composed of one carrier battle group, an amphibious task group and a surface action group, an air component capable of 200 combat sorties a day, and a special forces component.[16]

The NRF has several possible missions:

1. A stand-alone force for Article 5 collective defense or non–Article 5 crisis response operations, such as evacuation operations, disaster consequence management (including chemical, biological, radiological, and nuclear events), and support in a humanitarian crisis situation and counterterrorism operations;
2. An initial entry force facilitating the arrival of larger follow-on forces;
3. To show NATO determination and solidarity to deter crises (quick response operations to support diplomacy as required).

The NRF will be tailored to a specific operation so that a sufficient number of adequately prepared NATO forces are projected when and where necessary. Contributions will be drawn from combat-ready, interoperable units contributed by NATO member countries. This does not exclude support by partner countries, whose participation would be decided by the North Atlantic Council on a case-by-case basis for a specific operation.

Early Commitment, Distant Goals

In 2005, during the run-up to the Riga summit's declaration of NRF full operational capability in November 2006, General Lance Smith, Supreme Allied Commander, Transformation, offered a current view of NATO transformation capabilities in his command briefing, "Understanding NATO Transformation."[17] He described a NATO that in the twentieth century had been static, reactive, regional, and prone to use mass force in campaigns of attrition. During the Cold War and through the end of the century, the alliance aimed for deconfliction of forces at best, and depended on national supply-point logistics and national intelligence capabilities that were not designed to exchange information with alliance partners.

By contrast, the transformation goals for NATO in the twenty-first century were for alliance forces that would be agile, proactive, and global in reach. These forces would emphasize maneuver, precision, and coherent integration of effects, based on integrated logistics and fused intelligence. This meant, in reality, that early emphasis would be on fielding the force, and only when the NRF was established and in the field would attention then turn to the real work of transformation, such as the operational and transformational attributes of networking.

Richard Kugler points out that the bulk of transformational progress is yet to come for the NRF, although—and this is encouraging news—the way ahead is relatively clear, at least in concept:

> An especially important task will be ensuring that the NRF is equipped with the information networks needed to make it a properly transformed force. . . . A principal NATO weakness has been lack of mobile, deployable C4ISR systems and information networks. . . .
>
> A similar judgment applies to NRF capacity to employ other critical, new-era capabilities for expeditionary warfare. Many European militaries possess adequately modern weapon systems, for example, fighter aircraft, but they often lack combat enablers in several areas. This includes precision strike systems; close combat systems, such as light tanks and other light armored vehicles; force protection; tactical mobility; and logistic sustainability.[18]

The NRF has made significant strides toward effective force integration. Diverse national and service forces working together are the new standard for the NRF, and this capability has been demonstrated in NRF exercises. Common funding and effective intelligence and information sharing, as well as logistics integration, however, are still beyond reach. NATO national forces deploying to Afghanistan as part of the International Security Assistance Force (ISAF) are taking their own intelligence centers with them, as well as their own logistics and maintenance support. Reports are that there are four separate, redundant helicopter maintenance organizations in Afghanistan, a result of the nations' mandates for organic support.[19] Knowledge management is lacking, as are programs to interact with Afghan leaders, organizations, tribes, and international organizations (such as the International Red Cross and the United Nations) and nongovernmental organizations (Médecins Sans Frontières [Doctors Without Borders], HOPE, CARE, and so on) present on the battlefield.[20]

Push and Pull

Combining forces and capabilities in the same developmental package amounts to "getting out of the lab." Doing so effectively establishes a virtual cycle of technical push and operational pull. Realizing its potential and benefits requires pushing concept development and experimentation into the field with the operating forces.

There are certain protocols required. While operators are willing to experiment, even in combat, they have little patience for having thoughtless experiments and equipment pushed on them. They despise unfunded mandates. They will not be expert in knowing how to share results or provide feedback with laboratories or other units.

Jeffrey P. Bialos and Stuart L. Koehl provide another description of this cyclical push-pull effect:

> As the NRF's development proceeds in an iterative and interactive process, a combination operational (demand) pull and technology push will cause the migration of capability requirements, doctrines, operational methods, and tactics. Initial high-intensity mission requirements will drive development of a preliminary doctrine and operational method, mainly using existing technologies and capabilities. As it gains operational experience, the NRF will identify capability and interoperability shortfalls that in turn will drive new capability and interoperability requirements.[21]

This is, to a large degree, the approach taken by the alliance: first get the NRF in the field and, by so doing, integrate the various components of a joint force. Then, once the NRF is in the field, focus on transforming it and then transferring the effects and benefits to the larger force.

In essence, the NRF represents not only an operational capability, but an opportunity for an ongoing field experiment, combining the merits of both rigorous hypothesis experimentation and more reactive discovery experimentation. The Concept Development and Experimentation (CD&E) architecture of NATO provides a strong basis for NRF developments. By design, each CD&E venue adds to the development of the NRF concept, directly or indirectly. An example of this connectivity was Multinational Experiment 4 (MNE 4), which considered the distribution of a common operating picture to multiple locations. MNE 4 was designed, in part, to refine and assess processes, organizations, and technology to support the NRF, including Knowledge Base Development, Effects-Based Planning, Effects-Based Execution, and Effects-Based Assessment.[22]

Unfinished Business

It should be no surprise that both the concept and development of the NRF are inherently political within NATO, and that the achievement of political consensus among the NATO nations regarding the doctrine and objectives of the NRF remains a work in progress. Perhaps more surprising is the limited extent to which politics has interfered with NRF development so far. Politics may play a larger role from here on; since the purposes of the NRF remain inherently political, the nearer it gets to practical utility, the greater will be debates regarding its employment.

Technically, also, the NRF is a work in progress, unfinished in both emphasis and extent. So far, the compelling rationale for the NRF has resulted in real commitments of forces, organizations, deployments, operations, and results. The NRF is simultaneously a strategy, a scheme, a program of record, and an opportunity for transformation. In sum, it represents change at every level of the alliance, the final result of which cannot yet be seen but which can be imagined.

The NRF nevertheless is incomplete as an entity, despite declarations of full operational capability. It has served to modernize the alliance but not yet transform it. This pervasive delay in making fundamental changes represents propensities for debate that run deep in the alliance and the incomplete, and controversial, work plan for transformation that encompasses jointness, networking, and mobility. The difficulties inherent in resolving them so far are emblematic of the less than unanimous determination to rationalize alliance decisionmaking and operations.

Most troubling for the NRF has been the challenge of funding, which amounts to a plebiscite on consensus. During the NRF mission that brought earthquake relief to Pakistan, Spain won what many call the reverse lottery; by NATO's rules, the country that happens to be in rotation when the NRF deploys ends up paying the deployment's full costs. Under these circumstances, few nations will embrace expansive NRF operations. General James Jones worried about the policy's long-term implications. "I continue to have questions about the willingness of nations to contribute forces to each rotation in the amount necessary to be confident that we can meet all of the mission sets that are assigned to the NATO Response Force."[23]

Financial and political obstacles obscure the fact that, by every measure, the more time the NRF spends in the field, the more successful it will be. General Jones, its greatest military proponent, understood this intrinsically; every US marine knows that excellence comes from constant training, routine deployments, and frequent operations. From here on out, in combination with the support of laboratory experimentation and concept development, successes for the NRF will come from field experimentation and operational lessons that are internalized into NATO doctrine and culture.

NRF Exercises and Operations

Initial rotations up to NRF 6 were viewed as prototypes. NRF rotations (as of this writing) filled the "on-call" periods outlined below. Contrary to declarations of frequent NRF operational activity, actual deployments have been episodic and exercises tend to be more like demonstrations.

1. Prague summit (21–22 November 2002): NRF approved as a new alliance capability.
    - NRF established 15 October 2003.
    - NRF 1 (15 October–end 2003) and NRF 2 (January–mid-July 2004), Joint Force Command Brunssum, Netherlands.
2. NRF 3 (15 July–end 2004) and NRF 4 (January–mid-July 2005), Joint Force Command Naples, Italy.
    - NRF IOC declared at Exercise Destined Glory, 13 October 2004, a live-fire amphibious exercise. During Destined Glory, NRF forces combined with STRIKFORNATO maritime and amphibious forces.[24]

3. NRF 5 (15 July–end 2005) and NRF 6 (January–July 2006), Joint Headquarters Lisbon, Portugal.
   - NRF command and control capabilities were demonstrated twice. Joint Headquarters Lisbon commanded an alliance air transport operation in support of Hurricane Katrina disaster relief (September–October 2005).
   - JHQ Lisbon also commanded the deployment of tailored NATO forces in support of Pakistan's earthquake disaster relief (October 2005–February 2006).[25]
4. NRF 7 (mid- to end 2006) and NRF 8 (January–mid-July 2007), Joint Force Command Brunssum.
   - NRF FOC declared at the Riga summit, 29 November 2006. SACEUR (Supreme Allied Commander, Europe) declared all necessary NRF capabilities in place.[26]
5. NRF 9 (mid-July 2007) and NRF 10 (January–July 2008), Joint Force Command Naples.
   - JFC Naples and Component Commands were certified as an able and credible force for NRF 9 during exercise Steadfast Jackpot 2007.[27]
   - Three linked exercises, Noble Mariner, Noble Award, and Kindred Sword (19–24 May 2007), gave forces the opportunity to train together to increase coherence of the force as a whole, in a joint response to a complex scenario.[28]
   - Noble Midas 07 (27 September–12 October 2007), a live maritime and amphibious NATO and partner nations (Albania and Croatia) Crisis Response Operation exercise in the Adriatic Sea, focused on NRF operations supported from the sea, in the waters adjacent to Split, Croatia.[29]
   - Steadfast Jaw 07 (1–4 December 2007), an NRF command post and computer-assisted exercise in Ulsnes, Norway, simulated activity across a wide geographical area to test and develop NATO's expeditionary capabilities while certifying NRF 10.[30]
6. NRF 11 (mid-July 2008) and NRF 12 (January–July 2009), Joint Headquarters Lisbon, Portugal.

Forces in the Field Focus Capabilities Requirements

If General Jones was right about frequent operations shaping success, one way to facilitate the experimenter-operator relationship is to leverage the rapacious demand from the field for solutions to operational requirements.

Before the Riga summit, retired admiral Mario Bartoli, NATO deputy assistant secretary-general for armaments and the NATO Counter-terrorism Technology coordinator, said this in a different way:

> NATO now needs to acquire the right capabilities to fulfill its mandate and match its political transformation. . . . The NRF is the most viable transformation vehicle available to the Alliance today. It will prove indispensable for improving NATO's expeditionary capabilities in key areas. . . . It is no longer a question of transforming into a new organisation with new purposes and mandates. It is rather a question of acquiring the right capabilities to fulfill these mandates.[31]

In a period of rapid change in the art of war, commanders and troops can be conservative and skeptical regarding improvements artlessly forwarded from the rear echelon. They will respond with alacrity, however, to organizational, technical, and doctrinal solutions that improve their chances of success on the battlefield, especially if they are brought to accept their role as part of the solution. Given sufficient experimentation emphasis, the NRF offers a remarkable opportunity to bring operational and strategic transformation to the next level.

Heretofore, despite two headquarters command and control exceptions, the NRF generally has been limited to exercising and demonstrating new capabilities, and has not deployed for alliance operations. Without a significant commitment to operations, it stands to lose the operational imperative for change and reason for continuation. If political leaders and military commanders are serious about NATO transformation, they will want to emphasize the importance of routine NRF operations as a political, technical, and transformational force multiplier.

Afghanistan as an Opportunity and an Opportunity Cost

NATO's UN-mandated International Security Assistance Force operations in Afghanistan, and the alliance's "substantial programme of cooperation with Afghanistan, concentrating on defence reform, defence institution-building, and the military aspects of security sector reform,"[32] offer many of the same opportunities as does the NRF for operationally driven transformation. At this writing, NATO operations in Afghanistan overshadow what the NRF has been able to deliver, just as the politics surrounding operations in Iraq have begun to dominate US security thinking, to the exclusion of transformation priorities.

NATO's role in Afghanistan is beyond the scope of this review, but it is where NATO troops are in the field. In the final analysis, the alliance's commitment to field operations is a powerful rationale for carrying through on transformational goals. It compels attention, thoughtful and pragmatic review, and funding in the best sense of the word; provides the basis for effective operational experimentation; and eventually will prove to be the sine qua non of transformation.

While the International Security Assistance Force (ISAF) would appear to be a significant opportunity cost for the NATO Response Force, NATO spokespersons deny that the NRF has been abandoned:

> The concept of a highly ready and technologically advanced force at the Alliance's disposal remains firmly in place. Its training, transformation and expeditionary goals continue to be relevant and applicable. What we are conducting now in NATO are deliberations on the easing of the burden that many Allies suffer as a consequence of significant operational commitments in NATO and other organisations-led operations.[33]

These deliberations culminated at the informal defense ministers' meeting in Noordwijk, Netherlands, in October 2007, where NATO decided to reorient NRF force levels toward a concept of graduated response:

> On Thursday morning the focus of Ministers' attention will switch to defence transformation capabilities issues. . . . They'll want to give guidance on the development of the graduated force option for the NATO Response Force to ensure that the NATO Response Force remains capable of dealing with the full range of scenarios envisaged in the NATO Response Force concept and to ensure that the NATO Response Force retains its value in training and transforming national defence forces.[34]

At the Noordwijk final press conference, NATO secretary-general Jaap de Hoop Scheffer rationalized the modified NRF force generation method agreed upon by the twenty-six NATO ministers in this way:

> Let me tell you at the outset, the concept of the NATO Response Force is not going to change. . . . We'll generate a core force for the NATO Response Force and if and when the situation arises that we have to generate more, we'll force generate. The call will be there; the concept doesn't change and the NATO Response Force will be able to perform all the missions it should perform. . . . The bottom line here is that the NRF will stay the same, but the number of forces we'll have on permanent stand-by (as you know at the moment 25,000) will decrease.[35]

The NRF and ISAF: Both Engines for NATO Transformation

As HQ SACT (Headquarters Supreme Allied Commander, Transformation) chief of staff Lieutenant General Michel Maisonneuve has put it, with missions such as its operations in Afghanistan, NATO has gone from "preparing" to "doing."[36] This means that the alliance must use these deployments to evaluate whether organization, processes, systems, and capabilities are adequate for the current operational environment. He specifically cites the International Security Assistance Force (ISAF) as perhaps serving as "the greatest transformational test ever for the Alliance." This applies equally to the NRF, where "doing" equates to the push and pull of transformation, and operations are not simply a test but an opportunity for change as well.

US Ambassador to NATO Victoria Nuland explained how the practical demands of NATO operations in Afghanistan pushed the alliance beyond its theoretical transformation limitations, illustrating the Afghanistan commitment's parallel role as an engine for change:

> Afghanistan today provides the "why" for all of the previously mentioned initiatives and for NATO's continuing transformation. Few would have predicted, even five years ago, that all 26 Allies and 11 Partners would support more than 30,000 troops 3,000 miles from Alliance territory in making a long-term commitment to the peace and stability of that country.[37]

Furthermore, humanitarian assistance/disaster relief (HADR) operations have proved to be "good enough" for transformation experimentation. While it is true that the application of force generally is not included in HADR operations, virtually every other operational element is present for experimentation, including force protection, command and control, intelligence, logistics, medical operations, combat support, and combat service support.

Will the NRF Survive?

How much of an opportunity cost for the NRF are NATO's operations in Afghanistan? In the face of pressing ISAF requirements, can NATO do both? Will the NRF even survive, let alone remain an engine for transformation?

The clear answer from Brussels, Mons (Belgium), and Norfolk is yes. The NRF Graduated Force Core Model "provides a structure and force that enables NATO to respond to the initial phase of a crisis situation during times of high operational tempo with a credible, balanced, capable force. The Core can expand and be capable of performing missions at a fuller scale dependent on additional force offers. Additional forces may be generated from nations' High Readiness Forces (HRF)."[38] The Core will consist of command and control forces, enabling forces, and tailored combat forces. This expandable and adaptable approach is credible not least because it is both realistic and a better utilization of NATO's limited resources than having large numbers of forces on permanent standby.[39]

The Military Committee Guidance for Transformation (MC 477) reiterates that the NRF is "a catalyst for transformation." MC 477 sets the following priorities: (1) focus alliance initiatives to improve military capabilities and interoperability; (2) adapt the NRF to emerging technologies and concepts; and (3) support the NRF command training program.[40] Specifically, MC 477 states that "national forces committed to the NRF should receive, as appropriate, the focus of effort for capabilities enhancement to reach predetermined standards of military capability and interoperability," reemphasizing that national efforts should place the priority for transformation on NRF forces.[41]

Despite the recognized transformational successes brought about by the NRF, the Force Generation Conference that took place in September 2008 clearly demonstrated that even the Graduated Force construct is struggling to remain operationally relevant due to significant and persistent force generation shortfalls. At the time of this writing, the Deployable Force Coordination Group in Allied Command Operations has proposed a way ahead that presents a logical argument for adopting a more realistic set of missions and a less restrictive force commitment structure for the NRF. The proposal also correctly points out that a healthy rotation of national forces through the NRF is extremely important to both nations and Allied Command Transformation for ensuring that the NRF remains a catalyst for transformation.[42]

Conclusion

The end of the Cold War left NATO leaders searching for a way to redefine the alliance as a force for stability and security in a world no longer characterized by a common enemy or clear and unifying ideologies. Potential new roles and missions such as conflict prevention, humanitarian operations, and peacekeeping came to the fore during the Balkan Wars of the 1990s, but it was the rise of international terrorism that catalyzed the organization into transforming itself to meet emerging new threats. The NRF was created both as a means to fight the kinds of limited, asymmetric wars that are actually happening in places like Afghanistan and as the driver for transformation of the entire alliance. Even so, change comes hard to all bureaucracies, and NATO has yet to exploit the full potential of the NRF for either operations or experimentation.

The NRF nevertheless has become a powerful developmental tool. Having brought the NRF to full operational capability is a major achievement, not least because NATO now has a rather dramatic opportunity to accelerate change. Operational experimentation is such a powerful process that incorporating it as a fundamental asset in NRF transformation and development should be a high political and command priority. The very process of pushing experimentation into the field, and consciously incorporating experimental capabilities into small specially chartered formations responsible for concept development and experimentation, has the potential to transcend the NRF vehicle.

The specifics of process enhancement and the mechanisms of change are important. A full NRF experimentation program would encompass both discovery and hypothesis experimentation, including constructive, human-in-the-loop, and field experiments. Current practice has been to supplement field experimentation with an extensive parallel program in war-fighting laboratories, which has tended to overshadow the fieldwork. This practice is inefficient and gives rise to redundant and contradictory efforts. Given the power of operational experimentation to provide military solutions, NATO has the opportunity to press the advantages of field experimentation—including in Afghanistan—by exploiting the NRF's capacity for command-driven experimentation, thoughtful lessons learned, and insightful requirements. The fact that the concept of the NRF as an engine for alliance transformation has survived the limitations on NRF force generation imposed by ISAF operations speaks positive volumes about the alliance's continuing commitment to engineering its own transformation.

Notes

1. Henning Riecke, "The Need for Change," in "Examining NATO's Transformation," a special issue of the *NATO Review* (Spring 2005), http://www.nato.int/docu/review/2005/issue1/english/main.htm.

2. Jeffrey P. Bialos and Stuart L. Koehl,"The NATO Response Force: Facilitating Coalition Warfare Through Technology Transfer and Information Sharing" (Washington, DC: Center for Technology and National Security Policy, National Defense University, 2005).

3. David C. Gompert, Richard L. Kugler, and Martin C. Libicki, *Mind the Gap* (Washington, DC: National Defense University Press, 1999), 3–8.

4. Hans Binnendijk and Richard Kugler, "Transforming European Forces," *Survival* 44, no. 3 (Autumn 2002): 121.

5. *RMA* stands for "revolution in military affairs." Gompert et al., *Mind the Gap,* Chapter 6.

6. President George W. Bush, "President Bush Thanks Germany for Support Against Terror," remarks by the president to a special session of the German Bundestag, Berlin, 23 May 2002, Office of the White House Press Secretary, Washington, DC.

7. Donald Rumsfeld, press conference, Warsaw, 25 September 2002, http://www.nato.int/docu/speech/2002/s020925c.htm.

8. NATO Office of Information and Press, "NATO After Prague" (Brussels: NATO Press Office, 2002), 1, http://www.nato.int/docu/after-prague/html_en/after_prague01.html.

9. Ibid.

10. Ibid.

11. Richard Kugler, "The NATO Response Force 2002–2006: Innovation by the Atlantic Alliance," *Case Studies in Defense Transformation,* no. 1 (Washington, DC: Center for Technology and National Security Policy, National Defense University, 2007), 9–10, http://www.ndu.edu/ctnsp/casestudies.html.

12. NATO, North Atlantic Council, "NATO Response Force Moves Forward," press statement, Defense Ministers Session, Istanbul, 27–28 June 2004; available from the NATO Online library: http://www.nato.int/docu/rdr-gde-ist/html_en/ist-sum-rg-4.html.

13. Article 5 reads in part: "The Parties agree that an armed attack against one or more of them in Europe or North America shall be considered an attack against them all" (North Atlantic Treaty, 4 April 1949). See http://www.nato.int/docu/basictxt/treaty.htm.

14. NATO, North Atlantic Council, "Statement on Capabilities," press release (2003) 066, Defense Ministers Session, Brussels, 12 June 2003.

15. NATO Allied Command Transformation Public Information Office (ACT PIO), Statement of Work, Contractor Support for Experimentation Program of Work at HQ SACT, 2003, Norfolk, Virginia; contact ACT PIO: pio@act.nato.int.

16. "NATO Response Force Moves Forward," Istanbul Summit Reader's Guide, available from the NATO online library: http://www.nato.int/docu/rdr-gde-ist/html_en/ist-sum-rg-4.html.

17. General Lance Smith, US Air Force, Supreme Allied Commander Transformation, "NATO Military Transformation," Norfolk, Virginia, 3 May 2005; contact ACT PAO: pio@act.nato.int.

18. Kugler, "The NATO Response Force 2002–2006," 11–14. For additional analysis, see Gordon Adams et al., "Bridging the Gap: European C4ISR Capabilities and Transatlantic Interoperability," Defense and Technology Paper Number 5, National Defense University Center for Technology and Security Policy, Washington, DC, October 2004, http://www.ndu.edu/ctnsp/Defense_Tech_Papers.htm.

19. NATO Parliamentary Assembly, "Assessing Progress and Key Challenges for the Alliance," Committee Reports, 037 DSC 07 E—AFGHANISTAN, spring session, 2007, http://www.nato-pa.int/Default.asp?SHORTCUT=1166.

20. Supreme Allied Commander, Transformation, "The NATO Response Force: Beyond Full Operational Capability," Allied Reach 2006 Final Report, Norfolk, Virginia, 24–26 January 2006.

21. Jeffrey P. Bialos and Stuart L. Koehl, "The NATO Response Force: Facilitating Coalition Warfare Through Technology Transfer and Information Sharing" (Washington, DC: National Defense University Center for Technology and National Security Policy, 2005), http://www.ndu.edu/ctnsp/Defense_Tech_Papers.htm.

22. USJFCOM Multinational Experiment 4 (MNE 4) Fact Sheet, http://www.jfcom.mil/about/experiments/mne4.htm.

23. "Jones: NATO Response Force Should Be Fully Operational This Year," *Inside the Navy* 19, no. 33 (21 August 2006); quoted in Julianne Smith, "Transforming NATO (. . . Again): A Primer for the NATO Summit in Riga 2006," Center for

Strategic and International Studies, November 2006, http://www.csis.org/index.php?option=com_csis_pubs&task=view&id=3590.

24. "NRF Demonstrates IOC at Exercise Destined Glory in Sardinia," *SHAPE News,* 13 October 2004, http://www.nato.int/shape/news/2004/10/i041012a.htm.

25. "Support to the US in Response to Hurricane Katrina," *SHAPE News,* 10 October 2005, http://www.nato.int/shape/news/2005/09/katrina.htm.

26. NATO, "NATO Response Force Declared Fully Operational," NATO update, 29 November 2006, http://www.nato.int/docu/update/2006/11-november/e1129c.htm.

27. Allied Joint Forces Command Naples, JFC Naples Articles, "STEADFAST JACKPOT 07," 24 July 2007, http://www.jfcnaples.nato.int/JFCN_Articles/articles07/JFCN_06_07.htm.

28. "NATO's Response Force to Conduct Live Exercises in Baltic Region," *NATO News,* 2 May 2007, http://www.nato.int/docu/update/2007/05-may/e0514a.html.

29. Allied Maritime Component Command Naples, "NATO NRF Exercises Peace Enforcement in Adriatic Sea," CC-MAR Press Release 16, 27 September 2007, http://www.jfcnaples.nato.int/organization/CC_MAR_Naples/PressReleases/CC-MAR/pressreleases07/PR_16_07.htm.

30. "NATO's Response Force Prepares for Future Missions, 1–14 December 2007," *NATO News,* 18 December 2007, http://www.nato.int/docu/update/2007/12-december/e1201a.html.

31. Mario Bartoli, "NATO's Continuing Transformation," in "Assessing NATO Transformation," special issue of *NATO Review* (Autumn 2006), http://www.nato.int/docu/review/2006/issue3/english/art3.html.

32. NATO Headquarters, "NATO in Afghanistan," NATO Topics online, 10 August 2007, http://www.nato.int/issues/afghanistan/index.html.

33. NATO Headquarters, "The NATO Response Force: Questions and Answers," NATO Opinions online, 21 September 2007, http://www.nato.int/docu/speech/2007/s070921a.html.

34. John Colston, assistant secretary-general for Defence Policy and Planning, press briefing, NATO Headquarters, 22 October 2007, http://www.nato.int/docu/speech/2007/s071022a.html.

35. Remarks by NATO secretary-general Jaap de Hoop Scheffer, final press conference at the informal meeting of NATO defense ministers, Noordwijk, Netherlands, 25 October 2007, http://www.nato.int/docu/speech/2007/s071025b.html.

36. NATO, "Assessing Progress and Key Challenges for the Alliance," NATO Parliamentary Assembly, committee reports, 037 DSC 07 E—AFGHANISTAN, spring session, 2007: paragraph 44, http://www.nato-pa.int/Default.asp?SHORTCUT=1166.

37. Ambassador Victoria Nuland, "NATO's Mission in Afghanistan: Putting Theory into Practice," in "Road to Riga," special edition of *NATO Review* (Winter 2006), http://www.nato.int/docu/review/2006/issue4/english/art3.html.

38. Colonel Gianmarco Bellini, Allied Command Transformation, "NATO Response Force: A Catalyst for Alliance Transformation," presentation to the International Defense Transformation Seminar, Podgorica, Montenegro, 15 May 2008: 3.

39. Ibid., 5.
40. Ibid., 9.
41. Ibid., 10.
42. Colonel Gianmarco Bellini, Allied Command Transformation, "NRF: A Catalyst for Transformation," presentation to the International Defense Transformation course, Monterey, California, 7 November 2008: 12.

11

Pacific Theater Assessments

Mel Chaloupka and Mike Solomon

Transformation of military forces and defense capabilities relies on the introduction of new concepts, technologies, and procedures for the war fighter. For almost a decade, US Pacific Command (USPACOM) has actively pursued transformation by inserting new concepts, technologies, and procedures into joint and coalition exercises and operations. As a result, these innovations are immediately assessed for their utility by military units in an operational environment, rather than solely in a laboratory or test environment. The feedback from the war fighter in the field does more to improve performance and save lives when compared with acquisition without a rigorous military utility assessment. This kind of direct feedback also enables rapid changes and spiral development of capabilities, sometimes within months rather than years.

The USPACOM area of operational responsibility covers literally half the world's surface and encompasses forty-three nations. Unlike the North Atlantic Treaty Organization (NATO), whose militaries adhere to common guidelines codified in standardization agreements, the relationships within the Pacific region are predominantly bilateral. The resulting complex military interrelationships give rise to unique interoperability issues and solutions that do not manifest in other regions of the globe. Although the United States Joint Forces Command (USJFCOM), as executive agent, has responsibility for joint experimentation within the Department of Defense (DoD) USJFCOM focuses on common solutions rather than operational applications that are unique to a theater. Therefore, guidance from the chairman of the Joint Chiefs of Staff underscores the vital role of the geographic and functional combatant commands in conducting and leveraging joint experimentation.[1] The interoperability of US and coalition forces within the Pacific region relies on commonality with other US joint and service systems, as well as the alignment of procedures with coalition partners who participate in Pacific theater exercises and operations. These conditions make clear the need for a specific USPACOM role in joint experimentation.

The Joint Mission Force

> The way ahead is to conduct frequent joint and combined exercises, both at command posts and with forces in the field—exercises that involve advanced concepts and technologies. Determine the system deficiencies that impede joint operations. Then fix them in months, and start the cycle again.
>
> —*Admiral Dennis C. Blair,*
> *US Navy, commander, US Pacific Command*[2]

The USPACOM senior leadership convened in 1999 to study the means to achieve greater speed of action, precision, and mission effectiveness for Pacific region joint and combined task forces (JTFs and CTFs). A series of workshops and war games attended by theater service and component commanders, their staffs, and functional experts resulted in the implementation of a revolutionary concept entitled Joint Mission Force (JMF). The Joint Mission Force was defined as a force package of approximately 20,000 personnel, drawn from designated USPACOM component-ready reaction forces, augmented by capabilities provided by supporting commanders, coalition partners, and international or nongovernmental organizations, from which a JTF commander could build tailored task forces for the accomplishment of a wide range of missions.[3]

Development of the Joint Mission Force concept started with the identification of the top ten obstacles to rapid, seamless joint and combined operations. Drawing from this list, the JMF initiative ultimately achieved four key objectives designed to improve interoperability: (1) refine and package the joint mission essential task list for USPACOM joint task forces; (2) develop the first standing operating procedures for USPACOM joint task force headquarters; (3) develop an effective C4I architecture[4] linking the joint task force commander's headquarters and component commands; and (4) provide focus for joint experimentation on concepts, technologies, and procedures that would improve existing capabilities or introduce new ones.[5]

Dramatic improvements were made in the time required to plan, establish, and employ a JTF; synchronous collaboration for command and control and targeting as well as information management down to the level of the individual were just a few of the many contributions earlier experiments made to JTF operations through the Joint Mission Force concept. Since then, the approach to joint experimentation within USPACOM has been refined and has become more capability-based. To ensure that operational, concept, and contingency plans are credible and executable, joint experimentation now (at this writing) focuses on the requirements for executing these plans, overcoming gaps in the capabilities needed to achieve desired outcomes, and the dissemination of lessons learned in order to improve existing capabilities through the adoption of new technologies and procedures.

The Capabilities-Based Approach

> I am impressed . . . with PACOM's efforts to link their plans to expected resources. This is a capabilities-based analysis process that helps PACOM identify capability gaps that are traceable to operational plans and missions. This strong analytic approach . . . helps all of us consider specific investments in terms of the capabilities they support.
>
> —*Kenneth J. Krieg, undersecretary of defense for Acquisition, Technology and Logistics*[6]

To accomplish operational, concept, and contingency plans, USPACOM uses a capabilities-based approach to assess plans and set priorities for resources allocation. Through the Plans to Resources to Outcomes Process (known as PROP), the annual integrated priority list promulgated by USPACOM and the service components focuses on minimizing gaps in the capabilities required to implement operational, concept, and contingency plans. As a result of PROP, USPACOM joint experimentation activities emphasize the command's top priorities, with a goal of bridging capability gaps. The command's experimentation requirements in turn are mapped to DoD Joint Capability Areas, developed by the Office of the Joint Chiefs of Staff, and are connected to joint military forces through joint mission essential tasks (JMETs). This process helps ensure that USPACOM plans are credible and executable.[7]

Because resources for new concept development and technology application are limited, the Joint Requirements Oversight Council (JROC) prioritizes those military issues that demand immediate attention and resolution. Derived from combatant command integrated priority lists and operational lessons learned, the JROC list of most pressing military issues feeds the catalog of war-fighter challenges (WFCs), which becomes the template for resource allocation for USJFCOM joint experimentation. Technological and conceptual WFCs differ in priority from one combatant command to another, so a standard list of priorities from throughout the DoD does not entirely satisfy USPACOM requirements or those of other combatant commands.

The Pacific region is predominantly water, with landmasses that vary from dense jungle to frozen tundra; its vast language and cultural differences are the most diverse on the planet. In view of these facts, USPACOM's top priorities are not necessarily the most pressing concerns of other combatant commands. Yet some commonality exists, especially in the area of concept development, such as a joint concept on cooperative security and engagement that can be applicable to USPACOM as well as to US European Command. Similarly, tools and techniques for intelligence, surveillance, and reconnaissance in dense foliage areas are extremely important to US Southern Command, as well as to USPACOM. Consequently, USPACOM is an active participant in the Joint Concept Development and Experimentation (JCD&E) enterprise, a body of science and technology–focused researchers representing the combatant commands, armed services, defense agencies, Joint Staff, Office of the Secretary of Defense, other government departments and agencies, and the international community, as discussed in Chapter 6 of this volume.

Collectively, USPACOM and other enterprise members articulate, prioritize, and collaborate on both joint war-fighter challenges and the allocation of the enterprise's experimentation resources. The JCD&E enterprise fosters awareness among members of joint experimentation initiatives that are planned or ongoing in other organizations or commands, including the services and their components. Participation in the enterprise also helps avoid duplication of effort on concept and technology experimentation at multiple organizations. As a result, although USPACOM does not control JCD&E activities, USPACOM priorities are reflected in the entire joint experimentation community's identified war-fighting agenda. This process allows USPACOM to ensure that its very limited joint experimentation resources are applied to unique limited-objective experiments that relate specifically to USPACOM capability needs and gaps, or that prove the applicability of DoD-wide proposed solutions for the Pacific region.

Service experimentation often expands beyond service boundaries to focus on cross- or multiservice requirements in areas such as operational fires, combat search and rescue, or JTF operations at the Joint Force Maritime Component, Land Component, or Air Component Commands. USJFCOM joint experimentation must address the common elements of "jointness" that are applicable to all combatant commands (COCOMS), such as Standing Joint Force Headquarters (SJFHQ), Joint Automated Deep

Operations Coordination System (JADOCS), and logistics in-transit visibility issues.[8] Both service and USJFCOM experimentation focuses on mid- to far-term requirements, concepts, and solutions. The USPACOM joint experimentation addresses the near-term, theater-unique requirements that may not be applicable to other COCOMS or enjoy a broad enough support base for USJFCOM interest—areas such as maritime domain awareness or theater-unique antisubmarine warfare or air superiority requirements against specific threats.[9] USPACOM joint experimentation also addresses theater-specific applications (or lack of application) for the broader, USJFCOM experimentation products, such as SJFHQ and JADOCS.

Credible Plans and War-Fighting Readiness

> The USPACOM joint training plan is specifically designed to mature joint and combined warfighting capabilities and readiness and to advance security cooperation while using resources more effectively.
>
> —*Admiral William J. Fallon,*
> *US Navy, commander, US Pacific Command*[10]

The PROP progression described earlier is a means to identify and mitigate capability gaps within contingency, concept, and operational plans. When observations and lessons learned, joint quarterly readiness reviews, and issues for resolution are formalized from exercises and real-world operations, a clear picture emerges of areas where new technologies or concepts might benefit the war fighter most. Extensive research and comparative analysis then help to identify proposed capability solutions that can be inserted into appropriate exercises, where the war fighters themselves can carry out a military utility assessment.

The high operational tempo (OPTEMPO) of military units within USPACOM does not allow separate venues for experimentation, so the command philosophy is to "experiment while we exercise." Guidance on the integration of transformation and mature joint experimentation initiatives into appropriate exercises is contained in the USPACOM Joint Training Plan, applicable to all personnel and organizations that participate in USPACOM joint training events.[11] The resulting realism experienced by air, land, and sea forces in joint and coalition operations provides the ideal assessment venue in which to determine whether prospective new technologies and concepts should be integrated into the operational force.

The command's operational and concept plans are each tested in one or more major joint exercises: TERMINAL FURY; NORTHERN EDGE; VALIANT

SHIELD; ULCHI-FOCUS LENS; Reception, Staging, Onward movement, and Integration; FOAL EAGLE in Korea; COBRA GOLD in Thailand; BALIKATAN in the Philippines; TALISMAN SABER in Australia; ELIPSE CHARLIE, AKELE; and other homeland security or homeland defense exercises. After-action reviews and lessons learned during the exercises highlight readiness issues that require additional training, the application of new technology, or new tactics, techniques, or procedures in order to close capability gaps. Additionally, unit-generated joint quarterly readiness reviews highlight shortfalls that must be addressed in order to accomplish JMETs. USPACOM applies technologies such as unmanned aerial vehicles (UAVs), tactical satellites, language translation tools, and comprehensive maritime awareness sensor and tracking technologies to improve capability. The command also experiments with concepts such as persistent intelligence, surveillance, and reconnaissance (ISR), operationally responsive space (space power focused on timely satisfaction of Joint Force Commanders' needs),[12] and maritime domain awareness (the effective understanding of anything associated with the global maritime domain that could affect security, safety, economy, or environment)[13] to close capability gaps and improve war-fighting readiness.

Linking Experiments to Exercises

> Transformation widens the technology gap [among the United States, regional allies, and potential partners], but the key in every case is that you first recognize the gap exists. Then, in training and exercises together, you work out procedures that allow you to overcome these differences.
>
> —*Lieutenant General John Brown III, commander, US Army Pacific*[14]

Over the course of a year, USPACOM plans and participates in forty-three or more exercises. Some, like search and rescue exercises, are small-scale events involving only a few individuals or tactical-level units. Others, like TALISMAN SABER with Australia, involve as many as 20,000 US personnel and a third of the Australia Defence Force. Regardless of size, each joint (multiservice) or combined (multinational) exercise is designed to improve those skill sets required to accomplish one or more JMETs. As specific training objectives are developed for each exercise, experimental technologies and concepts are matched to the training objectives to ensure USPACOM joint experimentation is relevant to the operational or contingency plan being exercised.[15]

Some venues, such as the Combined Warrior Interoperability Demonstration (CWID), are designed exclusively for the United States and other nations to showcase new or emerging capabilities against a plausible scenario developed to demonstrate the value and interoperability of those capabilities. Functioning as lead combatant command for CWID in 2002 and 2003 (then called Joint Warrior Interoperability Demonstration, or JWID), USPACOM introduced the capabilities of a Joint Task Force Wide Area Relay Network (or JTF WARNET) and a Coalition Operations Wide Area Network to enhance interoperability at the operational and tactical levels of action. As a result of their introduction during JWID and further experimentation and assessment in subsequent operational exercises, those interoperability technologies are now being used by war fighters as part of the Intra-Battle Group Wide Area Network and the Combined Enterprise Regional Information Exchange System (called CENTRIXS).[16]

Although most nations within the Asia-Pacific region still segregate military testing, experimentation, and assessment from their operational forces, exercises such as COBRA GOLD with Thailand and Singapore have sparked interest among coalition partners for cooperative development or collaborative experimentation with new technologies and concepts.[17] Exercise TALISMAN SABER with Australia in June 2005, in which Australia's Defence Science and Technology Organisation (DSTO) identified areas where Australia's defense forces could participate more fully, marked a turning point for collaborative experimentation with coalition partners.[18] Figure 11.1 provides an assessment of joint and combined experimentation initiatives in TALISMAN SABER 2005.

Due in part to the success of joint experimentation during the first TALISMAN SABER exercise in June 2005, the USPACOM, DSTO, and Australia Defence Force experimentation staffs launched a more collaborative experimentation effort for TALISMAN SABER in 2007. The result was a final set of thirteen US and ten Australian initiatives for experimentation and study during the exercise. All of these initiatives were tied closely to the US JMETs and Australian Joint Essential Tasks to help close capability gaps. In Figure 11.2, which is divided into the four joint experimentation themes for TALISMAN SABER, all the initiatives had a host or sponsoring unit to ensure successful integration into the exercise scenario and military utility assessment.

As USPACOM joint experimentation experience has grown, the command has shared its technology and concept insertion and assessment process with coalition partners to promote greater interoperability and force effectiveness. Interaction with Thailand's Defense Technology Organization, for example, is furthering collaboration on the detection and neutralization of improvised explosive devices. Innovative two-way speech-to-speech and

Figure 11.1 TALISMAN SABER 2005 Experimentation Assessment

Initiative	Results
Combined Coordinated Fires	80% success rate; time-sensitive targeting coordination time ~5 min. Tactics, techniques, and concept of operations training were key to success; combined coordinated fires system workstations were excellent; persistent chat for collaboration was operationally useful.
Joint Datalink Information Sharing for Combat Execution	Tactics and techniques tested and validated for Blue Force Tracking and Link 16 datalink operations; concept of operations and procedures partially validated for Special Operations Forces.
Theater High-Speed Vessels	Combined operations with Australia's Special Operations Forces for C2; some limitations in C2 suite.
Signals Intelligence Electronic Tracking	SIGINT Tracker test only partially successful.
Bandwidth Monitoring and Control	Functioned well to monitor bandwidth aboard USS *Blue Ridge;* arrived too late for installation and operation at Williamtown, Australia.
Tactical Satellite	Demo and operations experiment aboard USS *Blue Ridge;* satellite launch delayed; simulated data only.
Blue Force Friendly Trackers	About 35 tracking devices distributed to US and Australian personnel; continuous tracking was problem due to limited satellite coverage.
Combined Secure Operations Network	First use of secure enclave for shared access to national systems; Cumbersome Mail Guard; distribution of voice-over-internet-protocol; file transfer procedures need improvement.

Source: Mike Solomon, USPACOM J81, "Warfighting Innovation in the Pacific," presentation to students at the Naval Postgraduate School, Monterey, California, 30 January 2007: 8.

text-to-text language translation tools are emerging from collaborative exercises such as YAMA SAKURA with the Japanese Self Defense Force[19] and Exercise ULCHI-FOCUS LENS with the Republic of Korea.[20]

A science and technology (S&T) initiative in the recent exercise TERMINAL FURY has also become a key component in headquarters staffing for joint exercises and operational responses.[21] Collaboration between the Science and Technology Advisor and the Joint Experimentation and Transformation Division resulted in the formation of an S&T cell during operations and exercises involving the USPACOM headquarters staff. Ideally, this cell comprises four to eight experienced scientific engineers from DoD or service labs, nongovernmental organizations, and private industry who are knowledgeable

Figure 11.2 TALISMAN SABER 2007 Experimentation Initiatives

Persistent Intelligence, Surveillance, and Reconnaissance

United States

- Tactical Satellite (TACSAT-2) for responsive tasking by the operational commander
- Multi-Intelligence Ship Tracking reach-back to a database of ship characteristics
- "COUNTER" small unmanned aerial vehicles (UAVs) for surveillance in urban operations
- Small unmanned aerial vehicles for long-range surveillance over the battlefield
- Cognitive Network for Atmospheric Sensors for battlefield and urban weather sensing

Australia

- Geospatial information coordination and display for the Australian Navy

Command, Control, and Communications

United States

- "COASTS" low-bandwidth, high-capacity short-range communications
- Multicast Video Streaming System for rapid, high data-rate video transmissions
- GPS Jamming for war-fighter training in a GPS-inhibited environment

Australia

- Airborne Early Warning and Control Operations in Joint and Coalition Operations
- Integrated Joint Operations Center Headquarters
- Multi-National Inter-Agency Group for Inter-Agency Operations
- Network Centric Warfare Systems Baseline Capture and Evaluation
- Amphibious Operations Information Management
- Operational and Tactical C2 of Joint and Coalition Forces in Amphibious Operations

Force Application

United States

- Information Operations Range: parallel network designed to train on computer network defense
- Joint Fires Coordination Measures to optimize firepower and reduce fratricide
- Joint Command and Control War on Terror Activities for clandestine C2 aboard a submarine

Australia

- Air Operations Research—Support to Combined Air Operations Centre Strike Operations
- Joint Combined Close Air Support (JC-CAS) in a Complex Urban Environment

(continues)

Figure 11.2 Cont.

Logistics

United States

- Node Management Deployable for efficiently tracking logistics during transit
- Coalition Mobility System for integrated logistics operations in multinational operations

Australia

- Field evaluation of 72-hour lightweight combat ration packs among Australian war fighters

Source: Mike Solomon, USPACOM J81, "Exercise TALISMAN SABER 07 Experimental Initiatives," presentation to commander, Seventh Fleet, 27 May 2007: 3, 4.

about emerging technologies and capabilities.[22] Through the observation of key events, challenges, and issues faced by command leaders during an exercise or operational response, the S&T cell members gain a greater understanding of USPACOM requirements. At the same time, they are able to advise the joint force commander on technology applications that can be implemented immediately to meet the commander's operational challenges.

The USPACOM senior leadership recognized the value of the S&T cell, thanks to the cell's introduction of two new technological capabilities to reduce command shortfalls—one related to tactical satellite coverage for more persistent intelligence, surveillance, and reconnaissance, and the other related to computer network defense. Both capabilities were available for integration into USPACOM forces within ninety days of first being introduced. The high OPTEMPO for USPACOM forces is expanding joint experimentation horizons in other dimensions as well. The USJFCOM-sponsored Joint National Training Capability (JNTC) is beginning to provide the operational architecture for greater training at less cost for more forces than previous simulations and field-training exercises could provide. Multiple sites and capabilities are interconnected via the Joint Training and Experimentation Network (JTEN) to provide more realistic training for joint and combined forces by integrating live, virtual, and constructive activities into the same training event.

The USPACOM joint experimentation staff is conducting interoperability and compatibility testing on the JTEN, and leveraging the JTEN for operational use during exercises to familiarize the joint forces with new technology. For example, during TALISMAN SABER in 2007, the JTEN was extended for the first time to an international partner (Australia) as part of the Joint Combined Training Capability proof of concept. As part of its overall live, virtual, and constructive training environment, the virtual Joint Information Operations Range provided a parallel capability for information operations (IO) staffs to conduct realistic training on network intrusions, viruses, and stealthy root-level cyber attacks.[23]

The JTEN, combined with modeling and simulation tools, promises to improve assessment of the military utility of technologies and concepts by consolidating the iterative data required for a full evaluation, despite the fact that the variables during exercises or operations cannot be precisely controlled. As USPACOM's joint experimentation processes and assessments mature, each outcome leads to a clearer decision path for the endorsement or acquisition of capabilities that enable the command to carry out its operational plans effectively. Whether operating unilaterally or in conjunction with one or more regional partners, USPACOM's joint experimentation is transforming regional capability.

Joint Experimentation as a Catalyst for Transformation

Some might argue that active military forces have too high an OPTEMPO to engage in joint experimentation with technologies and concepts that may never be fielded, and that such experimental activity is best suited for military labs and USJFCOM-orchestrated events. While OPTEMPO is certainly an important consideration, the objective of joint experimentation is not just to train current forces and capabilities but also to provide the means to improve future USPACOM forces—in other words, to transform military capabilities for greater speed of action, precision, and mission effectiveness. For the war-fighting combatant commands concerned with immediate and near-term engagement, the traditional decade or longer research, development, and acquisition cycle is an unacceptable means of transforming capability.

A well-run experimentation program that includes thorough domain research along with modeling and simulation will ensure that potential new technologies and procedures are fully vetted before advancing to the crucible of the joint exercise or field experiment venue. Only the most promising and carefully screened technologies will undergo a military utility assessment in a field exercise with operating forces in order to avoid unwanted impact on the activity.

Through military utility assessment, USPACOM war fighters are able to provide early feedback to technology and concept developers, and facilitate the rapid spiral development of needed capabilities.[24] The result is expedited fielding of important technologies. In 2001, for example, US forces in Korea were faced with the difficulty of identifying and selecting the most suitable weapon to counter potential enemy ground fire. Through development of the Automated Deep Operations Coordination System (ADOCS), US forces are better able to coordinate firing on ground targets with the right munitions, by the service component best able to deliver, while preventing friendly-force fratricide.

Applying the lessons learned from using ADOCS in joint and coalition experimentation over a three-year period, USPACOM partnered with USJFCOM on the Joint Fires Initiative for improving hardware, software, tactics, techniques, procedures, and training to conduct joint and combined fires. The resulting Joint Automated Deep Operations Coordination System (JADOCS) is a joint-mission management software application that facilitates horizontal and vertical integration across the battle-space functional areas.[25] JADOCS was fielded throughout USPACOM and other combatant command war-fighting units in less than four years. The operational time required to coordinate the execution of a time-sensitive target among JADOCS users dropped from two hours to as little as two minutes. Rapid spiral development of an emerging capability transformed the way the US military conducts fires missions.

Robust Military Utility Assessments

Assessing the military utility of initiatives during joint and combined exercises requires a significant commitment by the units that make up the training audience. Because technology and concept initiatives are self-funded by the technology provider or sponsor of the initiative (typically a private contractor such as Raytheon or Northup Grumman), and the USPACOM joint experimentation staff facilitates their integration into the exercises, there is no direct cost to the training audience. The units, however, provide the chief source of feedback for measuring system performance and effectiveness, and for evaluating how the proposed systems or concepts will impact USPACOM war-fighting capabilities.

Figure 11.3 depicts the flow for military utility assessments (MUAs) of experimentation initiatives. Assessments also provide the war fighter with an early understanding of how to employ the residuals—those assets remaining after the assessment is complete. Measures of effectiveness (MOEs) are drawn from the strategic-, operational-, or tactical-level JMETs required by the unit to accomplish the mission plan. The experimentation initiatives are graded on how they aid the unit in performing the JMETs, compared with accomplishment without the experimentation initiatives. Measures of performance (MOPs) grade the experimentation initiatives on how well they meet war-fighter expectations and requirements for key performance parameters, such as reliability, supportability, accessibility, usability, and functionality. USPACOM joint experimentation staff predetermine the MOEs, in coordination with the technology or concept provider. The MOEs and MOPs are quantified based on a staff analysis of the initiative's ability to fulfill one or more joint-mission essential tasks. Parameters and their variance determine whether the joint experimentation staff will endorse the successful technology or concept for immediate acquisition, limited acquisition, or further testing and development, or will recommend no further investment in the technology. The transparent grading process prevents undue influence by contractors lobbying for endorsement of their initiative.

Furthermore, an intuitive assessment of the technologies and concepts by experienced senior leadership provides an important balance for the technical data and analyses of the MOEs and MOPs, especially in an exercise environment where there is limited control over test conditions. In addition to providing insight and discovery during the test, the opportunity to assess the technology or concept with the war fighter in an operational environment will potentially shorten the test-to-acquisition cycle and field a needed capability much sooner than the standard procurement process.

During TALISMAN SABER 2007, the military utility assessment of persistent ISR options was not able to assess the UAV systems specifically in an urban environment as planned, owing to bad weather and force posturing. Yet use of the UAVs resulted in favorable effects on opposing force operations at greater distances and with fewer resources than thought possible. The observations and results have led senior leaders to consider additional study and testing, as well as a cost-benefit analysis of UAVs for tactical reconnaissance in addition to, or instead of, reliance on space-based means.

In Figure 11.3 the USPACOM military utility assessment process combines data collection, analysis, and system performance ratings with the operational experience of subject-matter experts to put system performance within the context of intended military operations. Experimental technologies or procedures are assessed quantitatively and qualitatively against how well they enable the war fighter to perform selected critical support tasks that are required to accomplish the JMETs of a military operation. Through the use of questionnaires and subject-matter experts who serve as observers for the experiments, and in collaboration with training and operations

Figure 11.3 Military Utility Assessments (MUAs)

Legend
Acceptable
Marginal
Unacceptable

MOEs	1	2	3	4	5	6	7	8	9	10
MOPs	1	2	3	4	5	6	7	8	9	10
Senior Leader Assessment	1	2	3	4	5	6	7	8	9	10

Questionnaires

How desirable	1	2	3	4	5	6	7	8	9	10
How contributes to objectives or effects	1	2	3	4	5	6	7	8	9	10
Troop Acceptance	1	2	3	4	5	6	7	8	9	10
Comments/Insights										
Challenges/Opportunities										

Measures of Effectiveness (MOEs)

	JMETs	Staff/Commands				
Joint Mission	OP XX.1	✓			✓	
Essential Tasks	OP XX.2			✓		
Completed	OP XX.3		✓			✓
	OP XX.4	✓				

CSTs	Critical Elements			
CST XX.1		✓		✓
CST XX.2	✓	✓	✓	✓
CST XX.3	✓	✓		✓
CST XX.4	✓	✓	✓	

Measures of Performance (MOPs)

Reliability	1	2	3	4	5	6	7	8	9	10
Supportability	1	2	3	4	5	6	7	8	9	10
Accessibility	1	2	3	4	5	6	7	8	9	10
Usability	1	2	3	4	5	6	7	8	9	10
Functionality	1	2	3	4	5	6	7	8	9	10

Source: Mike Solomon, USPACOM J81, "Experimentation and Transformation Linkage to USPACOM Joint Exercise Program," presentation to students

analysts, the joint experimentation staff scores the actual performance of a new technology against predetermined measures important to the military operation. The score is based on how the technology affects time, quantity, and quality in accomplishing joint-mission essential tasks. Generally, technologies or procedures that score 40 percent or less against predetermined MOPs or MOEs are discarded as having little or no military utility. Technologies and procedures that score between 40 and 60 percent are likely to have some military utility and may be recommended for further assessment in another exercise or venue. Experiments that score 70 percent or higher merit serious consideration for endorsement and rapid acquisition, perhaps with minor modifications or additional development.

Metrics are *interesting* in relation to the comparative performance of a specific task, but they are *useful* if they provide commanders and senior decisionmakers with the evidence they need to make a decision or take action to (1) endorse the technology or concept for immediate procurement; (2) support limited acquisition to address an urgent need while continuing spiral development; or (3) eliminate the technology or concept from continued experimentation, owing to lack of value for the war fighter.

Perhaps the most difficult step in the joint experimentation process is moving the successful technologies—the winners—into production and operational use among the USPACOM war fighters. Current DoD processes hinder the transition of successful experiments and demonstrations to DoD-wide use. The fact that the services and contractors often monopolize the rights to new capabilities means information may not be shared as required for system interface or interoperability, such as happened with simulation training systems.[26] Additionally, the process to change and coordinate Doctrine, Organization, Training, Material, Leadership and Education, Personnel, and Facilities (DOTMLPF) is slow and cumbersome. Often a truly joint program, particularly a joint command and control system, lacks a champion to coordinate the DOTMLPF requirements and sustain the winning system through the transition period, known as the valley of death; during this period, some successful programs die or atrophy because of a lack of sponsorship for logistics and training.[27]

It must be noted that even when an initiative has the sponsorship it needs to make the transition from experimentation to deployment, the procurement process is not always as smooth as a flowchart might envision, especially when a new concept or technology is adapted from civilian use to the more rigorous standards of the military. One recent example of a spiral development process gone awry is the Littoral Combat Ship (LCS) (see Chapter 10 in this volume). The development plan, based on "off-the-shelf" civilian ferry designs and projected to take half the time at half the cost of a traditional program, was touted as a new shipbuilding paradigm for the navy.[28]

In this case, however, the imperative for "faster, better, cheaper" procurement put one contractor in the position of trying to build a prototype even as the navy was redefining its specifications, and construction on subsequent hulls was suspended while the program was reevaluated.[29] Taken as a cautionary tale, the LCS highlights the need for rigor and oversight in the development process.

Though often very difficult, sustaining and integrating the winners are vital for putting innovative capabilities into the hands of military personnel within the near term, and USPACOM is taking a more proactive role in the outcome in order to close capability gaps. Technologies and concepts that are identified and assessed as "winners" are sometimes deployed through a service proponent, such as the US Pacific Fleet's operational management of a program known as the comprehensive maritime awareness joint capability technology demonstration, in partnership with Singapore.[30] In other cases, a service program of record successfully carries the winners through the transition for DoD-wide distribution; one example is the Defense Advanced Research Projects Agency Phraselator language translation tool, an outgrowth of an advanced concepts technology demonstration and part of the army's Sequoyah program of record.[31] An active proponent of the DoD Joint Rapid Acquisition Cell (JRAC), USPACOM solicits Joint Urgent Operational Needs or Immediate Warfighting Requirements from the headquarters staff and service components, so that needed capabilities get immediate funding and rapid fielding. Moving the winners through a component, a service program of record, or the JRAC completes the joint experimentation and assessment process, and rapidly provides capability to the combatant command joint and coalition forces in the field.

Conclusion

> First and foremost, USPACOM is a warfighting command committed to maintaining preeminence across the full spectrum of operations. We are ready to fight and win, and to dominate in any scenario, in all environments, without exception.
>
> —*Admiral Timothy J. Keating, commander, USPACOM*[32]

Since its establishment as a unified command on 1 January 1947, US Pacific Command has taken advantage of new technologies and concepts to transform US joint forces drawn from the army, navy, marine, air force, and Coast Guard, as well as coalition forces from partner nations throughout the Asia-Pacific area of operation. As a combatant command, USPACOM's focus is on near-term transformational opportunities that can counter any potential adversary tomorrow. The transformational focus within the command, particularly since 2000, has resulted in dramatic improvements to joint and combined operations.

This chapter has outlined the process by which USPACOM identifies needed capabilities and then evaluates potential solutions for rapid, in-theater deployment. Beginning with the capability-based analysis, the joint experimentation staff researches and selects candidate solutions that are likely to address capability gaps that have been identified from contingency and operations plans, as well as from lessons learned and readiness reports. These candidates are then screened to make sure they complement proposed solutions to the war-fighter challenges, and also to preclude duplication with other experimentation efforts. The technologies and concepts that have been selected for further development are matched to exercises that provide the best venues for limited objective experiments in an operational environment. Once a team of subject-matter experts and war fighters have made their military utility assessments based on experiences gained during the exercise, the commander will give his or her endorsement and recommend immediate procurement, suggest limited acquisition, or recommend the elimination of the losers. Finally, the USPACOM staff sends the winners through one of several courses for joint rapid acquisition. This streamlined procedure can cut the typical ten- to thirteen-year procurement cycle down to months, once an initiative has been shown through rigorous assessment to provide measurable value to its potential end-users.

Following are a few examples of how the process described above has helped USPACOM promote transformation internally and in collaboration with its partners in the Pacific region. USPACOM has made transformational changes to the conduct of joint and combined fires, machine language-translation capabilities, use of nonlethal capabilities, and an array of command and control tools and procedures. The innovative use of high-speed vessels during TALISMAN SABER in 2005 and other joint exercises resulted in command endorsement of their purchase or lease for continuous theater operations.[33] Exploitation of open-source situational awareness on the Internet through the Virtual Information Center continues to heighten USPACOM awareness and sensitivity to world movements and reactions.[34] Expanded use of the Asia-Pacific Area Network among USPACOM and the nations and organizations with which the command operates provides a common, day-to-day collaborative environment for the effective planning and execution of exercises, contingencies, and disaster response.

Operation Iraqi Freedom and Operation Enduring Freedom–Philippines, as well as other commitments in the region, pose continuous stress and challenge to the availability of forces for joint experimentation. Expanding partnerships with allies and nations of mutual interest in the region—Australia, Thailand, Singapore, Malaysia, Japan, South Korea, and others—in areas such as ballistic missile defense, maritime domain awareness, and collective intelligence, surveillance, and reconnaissance will promote development and experimentation and potentially greater interoperability and combined force capability than previously thought possible. The products of the joint experimentation process used within USPACOM are helping to transform joint and combined war-fighting forces and increase their effectiveness in ways that much of the world is still striving to attain.

Notes

1. General Peter Pace, US Marine Corps, "Memorandum for Chiefs of the Services, Commanders of the Combatant Commands, Directors, Joint Staff Directorates. Subject: Joint Experimentation (JE) Guidance for FY 2007 and FY 2008," 3 December 2006.

2. Admiral Dennis C. Blair, "Force Transformation in the Pacific," remarks at the US Naval Institute/Armed Forces Communications and Electronics Association Western Conference, San Diego, California, 15 January 2002: 5.

3. Blair, "A Status Report on the Joint Mission Force and Transformation in the U.S. Pacific Command," White Paper Version 2.0, 1 May 2002: 1–8.

4. C4I: command, control, communications, computers, and intelligence.

5. Scott E. Jasper, "Transforming Joint Warfighting Capabilities," *Joint Forces Quarterly* 35 (Autumn 2004): 69–76, http://www.dtic.mil/doctrine/jel/jfq_pubs/1435.pdf.

6. Kenneth J. Krieg, "Facing the Future with Innovation and Cooperation," speech to the US Pacific Command Operational Science and Technology Conference, Honolulu, 9 March 2006: 4–5, http://www.acq.osd.mil/usd/previous_krieg_speeches/03_09_06_NR_USPACOM_S_and_T_Conf_final.doc.

7. Joint Capability Areas provide a framework for capability management. See Honorable Gordon England, deputy secretary of defense, "Memorandum for Secretaries of the Military Departments, Joint Capability Areas (JCAs)," 14 February 2008, http://www.dtic.mil/futurejointwarfare/strategic/depsecdef_jca.pdf. JMETs are those mission tasks deemed by a joint force commander to be essential to mission accomplishment, and defined using the common language of the Universal Joint Task List in terms of task, condition, and standard. See "Universal Joint Task List (UJTL)," Chairman of the Joint Chiefs of Staff Manual (CJCSM) 3500.04D, Change 1, 15 September 2006, http://www.dtic.mil/cjcs_directives/cdata/unlimit/m350004.pdf.

8. See US Joint Forces Command, "Standing Joint Force Headquarters Core Element," fact sheet, http://www.jfcom.mil/about/experiments/mc02/sjfhq.htm.

9. Mel Chaloupka, "Disruptive Technologies: A Combatant Command Faces the Challenge," brief for USPACOM J81, 4 September 2007, http://www.dtic.mil/ndia/2007disrupt/Chaloupka.pdf.

10. Admiral William J. Fallon, statement before the House Armed Services Committee on US Pacific Command Posture, 7 March 2007: 26, http://armedservices.house.gov/pdfs/FCPACOM030707/Fallon_Testimony030707.pdf.

11. "USPACOM Pacific Joint Training Strategy, Tab A, Commander's Training Guidance," USPACOM Joint Training Plan, FY 2008–2013, 2 August 2007: B-A-2, paragraph 2.b, https://www1.apan-info.net/j7/J7/J71/J712/JTRG/tabid/207/Default.aspx.

12. US Department of Defense, "Plan for Operationally Responsive Space: A Report to Congressional Defense Committees," 17 April 2007: 2, http://www.acq.osd.mil/nsso/ors/ors.htm.

13. Office of the President, "National Plan to Achieve Maritime Domain Awareness for the National Security Strategy for Maritime Security," October 2005: ii, http://www.dhs.gov/xprevprot/programs/editorial_0753.shtm.

14. Quoted in Robert Karniol, "Pacific Partners," *Jane's Defence Weekly,* 25 April 2007: 20–21, http://www.jdw.janes.com.

15. US Pacific Command, *USPACOM Joint Exercise Programs,* USPACOMINST 0508.2A, 24 July 2007: 4–15, paragraph 4.6.q, and Annex 2 to Appendix A: A2-1 to A2-5; available through USPACOM J7, Camp H. M. Smith, Honolulu, Hawaii 96861.

16. Maryann Lawlor, "JWID: The Next Generation," *SIGNAL Connections* 1 (17 May 2004): 8.

17. Jasper, "Transforming Joint Warfighting Capabilities," 69–76.

18. Rick Chernitzer, "Rapid Spiral Transformation Plays Big Role in Talisman Saber," US Navy Seventh Fleet public affairs press release, 19 June 2005, http://www.c7f.navy.mil/TS05/radio/June_19_2005_Rapid_%20Spiral_Transformation_plays_a_big_role_at_Talisman_Saber.doc; Aarti Shah, "Talisman Saber '05 Tests Combined Fires Initiative for Joint Ops Picture," *Inside the Navy,* 20 June 2005; available with permission from the "Inside Defense" website: http://www.insidedefense.com.

19. US Marine Forces Pacific Experimentation Center, "Language Translation Systems Demonstration and Assessment Report: Limited User Evaluation Yama Sakura 45," January 2004, https://www.mfp.usmc.mil/TeamApp/MEC_laser/Topics/20050107071101/Yama%20Sukura.pdf.

20. Major Michael Shavers, "Ulchi Focus Lens Kicks Off in South Korea," *Air Force Link,* 25 August 2006, http://www.af.mil/news/story.asp?storyID=123025849.

21. Navy Warfare Development Command, "Navy Simulation Meets the Challenge," *CHIPS* 25, no. 2 (April–June 2007): 34–35.

22. USPACOM, FY 2008–2013: B-A-4–5, paragraph 4, https://www1.apan-info.net/j7/J7/J71/J712/JTRG/tabid/207/Default.aspx.

23. Lt. Penny Cockerell, "Talisman Saber 2007 Comes to a Close," US Seventh Fleet Public Affairs website, http://www.c7f.navy.mil/ts07/News/27.htm.

24. John Hanley, "Rapid Spiral Transformation," *Transformation Trends* (Washington, DC: Government Printing Office, 2003), 1–9.

25. Joint Programs Sustainment and Development (JPSD) Integration and Evaluation Center (IEC) Web Portal, JADOCS, https://www.iec.belvoir.army.mil/jadocs/index.htm.

26. Christopher Paul et al., "Implementing and Evaluating an Innovative Approach to Simulation Training Acquisitions," RAND National Defense Research Institute, 2006: 2.

27. Kenneth J. Krieg, undersecretary of Defense for Acquisition, Technology, and Logistics, "Facing the Future with Innovation and Cooperation," remarks to the US Pacific Command Operational Science and Technology Conference, Honolulu, 9 March 2006, http://www.acq.osd.mil/usd/previous_krieg_speeches/03_09_06_NR_USPACOM_S_and_T_Conf_final.doc.

28. Philip Taubman, "Lesson on How Not to Build a Navy Ship," *New York Times,* 25 April 2008, http://www.nytimes.com/2008/04/25/us/25ship.html. See also "The USA's New Littoral Combat Ships (Updated)," *Defense Industry Daily,* 29 April 2008, http://www.defenseindustrydaily.com/the-usas-new-littoral-combat-ships-updated-01343/#controversies.

29. Office of the Assistant Secretary of Defense (Public Affairs), "Navy Terminates Littoral Combat Ship (LCS 4) Contract," News Release No. 1269-07, 1 November 2007, http://www.defenselink.mil/releases/release.aspx?releaseid=11449.

30. Michael S. McGrath, "Quantitative Methods in Defense and National Security," brief to the Department of the Assistant Secretary of the Navy for Research, Development, Testing, and Evaluation conference, 7 February 2007: 27, www.galaxy.gmu.edu/QMDNS2007/WebPages/pres/keynote.pdf.

31. Bryon Greenwald, "Joint Capability Development," *Joint Forces Quarterly* 44 (1st Quarter 2007): 52, www.ndu.edu/inss/Press/jfq_pages/editions/i44/15.pdf.

32. Admiral Timothy J. Keating, "U.S. Pacific Command Posture," testimony before the House Armed Services Committee, 12 March 2008: 7, http://armedservices.house.gov/pdfs/FC031208/Keating_Testimony031208.pdf.

33. Solomon, "Experimentation Activities Key Results," presented at Future Joint Warfare Concept Development and Experimentation Day, Defense Technical Information Center, January 2007, http://www.dtic.mil/futurejointwarfare/strategic/cdeday2_pacom.ppt.

34. Thomas E. Potok, "Intelligent Software Agent Technology: USPACOM Success with Virtual Information Processing Agent Research (VIPAR) at the Virtual Information Center," US Department of Energy, Oakridge National Laboratory findings, March 2002, www.csm.ornl.gov/~v8q/Homepage/Presentations/USPACOM%203-21-2002.ppt.

Part 3

Conclusion

12

Measuring Progress

Scott Jasper

> This is a skilled and determined enemy. He's ruthless. He's got a thirst for blood like I've never seen anywhere in my life. And he's determined to do whatever he can.
>
> —*Major General Joseph F. Fil Jr., commander, US Forces in Baghdad*[1]

Around the globe, terrorists and insurgents are carrying out violent attacks that display increased levels of sophisticated intent. The fourth generation warrior is actively using or seeking asymmetric strategies that exploit the full range of traditional, irregular, catastrophic, and disruptive methods. Through terrorism, groups motivated by radical ideology (most notably Al-Qaida affiliates) wreak havoc on civilians and infrastructure to manipulate governmental policy; examples in the early 2000s are the bombings of the Algerian prime minister's office (April 2007),[2] the United Nations refugee agency's office in Algeria (December 2007),[3] and the US Embassy in Yemen (2008).[4] Terror attacks have become more organized over the last decade or so. The flaming SUV (sport-utility vehicle) attack on the Glasgow International Airport, linked to the discovery of two explosive-laden Mercedes Benzes found near Piccadilly Circus and Trafalgar Square in London, all occurred just days after the new British prime minister, a Scot, took office in June 2007.[5]

Through protracted campaigns of localized violence, insurgents in Iraq and Afghanistan seek to collapse the enemy from within by weakening public support and political will. Adaptive and cunning, the insurgents modify or shift guerrilla tactics (bombings, kidnappings, assassinations, and infiltrations) to achieve sensational effects, such as demolishing revered Iraqi shines and minarets in Baghdad and Samarra to fuel sectarian slaughter,[6] killing tribal sheiks that have turned against Al-Qaida,[7] using desperate or vengeful female suicide bombers to carry out explosive attacks in crowded areas of Iraqi cities,[8] and devastating Afghan police and troops through improvised explosive device bombings and guerrilla strikes.[9] Insurgents in Iraq have expanded infrastructure attacks beyond oil pipelines and power stations to highway bridge overpasses[10] and high-tension electrical lines[11] to inflict suffering and impede reconstruction.

Roadside bombs have made US forces in Iraq rely on helicopters to move supplies and troops, often at low altitude to avoid surface-to-air missiles. In a counter-airpower campaign, Al-Qaida-associated cells have used machine-gun ambush tactics to shoot or force down numerous US helicopters.[12] The Taliban in Afghanistan are using the same techniques against NATO (North Atlantic Treaty Organization) helicopters in an effort to disrupt security for reconstruction projects that could win the hearts and minds of the people.[13] In more sophisticated asymmetric approaches, international competitors are fielding advanced systems, such as diesel-electric submarines equipped with antiship cruise missiles, designed to destroy high-value units.[14] Their pursuit of anti-access strategies extends beyond the traditional land, sea, and air dimensions to include space—featuring direct-ascent antisatellite weapons, ground-based lasers, and satellite communication jammers—and cyberspace, featuring disruptive technologies for offensive operations against computer networks.[15]

An effective answer to these diverse challenges demands a capabilities-based force that can defeat any adversary and control any situation. This force should possess extraordinary speed and precision of response. The need to transform legacy service forces into an effective mission-oriented joint force is magnified by the loss of international faith and confidence in military operations. Even in Afghanistan, where NATO troops valiantly attempt to rebuild a war-torn nation, the leadership and populace have become outraged over civilian casualties caused by friendly fire on police, repeated airstrikes on homes, and indiscriminate firing on civilian vehicles.[16] In Iraq, leaders of US-backed anti-Al-Qaida groups condemn the killing of civilians by US soldiers as acts that cannot be justified.[17]

Measuring the progress of programs to create an appropriate capabilities-based force is a daunting challenge, requiring a transformational mind-set to ensure that the right capabilities are being produced. This concluding chapter will define succinctly the overarching direction of transformational change and the parameters by which to measure progress. It will offer methods to identify challenges that must be met to defeat adversary strategies, and match solutions that capitalize on available resources with concepts for future development. Finally, the chapter will offer frameworks by which to measure potential solutions as they are tested in operational experiments, and to decide what are the right transformational capabilities to field to the war fighter.

The Direction of Transformational Change

> When I talk about transformation, I'm referring to the way we do things. Transformation is a mind-shift.
>
> —*General August Van Daele, chief of defense, Belgium*[18]

The conduct of warfare by major powers has expanded in recent years to include smaller, more selective applications of power against nonstate actors in difficult urban, mountainous, and jungle terrain. This shift from third to fourth generation warfare has driven coalition service forces to work more synchronously together, often with interagency partners. The complexity of integrated joint and interagency operations mandates that multinational forces be truly compatible and interoperable.

The need to fight the fourth generation enemy beyond territorial borders has driven national militaries to transform from large, static, attrition-based formations to more precise, agile, deployable forces. To achieve synergy, these expeditionary forces must not rely merely on deconfliction of service or national boundaries but be able to operate in an effects-based, network-centric, and interdependent manner.[19] A transformed force with these characteristics will be

1. *Expeditionary:* Rapidly deployable from dispersed locations, ready on arrival, and sustainable in austere environments regardless of duration.
2. *Networked:* Connected by compatible systems and synchronized in time and purpose to facilitate integrated operations across the battle space.
3. *Interoperable:* Able to share and exchange knowledge and services between units and commands at all levels.
4. *Collaborative:* Capable of decentralized planning and sharing of data, information, knowledge, awareness, and understanding.
5. *Precise:* Ready to generate desired effects upon key elements to shape situations, while minimizing unintended effects and conserving resources.

6. *Resilient:* Able to withstand pressure or absorb punishment without losing focus, structure, momentum, or integrity.
7. *Agile and Adaptable:* Ready to move quickly and seamlessly to shift fundamental capabilities in a multiuse manner in any contingency.
8. *Lethal:* Able to destroy adversary systems in all conditions using kinetic or non-lethal means at both long ranges and in close combat.[20]

This detailed set of basic attributes can serve as a tool to measure the degree of transformational change in forces as they are developed, organized, trained, and equipped.

The transformed capabilities-based force must be able to conduct all missions effectively across the spectrum of conflict. Identifying the wide range of capabilities necessary to accomplish mission-related tasks requires a common language to discuss and describe capabilities. The US Joint Capability Areas (JCAs) provide a common framework for capability management across defense activities and processes.[21] The JCA lexicon can be used in capability portfolio management, strategy-to-task analysis, investment decisionmaking, and operational planning. JCAs can also be mapped to the US Universal Joint Task List for evaluation of capability performance according to designated standards under specified conditions, using transformational attributes (like those from the list above, derived from the "Capstone Concept for Joint Operations") to develop measures (i.e., measurements that provide the basis for describing varying levels of task performance) and criteria for adequate mission performance. The following are examples from the list of nine Tier 1 JCAs:

1. *Force Application:* The ability to integrate the use of maneuver and engagement in all environments to create the effects necessary to achieve mission objectives.
2. *Command and Control:* The ability to exercise authority and direction by a properly designated commander or decision maker over assigned and attached forces and resources in the accomplishment of the mission.
3. *Battle Space Awareness:* The ability to understand dispositions and intentions as well as the characteristics and conditions of the operational environment that bear on national and military decision-making.[22]

The Joint Capability Areas provide a means to prioritize the design, procurement, fielding, and sustaining of force capabilities. For example, the United States Joint Forces Command (USJFCOM) J-8 has been working many interoperability and integration issues in the early 2000s that relate to the sample JCAs above. To assist in the rapid creation of joint task force (JTF) headquarters, USJFCOM is developing JTF mission template playbooks that would identify the personnel, equipment, joint mission essential tasks, networks, and applications necessary to establish a core capability to accomplish major combat, disaster relief, or stability operations. To improve combat effectiveness and reduce fratricide, USJFCOM enhanced Joint Situational Awareness by tying Blue Force Tracking devices into one visible common operating picture and establishing common training and certification standards for joint terminal attack controller and joint forward air controller (airborne) personnel.[23]

War-Fighter Challenges in Defeating Adversary Methods

> I want to make sure that we are doing everything possible to help the combatant commanders as they fight this very difficult war. We are specifically looking at any technologies, concepts, or capabilities to see if we can shorten development and implementation timelines.
>
> —*General Lance L. Smith, US Air Force, Supreme Allied Commander, Transformation, and commander, US Joint Forces Command*[24]

The Allied Command Transformation Capabilities Development Process and the United States Joint Capabilities Integration and Development System, as described in Chapter 1 of this volume, provide systematic methodologies for moving from threat-based to capability-based planning. After determining capability needs for the predicted security environment and probable types of military missions, they identify potential solutions for capability gaps and redundancies. War-fighter challenges (WFCs), introduced by Mayes and Graham in Chapter 6, provide a complementary way to measure progress toward meeting immediate needs on the battlefield. Through careful study of what is needed to stay ahead in the fight against fourth generation opponents, the coalition force can hope to adjust and prevail even as the enemy changes and adapts. WFCs describe what the coalition force is unable to do in the midterm (the following two to eight years) because the joint concept, capability, or training is inadequate or missing. The JCAs provide a standard lexicon for articulating the challenge. The following is a sample WFC statement with embedded JCA elements:

> The *Joint Force* (1a) does not have the capability in the area of *Battlespace Awareness* (2a) to *analyze and disseminate* (2b) *time sensitive intelligence from integrated Intelligence, Surveillance and Reconnaissance assets to tactical level operators* (1b) in a timeframe that allows rapid,

effective *unified action against terrorists, weapons of mass destruction, and other time sensitive enemy targets in denied areas.* (3)

1. Capability Definition
   1a. Scope (Joint/Multinational/Interagency);
   1b. Specific Area Investigation;
   1c. Scenario/Environment (if specific)

2. Areas of Analysis/JCA Mapping
   2a. JCA Tier 1
   2b. JCA Tier 2/3

3. Strategic Guidance

WFCs can be solicited from combatant commanders, service commanders, and defense agencies. They are often based on operational lessons learned, integrated priority lists, and unit-generated joint quarterly readiness reviews. After collection, challenges need to be screened to eliminate those with limited joint value or lacking experimentation potential; the remainder are then consolidated to combine similar challenges into focus groupings that are mapped to the JCA categories. Challenges are prioritized by assessing the criticality of each one through a weighted methodology. Important factors for weighting include higher tasking, issue relevance, and conceptual capability gaps.[25]

Increased value is assigned if the challenge reflects a specified task or mission stated within a higher-authority directive or strategic guidance. Increased value is also placed on challenges that relate specifically to the Joint Requirements Oversight Council list of Most Pressing Military Issues:

1. Collect and fuse multi-source sensor data increasing situational understanding
2. Provide persistent surveillance in ungoverned/denied areas
3. Improve interagency coordination and planning to develop shaping strategies to assist nations at strategic crossroads
4. Improve information sharing to support operational forces and mission partners by providing adequate bandwidth and information sharing tools
5. Improve joint force management
6. Improve joint force projection and joint force sustainment
7. Increase and improve irregular warfare capacity in conventional forces (language, cultural, behavioral) and ability to model irregular challenges
8. Improve the ability to defeat improvised explosive devices (IED), mines, and other buried objects
9. Affordability of required capabilities
10. Enable joint forces to operate in a protected net-centric environment

11. Review and recapitalize joint force capabilities to maintain dominance across the full range of military operations[26]

Challenges also have increased value if they directly relate to capability gaps identified in the Joint Operations Concepts (JOpsC) family of joint future concepts. A Joint Operating Concept (JOC) is an articulation of how a Joint Force Commander will plan, prepare, deploy, employ, sustain, and redeploy a joint force against potential adversaries' capabilities or in crisis situations specified within the range of military operations. Joint Operating Concepts guide the development and integration of Joint Functional and Joint Integrating Concepts. The following JOCs cover the full spectrum of conflict:

1. Cooperative security and engagement
2. Strategic deterrence
3. Major combat operations
4. Irregular warfare
5. Military support to stabilization, security, transition, and reconstruction operations
6. Homeland defense and civil support

Finally, WFCs have additional merit if they are submitted by multiple commands or agencies. This comprehensive list provides a consolidated, consensus-based starting point for defeating adversary methods.

Aligning Solutions to Resources

> We have emphasized quality rather than quantity. Spearhead troops, manoeuvre forces and forces of all three services have received over 90 percent of the new acquisitions, whereas the territorial forces have received legacy equipment from the manoeuvre forces.
>
> —*Admiral Juhani Kaskeala, Finland's chief of defense*[27]

The prioritized war-fighter challenges must engender the widest possible range of solutions. Solutions may be evolutionary or revolutionary in nature. An evolutionary approach achieves transformational change through the cumulative effects of innovative modernization. A revolutionary transformation takes place through the nonlinear development of breakthrough capabilities. The difficulty lies in determining which approach can produce the best solutions, within limited fiscal budgets, to change the character of warfare. The choice is simplified, however, by remembering that the most effective transformation strategies exploit various combinations of emerging technologies, integrated organizational structures, innovative processes, and adaptive personnel developments.

History has shown that combinations of transformational elements can produce an overmatching competitive advantage. The explosive German breakthrough on the Meuse and its relentless exploitation that conquered France in 1940, as explored by Moran in Chapter 2, is a shining example of synergistic combinations. The German blitzkrieg strategy reengineered standard organizational processes to produce combined arms actions that incorporated the internal combustion engine, demoralizing encirclement tactics, and frontline initiative.[28] The blitzkrieg's tank divisions, with their organic motorized infantry, artillery, and supply echelons, were perceived by German officers as an evolutionary improvement in their doctrinal framework of decentralized tactics and rapid exploitation. For French and British officers in the summer of 1940, however, the integrated Panzer divisions, empowered by inspiring leadership and suicidal combativeness, were viewed as a revolutionary style of war.[29]

Quality can compensate for quantity to a significant degree, since a relatively small number of transformed forces can greatly improve the overall force. In the German western campaign of May 1940, the Wehrmacht consisted of 10 integrated Panzer divisions, 8 motorized infantry divisions, and 118 regular infantry divisions; thus, the Panzers, the heart of the blitzkrieg, made up only an astonishing 8 percent of the entire force![30] Just as the Panzers led the way for legacy forces, the US Navy is developing the Littoral Combat Ship, in support of the Sea Shield Concept, to defeat maritime anti-access threats (swarming boats, submarines, mines) and thus clear the way for follow-on legacy amphibious units. Although admittedly expensive, the US Air Force fielded the supercruise, stealthy F-22A Raptor, in support of the Global Strike Concept of Operations, to protect legacy bomber missions against land-based anti-access threats (advanced air defenses and fourth generation fighters).

In terms of military capability, modernization manifests in the technical sophistication of forces, units, weapon systems, and equipment. Therefore, an evolutionary approach to transformation might mean updating or replacing a legacy platform, such as installing the 250-pound GBU-39 Small Diameter Bomb (SDB) weapon system, which minimizes collateral damage, on F-15E Strike Eagles,[31] or replacing the F-16 Falcon with the internationally built, SDB-capable F-35 Joint Strike Fighter Lightning. Evolutionary changes might include the development of innovative capabilities that can be spun off to other legacy platforms. For example, the US Army is installing the Quick Kill Active Protection System on a Stryker wheeled armored vehicle as part of a developmental testing program.[32] The system is supposed to defeat rocket-propelled grenades and antitank guided missiles, such as were used with considerable effectiveness by Hezbollah forces against Israeli Merkava tanks in the 2006 Lebanon conflict. If successful, Active Protection Systems could be installed on the Abrams and Bradley legacy vehicles, and eventually on the lighter, thin-skinned Future Combat System family of Manned Ground Vehicles.[33] By contrast with these sorts of add-on or next-generation developments, a revolutionary approach leaps past modernization to provide breakthrough capabilities, like directed energy weapons. Examples might include the Active Denial System, designed to deter adversaries by intolerable heat from millimeter waves, or the Airborne Laser, designed to destroy enemy ballistic missiles during the primary boost phase of flight with an aircraft-mounted, high-energy laser.[34]

The injection of new technology like the Active Denial System or Airborne Laser into the military is certainly transformational; it is important to remember, however, that the most effective use of precious resources considers the coevolution of key, immutable transformational elements (technologies, organizations, processes, and people), as emphasized by Garstka in Chapter 4. Change in any one element necessitates change in all. The US Army's modernization strategy is a splendid illustration of this synergistic approach, as outlined by Butler in Chapter 9. "The Army is pursuing the most comprehensive transformation of its forces since the early years of World War II. This transformation is intended to produce evolutionary and revolutionary changes which improve both Army and Joint force capabilities to meet current and future full spectrum challenges."[35] Key army transformation efforts include the Future Force Capstone Concept (process), the Army Modular Force (organization), Future Combat Systems and Battle Command Systems (technology), and Army Force Generation (people). These complementary initiatives are meant to achieve a transformational effect far greater than the sum of their individual parts, and help achieve key transformational attributes, such as expeditionary, and Joint Capability Areas, such as Battlespace Awareness.[36]

Solution Experimentation in Exercises

> Military experimentation has long played a vital role in the search for new ways to gain advantage in war. Whether developing technologies . . . or polishing concepts . . . well crafted experimentation in advance of conflict has often made a critical difference.
>
> —*Rear Admiral James A. Winnefeld Jr., US Navy, director for Joint Forces Experimentation, US Joint Forces Command*[37]

After transformational solutions are matched to war-fighting challenges, they are allocated appropriately to rigorous laboratory trials or field experiments, as described by Hodermarsky in Chapter 8. Ideally, the most mature and promising experimentation initiatives are integrated into operational exercises where air, land, and sea forces can make military utility assessments during joint and coalition operations. The experimental concepts, technologies, organizations, and processes are integrated into the exercise scenario and matched to the exercise's training objectives. War-fighter feedback on the experimental initiative's contribution to task completion can enable rapid change and spiral development within months, rather than years, or can expedite fielding.

In the military utility-assessment processes, measures of effectiveness and performance (MOEs and MOPs) are predetermined and quantified by the joint experimentation staff in coordination with the technology or concept provider, as Chaloupka and Solomon note in Chapter 11. MOEs are drawn from the strategic-, operational-, or tactical-level joint mission essential tasks (JMETs) required by the unit to accomplish the mission plan. The experimentation initiatives are graded on how they aid the unit in performing the JMETs, compared with results without the experimentation initiatives. MOPs grade the experimentation initiatives on how well they meet war-fighter expectations and requirements for key performance parameters, such as reliability, supportability, accessibility, usability, and functionality. Based on the MOE and MOP scoring results, the commander will give his or her endorsement and recommend immediate procurement, suggest limited acquisition, or recommend elimination.

In TALISMAN SABER 07 (TS 07), for example, US Pacific Command fielded Cooperative Operations in Urban Terrain (COUNTER) small unmanned aerial vehicles (UAVs), to enhance persistency for intelligence, surveillance, and reconnaissance (ISR). COUNTER consisted of a small UAV flying at the altitude of 2,000 feet while collecting ISR video and working in concert with three smaller micro-UAVs flying at lower altitude, to carry out hard-to-reach surveillance in limited access areas. The following MOE was used for COUNTER's four experimental objectives:

1-1. Percentage of targets accurately detected and located by ground units using the COUNTER small UAV.

The staff used the following MOPs:

1.1.1. Functionality to support tasks to detect and locate.
2.1.1. Functionality to support identification tasks.

2.1.2. Number of occurrences of fratricide.
3.1.1. Functionality to improve battle-space awareness.
4.1.1. Ability for a single operator to simultaneously control a single small UAV and two micro-UAVs.
4.1.2. Ability of the autonomous control algorithms to place the desired targets within the sensor field of view.
4.1.3. Ability of the control station to display information to the operator in a timely and well-organized manner.[38]

As its name suggests, COUNTER was developed specifically to operate amid buildings and structures in an urban environment, and two of the experimental objectives were focused on ISR in that urban terrain; the scenario and overall topography of the training area, however, did not provide COUNTER with a strictly urban environment, so MOE data are mixed. Subjective and objective data integrated from surveys, interviews, war-fighter feedback, and expert observations resulted in a rough score of 65 percent for COUNTER—moderate, positive impact with collection of information that resulted in actionable intelligence for the operating forces. Waypoint navigation and extended range during COUNTER operations brought unexpected gains for the operating forces, resulting in favorable scores. The technology readiness level and supportability for COUNTER were evaluated as maturing. Integration of the micro-UAVs with the larger COUNTER UAV showed potential for meeting future tactical UAV requirements. Therefore, COUNTER could solve an identified war-fighting challenge by providing the Joint Force with needed capability in the area of Battlespace Awareness (Tier 1 JCA), while also contributing to the achievement of the precise and lethal attributes.

Multiple Solution Transition Approach

> Our ability to link commanders, sensors and shooters, to process information and acquire and engage targets in real time is going to be critical to success in future conflicts.
>
> —*General J. J. Singh, chief of the Army Staff, India*[39]

After experimentation, the winning solutions become lasting improvements through material acquisition or doctrine changes. Ideally, the solutions, like COUNTER, should solve war-fighting challenges, contribute to Joint Capability Areas, and further the goals of transformation. Given the sheer magnitude of these factors, however, a comprehensive Joint Concept Development and Experimentation (JCD&E) Campaign Plan must be developed to measure overall program progress across multiple solutions.[40] For example, achievement of the described capability in the above quote by General Singh, which applies across multiple JCAs (Net-Centric, Command and Control, Battlespace Awareness, and Force Application) and embodies multiple attributes (networked, collaborative, and lethal), might require integrated solutions across all elements of transformation. While the TS 07 COUNTER initiative could contribute ISR for engaging targets in urban terrain in real time, other improvements derived through joint functional concepts (like Net-Centric Environment[41]), enabling technologies (like the AGM-114 Hellfire missile-armed and GBU-12 laser-guided bomb-armed MQ-9 Reaper UAVs[42]), organizational adaptations (like tailored Combined Air Operations Centers), and training innovations (like Joint National Training Capability architectures) might be necessary to achieve the desired rapid sensor-to-shooter targeting that concentrates combat power.

A JCD&E Campaign Plan could map and prioritize war-fighter challenges for the JCAs. The JCD&E Campaign Plan would identify the full range of potential solutions for the war-fighter challenges and align them to the appropriate military experimentation activities. The results of this collective approach should be practical and usable prototype solutions matched to joint concept, capability, or training shortfalls. Ultimately, these multiple prototypes could be transitioned to programs of record that are fielded across services and nations. For true progress to be made toward defeating common threats, these prototypes must be interoperable with respect to matériel, doctrine, tactics, training, communications, and facilities so that units and systems from different military organizations can operate together.[43] An example of experimentation to enhance interoperability is the Advanced Concept Technology Demonstration (ACTD) Bold Quest 2007, designed to reduce friendly fire incidents, with emphasis on precise and discriminating air-to-ground engagement.[44] Multinational forces assessed the military utility of the ground friendly-force tracking device, which provides near-time location of friendly ground forces, for air command and control, from the air operations center, to the forward air controllers on the ground, and to the cockpits of aircraft. The prior Urgent Quest ACTD in 2005 focused on ground-to-ground combat identification solutions.

Prototypes must also be compatible in software and applications. As the commander of NATO's Regional Command–South in Afghanistan remarked, "We have chaotic C2 [command and control]—the Netherlands and France have the same radios but still can't talk to each other because they use different software. It's stupid."[45] A catalyst for improving interoperability and compatibility in allied forces is the NATO Response Force (NRF). As Giarra describes it in Chapter 10, the rapidly deployable NRF can serve as a stand-alone force for collective defense or crisis response operations or can act as an initial entry force. Multinational forces are committed to the NRF on a rotational basis, and undertake a NATO training program that culminates in a certification exercise validating readiness for deployment. The NRF certification exercises, like Steadfast Jaw 2007,[46] that test the ability of land, sea, and air forces to work seamlessly together also provide an opportunity for experimentation with prototype solutions. Thus, the NRF should drive nations to divest outdated legacy platforms and invest in compatible and interoperable capabilities.

Conclusion: Measuring Programs for Future Challenges

> The nexus of weapons of mass destruction (WMD) and terrorism poses one of the gravest potential risks to the national security of the United States and its global partners. A successful major WMD terrorist attack could result in mass casualty events and produce far-reaching economic and political consequences that would affect all members of the international community.
>
> —*Office of the Coordinator for Counterterrorism, US Department of State*[47]

This quotation from *Country Reports on Terrorism 2007* amplifies the NATO decree in the Comprehensive Political Guidance that "terrorism, increasingly global in scope and lethal in results, and the spread of weapons of mass destruction are likely to be the principal threats to the Alliance over the next 10 to 15 years."[48] Of greatest concern are terrorist acts that produce mass casualties, visually dramatic destruction, momentous economic aftershocks, and fear among the populace. Without concern for human suffering, some international competitors continue the proliferation of sophisticated weapons that fuel terrorism, insurgency, and sectarian violence.[49] This chapter has sought to explain how to measure program progress toward creating the appropriate capabilities-based force, primarily in the midterm (the next two to eight years), to prevail against a range of threats from irregular activities such as piracy and smuggling, to catastrophic events that include deadly pandemics and natural disasters, to traditional challenges from conventional militaries. But what about measuring program progress for the far term (eight to twenty years), in which future wars might be dominated by disruptive challenges?

Disruptive challenges emerge from states and nonstate actors who employ technologies and capabilities (such as biotechnology, cyber and space operations, or directed energy weapons) in new ways to counter current military advantages.[50] The difficulty in defending against these disruptive threats is that we are just now exploring their potential for ourselves. For example, as we develop futuristic directed energy weapons, like the Advanced Tactical Laser, an airborne high-energy chemical laser,[51] how vulnerable are we to laser weapons used by our adversaries?[52] This perplexing question is a reminder that transformation demands a radical and uncomfortable shift in the cultural mind-set. Rather than simply improving upon the status quo, a transformational frame of mind will anticipate security challenges, embrace unsettling innovation, accept analyzed risk, and encourage critical thinking. Therefore, transformation programs must factor in responses to disruptive challenges that we are not comfortable addressing today. The steps for measuring progress are basically the same, but it may be necessary to use more forward-thinking modeling and simulation, to generate creative scenarios that replicate disruptive challenges, in operational assessments.

The alarming emergence of new challenges to global security necessitates a unified, long-term commitment by the global community to the process of transforming defense capabilities. The US secretary of defense recently testified that in light of this strategic environment, we must make the choices and investments necessary to protect security, prosperity, and freedom for the next generation.[53] This chapter has provided conceptual frameworks for measuring progress in the continuing effort to sustain military preeminence. Ideally, transformational initiatives should solve war-fighting challenges, contribute to Joint Capability Areas, and promote transformational attributes. Through a rigorous Campaign Plan–led process of concept development and experimentation, the right capabilities to defeat adversary strategies can be fielded to the war fighter.

The present volume has strived to describe in clear terms *what* transformation means, *why* it is essential, and *how* to translate revolutionary concepts through experimentation into integrated defense capabilities. Its authors demonstrate how promising technologies can be combined with innovative processes, organizational improvements, and personnel development to achieve competitive military advantage across the range of traditional and emerging roles and missions. The practical insights and proven methodologies compiled here potentially will assist international security planners and policymakers to think and act in new ways to counter formidable challenges to national and collective security interests.

Notes

1. Quoted in Robert H. Reid, "Ambush Caps Deadliest Quarter in Iraq War," *Monterey County Herald,* 30 June 2007: A1.

2. Craig Whitlock, "Al-Qaeda Branch Claims Algeria Blasts," *Washington Post* online archive, 12 April 2007: A1, http://www.washingtonpost.com.

3. "UN Toll in Algiers Bombing Rises," BBC News online, 14 December 2007, http://newsvote.bbc.co.uk/mpapps/pagetools/print/news.bbc.co.uk/2/hi/africa/7145120.stm.

4. "Sixteen Killed in Attack on U.S. Embassy," *USA Today,* 18 September 2008: 9A.

5. Ian Stewart, "Glasgow Airport Terror Target," *Monterey County Herald,* 1 July 2007: A1.

6. Steven R. Hurst, "Truck Bomb Kills 78, Wounds 200 at Shiite Shrine," *Monterey County Herald,* 20 June 2007: A5.

7. "Suicide Bomber Kills Sunni Sheiks Who Opposed al-Qaeda," *USA Today,* 26 June 2007: A11; "Gen. Petraeus Suspects al-Qaeda in Assassination," *USA Today,* 14 September 2007: A6; and Kim Gamel, "Car Bombs Kill 22 in Baghdad," *Monterey County Herald,* 12 February 2008: A4.

8. Jomana Karadsheh, "Female Bomber Kills 16 Near Government Complex," CNN News online, 22 June 2008, http://www.cnn.com/2008/WORLD/meast/06/22/iraq.main/index.html; and "Female Bomber Kills at Least 22 at Police Celebration in Iraq," *USA Today,* 16 September 2008: 8A.

9. David Rohde, "Afghan Police Suffer Setbacks as Taliban Adapt," *New York Times,* 2 September 2007, http://www.nytimes.com/2007/09/02/world/asia/02taliban.html?; and Stephen Graham, "Bombings Kill 5 Foreign Troops in Afghanistan: Rebels Slay Five Afghan Soldiers in Another Attack," *Monterey County Herald,* 22 June 2008: A7.

10. Charles J. Hanley, "Suicide Bomber Topples Bridge; GIs Trapped," *Monterey County Herald,* 11 June 2007: A1.

11. Steven R. Hurst, "Iraq's Power Woes Mount; Grid Near Collapse," *Monterey County Herald,* 5 August 2007: A7.

12. Jim Michaels, "General Implicates al-Qaeda in Copter Crashes," *USA Today,* 23 February 2007: A5.

13. Sayed Salahuddin, "Taliban Fire May Have Caused Afghan Crash—NATO," *Reuters Alert Net,* 31 May 2007, http://www.alertnet.org/thenews/newsdesk/SP247132.htm.

14. Timothy Hu, "Marching Forward," China Report, *Jane's Defence Weekly,* 25 April 2007: 29–30, http://jdw.janes.com.

15. The Honorable Richard P. Lawless, deputy undersecretary of Defense for Asian and Pacific Affairs, "China: Recent Security Developments," prepared statement before the House Armed Services Committee, 13 June 2007: 3–8, http://armedservices.house.gov/pdfs/FC061307/Lawless_Testimony061307.pdf.

16. Noor Khan, "Airstrikes Kill 21 Civilians, Afghanistan Officials Say," *Monterey County Herald,* 10 May 2007: A7; Darmian Kemp, "Lack of Ground Forces Threatens to Undermine Afghanistan Mission," *Jane's Defence Weekly,* 24 October 2007: 29, http://jdw.janes.com; and Trefor Moss, "Taliban Winning War, Pakistani Presidential Candidate Warns," *Jane Defence Weekly,* 3 September 2008: 17, http://jdw.janes.com.

17. Kim Gamel, "More Civilians Die in Airstrikes on Iraq," *Monterey County Herald,* 6 February 2008: A5.

18. Quoted in Guy Toremans, "Interview," *Jane's Defence Weekly,* 28 February 2007: 34, http://jdw.janes.com.

19. General Lance Smith, US Air Force, Supreme Allied Commander, Transformation, and commander, US Joint Forces Command, "NATO Transformation: Meeting the 21st Century Challenges," presentation at the conference NATO Transformation: Towards the Riga Summit and Beyond, Royal United Services Institute (RUSI), 20–21 July 2006; available from the ACT (Allied Command Transformation) Public Information Office at pio@act.nato.int.

20. Department of Defense, "Capstone Concept for Joint Operations, Version 2.0," August 2005: 20–23.

21. Admiral E. P. Giambastianti, US Navy, vice chairman of the Joint Chiefs of Staff, "Joint Capability Areas (JCAs) Progress Report," Action Memo for deputy secretary of defense, 26 February 2007, http://www.dtic.mil/futurejointwarfare/strategic/vcjcsprogressreport_dsd.pdf.

22. Honorable Gordon England, deputy secretary of defense, Memorandum for Secretaries of the Military Departments, Joint Capability Areas (JCAs), 14 February 2008, http://www.dtic.mil/futurejointwarfare/strategic/depsecdef_jca.pdf.

23. Colonel Bryon Greenwald, US Army, chief of staff in the Joint Capability Development Directorate (J-8), US Joint Forces Command, "Joint Capability Development," *Joint Forces Quarterly* 44 (1st Quarter 2007): 51–52, http://www.ndu.edu/inss/Press/jfq_pages/editions/i44/15.pdf.

24. Quoted in "An Interview with General Lance Smith, USAF, Commander, U.S. Joint Forces Command," *Joint Forces Quarterly* 44 (1st Quarter 2007): 39, http://www.ndu.edu/inss/Press/jfq_pages/editions/i44/12.pdf.

25. Colonel Kelly L. Mayes, US Marine Corps, director, Campaign Plan Management and Integration, US Joint Forces Command, "CDE Campaign Plan Development," presentation for the Sixth Annual Multinational CDE Conference, Athens, Greece, 30 October 2006; available from ACT Public Information Office at pio@act.nato.int.

26. US Office of the Joint Chiefs of Staff, "Most Pressing Military Issues (MPMI)," JCS link, J8 Force Structure Resources and Assessment, May 2007, http://www.jcs.mil/j8.

27. Matthew Smith, "Interview," *Jane's Defence Weekly,* 20 June 2007: 34, http://jdw.janes.com.

28. Brett Steele, "Military Reengineering Between the World Wars" (Santa Monica, California, RAND Corporation, 2005): xiii–xix.

29. Williamson Murray, "May 1940: Contingency and Fragility of the German RMA," in MacGregor Knox and Williamson Murray, eds., *The Dynamics of Military Revolution 1300–2050* (Cambridge: Cambridge University Press, 2001), 155.

30. Williamson Murray and Thomas O'Leary, "Military Transformation and Legacy Forces," *Joint Forces Quarterly* 30 (Spring 2002): 20–27, http://www.dtic.mil/doctrine/jel/jfq_pubs/0630.pdf.

31. Bruce Rolfsen, "Precision, Power from Above—Smaller Bombs Guided by GPS," *Navy Times,* 2 October 2006: 28, http://navytimes.com.

32. Nathan Hodge, "US Army Installs Quick Kill on Stryker for Testing," *Jane's Defence Weekly,* 13 June 2007: 9, http://jdw.janes.com.

33. Nathan Hodge, "US Army Mulls Active Protection for Its Vehicles," *Jane's Defence Weekly,* 20 August 2008: 6, http://jdw.janes.com.

34. Tony Skinner, "Seeing the Light," *Jane's Defence Weekly,* 16 April 2008: 21–27, http://jdw.janes.com.

35. Lieutenant General Stephen M. Speakes, US Army, "2008 Army Modernization Strategy," 25 July 2008: B-6, http://www.g8.army.mil/G8site_redesign/mod Strat.html.

36. Ibid., 5–80, B-1–B-10.

37. Rear Admiral James A. Winnefeld Jr., "Joint Experimentation: Shaping Doctrine and Capabilities," *Joint Forces Quarterly* 44 (1st Quarter 2007): 47, http://www.ndu.edu/inss/Press/jfq_pages/editions/i44/14.pdf.

38. Mike Solomon, USPACOM J81, "Exercise TALISMAN SABER 07 Experimental Initiatives," presentation to commander, Seventh Fleet, 27 May 2007: 3, 4.

39. Quoted in Peter Felstead, "Mapping the Future—India," supplement to *Jane's Defence Weekly,* October 2006: 11, http://jdw.janes.com.

40. Brigadier General Michael E. Rounds, US Army, acting director for Operational Plans and Joint Force Development, the Joint Staff, *Joint Operations Concepts Development Process (JOPSC-DP) Pocket Guide* (Washington, DC: GPO, 2008), 13–15.

41. US Department of Defense, "Net-Centric Environment Joint Functional Concept," version 1.0 (Washington, DC: Joint Electronic Library, 2005), http://www.dtic.mil/futurejointwarfare/concepts/netcentric_jfc.pdf.

42. Tim Ripley, "UK Reaper UAVs Cleared for Combat Missions," *Jane's Defence Weekly,* 11 June 2008: 7, http://jdw.janes.com.

43. NATO, "Backgrounder: Interoperability for Joint Operations," NATO Publications, July 2006: 1–2; available from Public Diplomacy Division at natodoc@hq.nato.int.

44. Crystal M. Raner, "ACT, Nations Aim to Eliminate Friendly Fire at Bold Quest," NATO Multimedia Library News and Articles, 18 September 2007; available from ACT Public Information Office at pio@act.nato.int.

45. Tony Skinner, "Deficiencies in C4I Plague ISAF Operations," *Jane's Defence Weekly,* 23 May 2007: 6, http://jdw.janes.com.

46. NATO, "NATO's Response Force Prepares for Future Missions," North Atlantic Treaty Organization News, 18 December 2007, http://www.nato.int/docu/update/2007/12-december/e1201a.html.

47. US Department of State, Office of the Coordinator for Counterterrorism, "Country Reports on Terrorism 2007" (Washington, DC: GPO, 2008): 177, http://www.state.gov/s/ct/rls/crt/2007/.

48. "Comprehensive Political Guidance," endorsed by NATO Heads of State and Government at Riga, Latvia, 29 November 2006 (Brussels: NATO Online Library), 4, http://www.nato.int/docu/basictxt/b061129e.htm.

49. Christian Lowe, "CentCom Chief Tells of Iran Weapons Leak," *Navy Times,* 2 October 2006: 29, http://navytimes.com; Steven R. Hurst, "U.S. Military: Iran Arming Iraq Militias," Associated Press, 11 February 2007, http://www.topix.net; and Scott Gourley, "MNF-I Outlines Iranian Support for Iraqi Groups," *Jane's Defence Weekly,* 26 March 2008: 20, http://jdw.janes.com.

50. US Office of the President, "The National Security Strategy of the United States of America" (Washington, DC: GPO, 2006), 44, http://handle.dtic.mil/100.2/ADA448118; and http://www.whitehouse.gov/nsc/nss/2006/intro.html.

51. "Boeing Flight Tests and Laser Firings for Laser Gunship Program," Boeing News Releases, St. Louis, 13 October 2006, http://www.boeing.com/ids/news/2006/q4/061012b_nr.html.

52. Caitlin Harrington, "US Seeks to Protect Air-Launched Weapons Against Laser Defences," *Jane Defence Weekly,* 6 August 2008: 7, http://jdw.janes.com.

53. Secretary of Defense Robert M. Gates, "Testimony on Fiscal Year 2009 National Defense Budget," prepared statement before the House Armed Services Committee, 6 February 2008: 1–7, http://armedservices.house.gov/pdfs/FC020608/Gates_Testimony020608.pdf.

Acronyms and Abbreviations

ACT	Allied Command Transformation
ACTD	Advanced Concept Technology Demonstration
ADOCS	Automated Deep Operations Coordination System
AEFI	Association for Enterprise Integration
BCT	Brigade Combat Team
BFTS	Blue Force Tracking System
C2	Command and Control
CBA	Capabilities-Based Assessment
CCJO	Capstone Concept for Joint Operations
CD&E	Concept Development and Experimentation
CENTRIXS	Combined Enterprise Regional Information Exchange System
CEO	chief executive officer
CIACG	Combined Interagency Coordination Group
CJTF	Combined Joint Task Force
COCOMS	combatant commands
CONOPS	Concept of Operations
COUNTER	Cooperative Operations in Urban Terrain
CTF	Combined Task Force
CWID	Combined Warrior Interoperability Demonstration
DO	distributed operations
DoD	Department of Defense
DOTMLPF	Doctrine, Organization, Training, Material, Leadership and Education, Personnel, and Facilities
DSTO	Defence Science and Technology Organisation
EFP	explosively formed penetrator

FAA	Functional Area Analysis
FCS	Future Combat System
FFT	Friendly Force Tracking
FNA	Functional Needs Analysis
FOC	full operational capability
FSA	Functional Solutions Analysis
GCCS	Global Command and Control System
GPO	Government Printing Office
GPS	global positioning system
HADR	humanitarian assistance/disaster relief
HFN	hastily formed networks
HQ SACT	Headquarters Supreme Allied Commander, Transformation
HRF	High Readiness Forces
IBEPP	Infantry Battalion Enhancement Period Program
IED	improvised explosive device
IFTS	Interim Forces Tracking System
IO	information operations
IOC	initial operational capability
ISAF	International Security Assistance Force
ISR	intelligence, surveillance, and reconnaissance
IVO	international voluntary organization
JADOCS	Joint Automated Deep Operations Coordination System
JCA	Joint Capability Area
JCD&E	Joint Concept Development and Experimentation
JCIDS	Joint Capabilities Integration and Development System
JCRT	Joint Capabilities Requirements Tool
JFC	Joint Force Command
JIACG	Joint Interagency Coordination Group
JMET	joint mission essential task
JMF	Joint Mission Force
JNTC	Joint National Training Capability
JOC	Joint Operating Concept
JOPES	Joint Operation Planning and Execution System
JOpsC	Joint Operations Concepts
JRAC	Joint Rapid Acquisition Cell
JROC	Joint Requirements Oversight Council
JTEN	Joint Training and Experimentation Network
JTF	Joint Task Force

JTF WARNET	Joint Task Force Wide Area Relay Network
JWID	Joint Warrior Interoperability Demonstration
LCS	Littoral Combat Ship
LOE	limited objective experiment
M&S	modeling and simulation
MC	Military Committee
MCWL	Marine Corps Warfighting Laboratory
MNE	Multinational Experiment
MNIG	Multinational Interagency Group
MOE	measure of effectiveness
MOP	measure of performance
MTT	mobile training team
MUA	military utility assessment
NATO	North Atlantic Treaty Organization
NECC	Navy Expeditionary Combat Command
NGO	nongovernmental organization
NRF	NATO Response Force
OFT	Office of Force Transformation
OODA	observe, orient, decide, act
OPTEMPO	operational tempo
OSD	Office of the Secretary of Defense
PROP	Plans to Resources to Outcomes Process
PRT	Provincial Reconstruction Team
PVO	private voluntary organization
QDR	Quadrennial Defense Review
RFF	Request for Forces
RMA	revolution in military affairs
S&T	science and technology
SAC	Strategic Airlift Capability
SACEUR	Supreme Allied Commander, Europe
SALIS	Strategic Airlift Interim Solution
SDB	Small Diameter Bomb
SJFHQ	Standing Joint Force Headquarters
SUV	sport-utility vehicle
TPFDD	Time-Phased Force and Deployment Data
TPG	Transformation Planning Guidance
T3	Train-the-Trainer
UAV	unmanned aerial vehicle
UJTL	Universal Joint Task List
USAF	United States Air Force
USJFCOM	United States Joint Forces Command

USPACOM	United States Pacific Command
VMOC	Virtual Mission Operations Center
WFC	war-fighter challenge
WMD	weapons of mass destruction

Bibliography

Alberts, David S., and Richard E. Hayes (2003). *Power to the Edge: Command . . . Control . . . in the Information Age,* CCRP Publication Series. Washington, DC: Department of Defense.

——— (2002). *Code of Best Practices for Experimentation.* CCRP Publication Series. Washington, DC: Department of Defense.

———, with John J. Garstka, Richard E. Hayes, and David A. Signori (2001). *Understanding Information Age Warfare.* CCRP Publication Series. Washington, DC: Department of Defense: 66–72.

———, with John J. Garstka and Fredrick P. Stein (1999). *Network Centric Warfare: Developing and Leveraging Information Superiority,* 2nd ed. CCRP Publication Series. Washington, DC: Department of Defense.

Aliberti, Keith, and Thomas L. Bruen (2007). "Prediction and Cooperation," *Army Logistician* 39, no. 1.

Alkire, Brien, et al. (2008). "Getting the Most out of Littoral Combat Ships." Research brief RB-9301-NAVY. Santa Monica, CA: RAND Corporation.

Anderson, Gary W. (2004). "Fallujah and the Future of Urban Operations," *Marine Corps Gazette* (November): 52–58.

Badalan, Eugen (2006). "Transformation and Responsibility—Assuming Responsibility for Transformation," *Romanian Military-Thinking: Military Theory and Science Journal* (January–March).

Bailey, J. B. A. (2004). *Field Artillery and Firepower,* rev. ed. Annapolis, MD: Naval Institute Press: 207, 340–343.

Barnett, Thomas (2004). *The Pentagon's New Map: War and Peace in the New Century.* New York: Putnam: 3.

Barrett, Frank (2000). "Radical Aesthetics and Change: Jazz Improv as a Self-Organizing System," in Stephen Linstead and Heather Hopft, eds., *The Aesthetics of Organizations.* London: Sage Press: 237–255.

Bernstein, Peter L. (1996). *Against the Gods: The Remarkable Story of Risk.* New York: John Wiley & Sons: 304–328.

Bialos, Jeffrey P., and Stuart L. Koehl (2005). *The NATO Response Force: Facilitating Coalition Warfare Through Technology Transfer and Information Sharing.* Washington, DC: Center for Technology and National Security Policy, National Defense University.

Biddle, Stephen (2002). "Land Warfare: Theory and Practice," in *An Introduction to Strategic Studies.* New York: Oxford University Press: 104–107.

Binnendijk, Hans, and Richard Kugler (2002). "Transforming European Forces," *Survival* 44, no. 3.

Blair, Dennis C. (2002). *A Status Report on the Joint Mission Force and Transformation in the U.S. Pacific Command,* White Paper, version 2.0. Honolulu: 1–8.

Browley, Dean, Michael Brennan, and Stephen Cook (2001). *Military Experimentation: A Systems Engineering Approach to Force Development.* Salisbury: University of South Australia.

Buckman, T. (2005). *NATO Network-Enabled Capability Feasibility Study.* The Hague: NATO Consultation, Command, and Control Agency.

Burrows, Mathew J. (2007). "Intelligence Community Perspective on the Maturing URW Threat." *Proceedings on Combating the Unrestricted Warfare Threat: Integrating Strategy, Analysis, and Technology.* Baltimore: Johns Hopkins University: 97–106.

Cebrowski, Arthur K. (2007). "Criteria for Successful Experimentation." Internal memorandum for the Secretaries of the Military Departments et al. US Office of the Undersecretary of Defense for Policy, Office of Force Transformation: 2.

——— (2003). *Military Transformation: A Strategic Approach.* US Office of the Secretary of Defense, Office of Force Transformation. Washington, DC: Government Printing Office: 3, 10.

———, and John J. Garstka (1998). "Network-Centric Warfare: Its Origin and Future," *Proceedings.* Annapolis, MD: US Naval Institute.

Christenson, Clayton M. (1997). *The Innovator's Dilemma: When New Technologies Cause Great Firms to Fail.* Boston: Harvard Business School Press.

Churchill, Winston S. (1949). *The Second World War,* vol. 2: *Their Finest Hour.* Boston: Houghton Mifflin: 25–46.

Clarke, Arthur C. (1945). "The Space Station: Its Radio Applications," *Wireless World,* May 1945, reprinted in *Spaceflight* 10, no. 3 (March 1968): 85–86.

Cliff, Roger, et al. (2007). *Entering the Dragon's Lair: Chinese Antiaccess Strategies and Their Implications for the United States.* Santa Monica, CA: RAND Corporation: 1–50.

De Spiegeleire, Stephan, and Rem Korteweg (2006). "Future NATOs," *NATO Review* (Summer).

de Tocqueville, Alexis (2000). *Democracy in America,* ed. and trans. Harvey C. Mansfield and Delba Winthrop. Chicago: University of Chicago Press: 610.

Feickert, Andrew (2007). *U.S. Army's Modular Redesign: Issues for Congress.* Congressional Research Service. Washington, DC: US Library of Congress.

Foley, Robert T., trans. and ed. (2003). *Alfred von Schlieffen's Military Writings.* London: Frank Cass: 163–174.

Fontenot, Gregory, E. J. Degen, and David Tohn (2004). *On Point.* Fort Leavenworth, KS: Combat Studies Institute Press: 408–409.

Friedman, Norman (1981). *Carrier Air Power.* New York: Rutledge Press: 172–191.

Friedman, Thomas L. (2006). *The World Is Flat: A Brief History of the Twenty-First Century.* New York: Farrar, Straus and Giroux: 5.

Frieser, Karl-Heinz (1996). *Blitzkrieg-Legende: Der Westfeldzug 1940.* Munich: R. Oldenbourg: 72–73, 101.

Fugate, Bryan I. (1984). *Operation Barbarossa: Strategy and Tactics on the Eastern Front, 1941.* Novato: Presidio Press: 36.

Geer, Harlan, and Christopher Bolkom (2005). *Unmanned Aerial Vehicles: Background and Issues for Congress.* Congressional Research Service. Washington, DC: US Library of Congress.

Glantz, David M. (1998). *Stumbling Colossus: The Red Army on the Eve of World War.* Lawrence: University Press of Kansas: 154–159.

Gompert, David C., Richard L. Kugler, and Martin C. Libicki (1999). *Mind the Gap.* Washington, DC: National Defense University Press.

Goulding, Vincent J., Jr. (2008). "DO: More Than Two Words," *Marine Corps Gazette* 92, no. 4.

——— (2006). "Just DO It," *Proceedings* (United States Naval Institute) 132, no. 11: 32–35.

——— (2006). "DO Platoon," *Marine Corps Gazette* 90, no. 6: 57.

Government Accountability Office (2004). *Military Transformation: Clear Leadership, Accountability, and Management Tools Are Needed to Enhance DOD's Efforts to Transform Military Capabilities* (GAO-05-70). Washington, DC: Government Printing Office (GPO).

Greenwald, Bryon (2007). "Joint Capability Development," *Joint Forces Quarterly* 44: 51–52.

Griffith, David A., et al. (2006). *Coalition Airspace Management and De-Confliction.* White Paper. Wright-Patterson Air Force Base, OH: Information Directorate, Air Force Research Laboratory: 10–12.

Guderian, Heinz (2000). *Panzer Leader.* London: Penguin.

Guttieri, Karen (2003). "The Civil Dimension of Strategy," in Obiora Chinedu Okafor and Obijiofor Aginam, eds., *Humanizing Our Global Order.* Toronto: University of Toronto Press: 89.

Hammes, Thomas X. (2004). "4th-Generation Warfare: Our Enemies Play to Their Strengths," *Armed Forces Journal* (November): 41.

Hanley, John (2003). "Rapid Spiral Transformation," *Transformation Trends.* Office of Force Transformation. Washington, DC: GPO, 1–9.

Hone, Thomas C., Norman Freidman, and Mark D. Mandeles (1999). *American and British Aircraft Carrier Development: 1919–1941.* Annapolis, MD: Naval Institute Press.

Hu, Timothy (2007). "Marching Forward," in special edition of "China Report," *Jane's Defence Weekly,* 25 April: 29–30.

Hundley, Richard O. (1999). *Past Revolutions, Future Transformations.* Santa Monica, CA: RAND Corporation: 7–20.

Jasper, Scott E. (2004). "Transforming Joint Warfighting Capabilities," *Joint Forces Quarterly* 35: 69–76.

Karniol, Robert (2007). "Pacific Partners," *Jane's Defence Weekly,* 25 April: 20–21.

Kass, Richard A. (2008). *The Logic of Warfighting Experiments.* Washington, DC: Department of Defense (DoD) Command and Control Research Program.

Katzman, Kenneth (2008). *Iraq: Post-Saddam Governance and Security.* CRS Report for Congress RL31339. Washington, DC: GPO: 28–30.

Knox, MacGregor (2000). *Common Destiny: Dictatorship, Foreign Policy and War in Fascist Italy and Nazi Germany.* Cambridge: Cambridge University Press.

Krulak, Charles C. (1999). "The Strategic Corporal: Leadership in the Three Block War," *Marines Magazine* (January): 3.

Kugler, Richard (2007). "The NATO Response Force 2002–2006: Innovation by the Atlantic Alliance," *Case Studies in Defense Transformation,* no. 1. Washington, DC: Center for Technology and National Security Policy, National Defense University.

Lambakis, Steven J. (2005). "Reconsidering Asymmetric Warfare," *Joint Forces Quarterly* 36: 102–103.

Lash, Joseph P. (1976). *Roosevelt and Churchill, 1939–1941: The Partnership That Saved the West.* New York: Norton.

Lawlor, Maryann (2004). "JWID: The Next Generation," *SIGNAL Connections* 1, no. 8 (17 May).

Leonhard, Robert (1998). *The Principles of War for the Information Age.* Novato: Presidio Press.

Lind, William S. (1999). *Maneuver Warfare Handbook.* Boulder, CO: Westview.

———, et al. (2001, originally published in 1989). "The Changing Face of War: Into the Fourth Generation," *Marine Corps Gazette* 85, no. 11: 65–68.

Lindstrom, Gustav, et al. (2003). *Interoperability of U.S. and NATO Allied Air Forces: Supporting Data and Case Studies.* Santa Monica, CA: RAND Corporation.

Lissack, Michael, and Johan Roos (1999). *The Next Common Sense: Mastering Corporate Complexity Through Coherence.* London: Nicholas Brealey.

Macksey, Kenneth (1974). *Tank: Facts and Feats—A Record of Armored Fighting Vehicle Achievement.* New York: Two Continents.

Maier, Klaus A., et al. (1991). *Germany and the Second World War,* vol. 2: *Germany's Initial Conquests in Europe.* Trans. Dean S. McMurry and Ewald Osers and ed. P. S. Falla. Oxford: Oxford University Press: 101–150.

McCarthy, Peter, and Mike Syron (2003). *Panzerkrieg: The Rise and Fall of Hitler's Tank Divisions.* New York: Carroll & Graf.

McCormick, Gordon H., Steven B. Horton, and Lauren A. Harrison (2007). "Things Fall Apart: The Endgame Dynamics of Internal Wars," *Third World Quarterly* 28. no. 2: 321–324.

McLuhan, Marshall (1964). *Understanding Media: The Extensions of Man.* Cambridge, MA: MIT Press: 5.

Miller, David (2002). *The Great Book of Tanks.* St. Paul, MN: MBI.

Mintzberg, Henry (1983). *Structure in Fives: Designing Effective Organizations.* London: Prentice-Hall.

Morris, Chris (2004). "Experimentation: What's It All About Then?" *NITEworks* 1 (Spring): 6.

Mullen, Admiral M. G. (2007). *CJCS Guidance for 2007–2008.* Washington, DC: GPO: 3.

Murray, Williamson, and Thomas O'Leary (2002). "Military Transformation and Legacy Forces," *Joint Forces Quarterly* 30: 20–27.

———, and Macgregor Knox, eds. (2001). *The Dynamics of Military Revolution 1300–2050.* Cambridge: Cambridge University Press: 3n, 154–174.

———, and Allan R. Millett (1996). *Military Innovation in the Interwar Period.* Cambridge: Cambridge University Press.

Myers, Grover E. (2003). "MILLENNIUM CHALLENGE 2002: Setting the Mark," *Joint Forces Quarterly* 33: 26.

National Research Council (2007). *Strategy for an Army Center for Network Science, Technology, and Experimentation.* Washington, DC: National Academies Press: 15–38.

Newberry, Brian M. (2005). *To TPFDD or Not to TPFDD: Is the TPFDD Outdated for Expeditionary US Military Operations?* Fort Leavenworth, KS: School of Advanced Military Studies, United States Army Command and General Staff College: 15–35.

North Atlantic Treaty Organization (2008). "Bucharest Summit Declaration." Issued by heads of state and government participating in the meeting of the North Atlantic Council. Bucharest: NATO Press Office.

——— (2007). "Assessing Progress and Key Challenges for the Alliance." NATO Parliamentary Assembly, Committee Reports, 037 DSC 07 E—AFGHANISTAN, spring session. Brussels: NATO Press Office.

——— (2006). "Riga Summit Declaration." Issued by heads of state and government participating in the meeting of the North Atlantic Council. Riga, Latvia: NATO Press Office.

——— (2006). "The NATO Response Force: Beyond Full Operational Capability." Allied Reach 2006 Final Report. Norfolk, VA: Headquarters, Supreme Allied Commander, Transformation.

——— (2006). "Comprehensive Political Guidance." Brussels: NATO Online Library.

——— (2005). "Managing Transformation." ACT Directive 80-7. Norfolk, VA: Headquarters, Supreme Allied Commander, Transformation.

——— (2004). "Strategic Vision: The Military Challenge." Norfolk: Headquarters, Supreme Allied Commander, Transformation.

——— (2002). "NATO After Prague." Brussels: NATO Press Office.

Nuland, Victoria (2006). "NATO's Mission in Afghanistan: Putting Theory into Practice," in "Road to Riga," special edition of *NATO Review* 4 (Winter).

Owens, Bill (2001). *Lifting the Fog of War.* Baltimore: Johns Hopkins University Press.

Pace, Peter (2003). *An Evolving Joint Perspective: US Joint Warfare and Crisis Resolution in the 21st Century.* Office of the Chairman, Joint Chiefs of Staff. Washington, DC: GPO: 18–39.

Paul, Christopher, et al. (2006). "Implementing and Evaluating an Innovative Approach to Simulation Training Acquisitions." Santa Monica, CA: RAND National Defense Research Institute.

Pierce, Terry C. (2004). *Warfighting and Disruptive Technologies: Disguising Innovation.* London: Frank Cass: 19–27, 124.

Potok, Thomas E. (2002). "Intelligent Software Agent Technology: USPACOM Success with Virtual Information Processing Agent Research (VIPAR) at the

Virtual Information Center." US Department of Energy, Oakridge National Laboratory findings. Washington, DC: GPO.

Riecke, Henning (2005). "The Need for Change," *NATO Review* (Spring).

Roberts, Michael (1995). "The Military Revolution, 1560–1660," reprinted in *The Military Revolution Debate: Readings on the Military Transformation of Early Modern Europe,* ed. Clifford J. Rogers. Boulder, CO: Westview Press: 13–15.

Roberts, Nancy C. (2002). *The Transformative Power of Dialogue,* vol. 12. Oxford, UK: Elsevier Science: 10.

Schoomaker, Peter J., and Francis J. Harvey (2006). *2006 Army Transformation Roadmap.* Washington, DC: GPO.

Simmel, Georg (1968). *The Conflict in Modern Culture and Other Essays.* New York: Teacher's College Press: 45.

Simon, Herbert (1996). *The Sciences of the Artificial.* Cambridge: MIT Press.

Smith, Lance L. (2006). *Understanding NATO Military Transformation.* Norfolk, VA: ACT Multimedia Library.

Steele, Brett (2005). "Military Reengineering Between the World Wars." Santa Monica, CA: RAND Corporation.

Taylor, P. M. (2002). "Perception Management and the 'War' Against Terrorism," *Journal of Information Warfare* 1, no. 3: 16–29.

United Nations (2006). "Human Rights Report." UN Assistance Mission for Iraq. New York: United Nations.

US Army Center for Army Lessons Learned (2004). "Initial Impressions Report No. 04-13." Ft. Leavenworth: Combined Arms Center.

US Department of Defense (2007). "Joint Urban Operations: Joint Integrating Concept, Version 1.0." Washington, DC: Joint Electronic Library.

——— (2007). "Plan for Operationally Responsive Space: A Report to Congressional Defense Committees." Washington, DC: GPO.

——— (2006). "Major Combat Operations Joint Operating Concept, Version 2.0." Washington, DC: Joint Electronic Library: C1–C4.

——— (2005). "Capstone Concept for Joint Operations, Version 2.0." Washington, DC: Joint Electronic Library.

——— (2005). "Military Support for Stability, Security, Transition, and Reconstruction (SSTR) Operations." DoD Directive 3000.05. Washington, DC: Joint Electronic Library.

——— (2005). *The Implementation of Network-Centric Warfare.* Office of Force Transformation. Washington, DC: GPO: 3–24.

——— (2005). "Net-Centric Environment Joint Functional Concept, Version 1.0." Washington, DC: Joint Electronic Library.

US Department of State (2008). *Country Reports on Terrorism 2007.* Office of the Coordinator for Counterterrorism. Washington, DC: GPO.

US Department of the Army (2008). *Future Combat System (Brigade Combat Team) (FCS [BCT]): Systems Overview.* Washington, DC: GPO.

——— (2007). *Future Combat Systems Spin Out.* Washington, DC: GPO.

US Joint Forces Command (2008). "Department of Defense Joint Concept Development & Experimentation Campaign Plan, 09/10." Suffolk, VA: USJFCOM Public Affairs.

——— (2008). "The Joint Concept Development and Experimentation Enterprise Process Guide 2008." Suffolk, VA. (Distribution limited; refer requests for document to Command and Operations Group, US Joint Forces Command, 115 Lake View Parkway, Suffolk, VA 23435-2697.)

——— (2007). "Innovation and Experimentation Enterprise (IEE) Business Plan Vision." Suffolk, VA: USJFCOM Public Affairs: 2–3.

——— (2007). *Joint Operating Environment—Trends and Challenges for the Future Joint Force Through 2030.* Suffolk, VA: USJFCOM Public Affairs: 19.

US Marine Corps Warfighting Laboratory (2007). "Marine Corps Operating Concepts for a Changing Security Environment." Quantico, VA.

——— (2007). "MCWL Analysis Reports." Fact sheet. Quantico, VA.

——— (2006). "Distributed Operations Limited Objective Experiment (LOE) 2, After Action Report (AAR)." Quantico, VA.

US Marine Forces Pacific Experimentation Center (2004). *Language Translation Systems Demonstration and Assessment Report: Limited User Evaluation Yama Sakura 45.* Twentynine Palms, CA.

US Office of the Joint Chiefs of Staff (2008). *Joint Operations Concept Development Process (JOpsC-DP) Pocket Guide.* Washington, DC: GPO.

——— (2007). "Joint Capability Areas (JCAs) Progress Report." Washington, DC: GPO.

——— (2007). *Joint Capabilities Integration and Development System.* Chairman Joint Chiefs of Staff Instruction 3170.01F. Washington, DC: GPO: A1–A10.

——— (2007). "Most Pressing Military Issues (MPMI)." Washington, DC: GPO.

——— (2007). *Operation of the Joint Capabilities Integration and Development System.* Chairman Joint Chiefs of Staff Manual 3170.01C. Washington, DC: GPO: A1–A18.

——— (2006). *Capabilities-Based Assessment (CBA) User's Guide, Version 2.* Joint Staff Force Structure, Resources, and Assessments Directorate (JCS J-8). Washington, DC: GPO.

——— (2006). *Joint Operations Concepts Development Process (JOpsC-DP).* Chairman Joint Chiefs of Staff Instruction 3010.02B. Washington, DC: GPO.

——— (2006). *The Universal Joint Task List.* Chairman Joint Chiefs of Staff Manual 3500.04D. Washington, DC: GPO.

——— (2000). *Joint Vision 2020.* Washington, DC: GPO.

——— (1999). *Joint Deployment and Redeployment Operations.* Joint Publication 3-35. Washington, DC: GPO.

——— (1997). *Joint Vision 2010.* Washington, DC: GPO.

US Office of the President (2006). *The National Security Strategy of the United States of America.* Washington, DC: GPO.

——— (2005). *National Plan to Achieve Maritime Domain Awareness for the National Security Strategy for Maritime Security.* Washington, DC: GPO.

US Office of the Secretary of Defense (2008). *Joint Capability Areas (JCAs).* Washington, DC: GPO.

——— (2006). *Quadrennial Defense Review Report.* Washington, DC: GPO.

——— (2005). *The National Defense Strategy of the United States of America.* Washington, DC: GPO.

——— (2005). *UAS Roadmap.* Washington, DC: GPO.

——— (2003). *Transformation Planning Guidance.* Washington, DC: GPO.
——— (2001). *Quadrennial Defense Review Report.* Washington, DC: GPO.
US Office of the Under Secretary of Defense for Acquisition, Technology, and Logistics (2004). *Report of the Defense Science Board Task Force on Integrated Fire Support in the Battlespace.* Washington, DC: GPO: 41–46.
——— (2003). *Phase 1 Report on the Defense Science Board Task Force on Joint Experimentation.* Washington, DC: GPO.
US Pacific Command (2007). "PACOM Joint Training Strategy, FY 2008–2013." Honolulu: Asia-Pacific Area Network.
——— (2007). "USPACOM Joint Exercise Programs." US Pacific Command Instruction 0508.2A. Honolulu. (Available through USPACOM J7, Camp H. M. Smith, Hawaii 96861.)
van Creveld, Martin (1991). *The Transformation of War: The Most Radical Reinterpretation of Armed Conflict Since Clausewitz.* New York: Free Press.
Wagley, John R. (2006). *Transnational Organized Crime: Principal Threats and U.S. Responses.* CRS Report for Congress, RL33335. Washington, DC: GPO: 1–6.
Winnefeld, James A., Jr. (2007). "Joint Experimentation: Shaping Doctrine and Capabilities," *Joint Forces Quarterly* 44 (1st Quarter): 47.

The Contributors

Dick Bedford is the branch head for Strategic Engagement and Vision at the Supreme Headquarters Allied Commander, Transformation in Norfolk, Virginia. A former US naval officer, Bedford served in a variety of command and staff jobs in the United States and Europe. He holds master's degrees in public administration from the John F. Kennedy School of Government at Harvard University, and in national security studies from the Walsh School of Foreign Service at Georgetown University. Captain Bedford is also a seminar graduate of the National Defense University's School for Information and Resources Management and a graduate of the Harvard University School for Senior Executive Fellows.

Rich Butler is a Surface Warfare officer in the United States Navy. His career includes tours on board various combatants as division officer and department head. He served in command of the patrol coastal gunboat USS *Firebolt* during two combat tours to Iraq. Lieutenant Commander Butler also served in a joint tour with US Army III Corps. He is a graduate of the National Security Affairs master's degree program at the Naval Postgraduate School and holds an undergraduate degree in history from the University of Rochester.

Mel Chaloupka is the head of Experimentation and Transformation at US Pacific Command, where he is actively engaged in revitalizing the Command Experimentation program. He developed the command's current Simulation Facility and future Pacific War Fighting Center, the Decision Support and War Gaming office, the Virtual Information Center, and the Asia Pacific Area Network. Chaloupka was previously assigned as a professor in the National Security Decision Making Department and later as program manager at the Center for Naval Warfare Studies in the Advanced Concepts Department. He received his master's degree in public administration from Loyola Marymount University with an emphasis on policy analysis.

Henrik Friman is the research director at the Swedish National Research Agency, Department of Information Systems, and a visiting professor at the US Naval Postgraduate School's Center for Innovation and Experimentation. Friman is a fellow of the Swedish Royal Academy of War Science, and the Swedish representative in the US Transformation Chair Network. He holds a doctorate degree in strategic management from Stockholm University, School of Business.

John J. Garstka is the special assistant for Capability Integration in the office of the Deputy Assistant Secretary of Defense for Forces Transformation and Resources in the Office of the Under Secretary of Defense for Policy, where he assists in the development and oversight of policy relating to Conventional Force Capabilities. Previously, he was the assistant director for Concepts and Operations in the Office of Force Transformation and chief technology officer in the Joint Staff Directorate for C4 Systems. Garstka has authored or coauthored multiple publications and reports, including *Network Centric Warfare: Developing and Leveraging Information Superiority*, with David S. Alberts and Frederick P. Stein; *Understanding Information Age Warfare*, with Alberts, Richard E. Hayes, and David A. Signori; and the 2001 "DoD Report to Congress on Network Centric Warfare." Garstka holds a Master of Science degree in engineering-economic systems from Stanford University, where he studied as a Hertz Fellow. He served as an officer in the active and reserve components of the US Air Force for twenty-five years, working as an acquisition professional, force structure analyst, and strategic planner.

Paul Giarra is the president of Global Strategies and Transformation, a defense consulting firm. Previously a senior program manager at Hicks and Associates, Inc., he has supported transformation and experimentation in the Office of the Secretary of Defense, at US Joint Forces Command, at NATO Headquarters, and at NATO Allied Command Transformation. During his naval career, Commander Giarra was a naval aviator, a strategic planner, and a political-military strategic planner for Far East, South Asia, and Pacific issues; he also managed the US-Japan alliance in the Office of the Secretary of Defense. He served as the leader of the 2006 NATO Allied Reach Data Analysis and Collection Team for the NATO Response Force. Giarra has a bachelor's degree in history from Harvard College and a master's in international relations from Salve Regina University, and is a graduate of the US Naval War College (Command and Staff) with Highest Distinction. He also has attended the National Institute of Defense Studies in Tokyo.

Scott Graham is an aviation officer in the US Army. He currently serves as a campaign analyst with the US Joint Forces Command, Joint Experimentation Directorate. Prior to this assignment, Lieutenant Colonel Graham served as a military analyst with the Army Training and Doctrine Command Analysis Center, developing high-resolution, closed-looped simulation models for analyzing future force scenarios. He is a former assistant professor at the US Air Force Academy, where he taught mathematics and engineering courses. He completed his Master of Science degree in industrial engineering at Texas A&M University.

Michael Hallett is a Surface Warfare officer serving at NATO's Allied Command Transformation (ACT). He has extensive experience in civil-military interaction, including service at the International Security Assistance Force Headquarters in Kabul, Afghanistan, as the forward lead for ACT's Civil Military Overview/Civil Military Coordination Fusion Centre project. He has also served as an Africa analyst and strategic concept developer at Commander Naval Forces/Commander Sixth Fleet (CNE/C6F) Operational Net Assessment directorate. Hallett has a Master of Arts degree in philosophy and a collaborative Master of Arts in international relations from the University of Toronto, and degrees from the Naval War College and Joint Forces Staff College. Recent publications include articles in the US Naval Institute Press *Proceedings*, NATO's *Transformer*, and the *Small Wars Journal*. He is a PhD candidate at the University of Toronto.

Susan Higgins is the deputy director of the Cebrowski Institute for Innovation and Information Superiority at the Naval Postgraduate School. As a lecturer in the Information Science Department, she has taught courses in Command and Control, Space Systems, Technology and Innovation, and Network Centric Operations. As the US Department of Defense Transformation cochair at the NPS from 2005 to 2008, she served as a node in a network of educators focused on growing the DoD's next generation of leaders. She also developed and taught one of the navy's first fully Web-based, interactive distributed learning courses—Introduction to Space Systems. She holds a master's degree in space systems operations from the Naval Postgraduate School.

George T. Hodermarsky is an assistant vice president and senior program manager for Science Applications International Corporation in Suffolk, Virginia. He has been actively engaged in defense transformation efforts, particularly concept development and experimentation, since 1999. In support of the Office of the Secretary of Defense, the US Joint Forces Command, and NATO Allied Command Transformation, Dr. Hodermarsky regularly contributed to major experimentation projects such as Millennium Challenge 2002 and the Multinational Experiment series. Prior to this, he served in operational and senior staff positions in the US Navy, retiring as a captain. His doctorate degree is in international studies from Old Dominion University.

Scott Jasper teaches courses in International Defense Transformation in the National Security Affairs Department and Center for Civil-Military Relations at the Naval Postgraduate School in Monterey, California. A captain in the US Navy, Jasper served as the deputy for Joint Experimentation at Headquarters, US Pacific Command. He promoted the creation and implementation of a revolutionary concept for joint warfare that produced standardized procedure sets, mission-focused training tasks, and routine technology integration exercises for Joint Task Force component commands. His most recent publications include defense-transformation-related articles in the Partnership for Peace Consortium of Defense Academies' quarterly journal *Connections,* the *Joint Forces Quarterly,* and the *Marine Corps Gazette*. Captain Jasper received his master's degree in national security and strategic studies from the Naval War College, and his MBA from San Jose State University.

James Mattox is a field artillery officer in the US Army. He served as an assistant operations officer (S3) and a headquarters and service battery commander in the 4th Infantry (Mechanized) Division during Operation Iraqi Freedom I in 2003. Major Mattox earned master's degrees in defense analysis from the Naval Postgraduate School and in international relations from Troy University. He is also a graduate of the US Army Command and General Staff College.

Kelly L. Mayes recently retired after thirty years as an infantry officer in the US Army. He currently serves as the director of Campaign Design, US

Joint Forces Command, Joint Experimentation Directorate. In this capacity, Colonel Mayes is responsible for the development and coordination of a Department of Defense–wide Joint Concept Development and Experimentation Campaign Plan. Prior to this assignment, Colonel Mayes was the chief of Concepts Development for J9 JFCOM, where he led the development of the Major Combat Operations Joint Operating Concept; the Stabilization, Security, Transition and Reconstruction Operations Joint Operating Concept; and the Joint Urban Operations Joint Integrating Concept. He is a graduate of the US Marine Corps Command and Staff College, the Marine Corps School of Advanced Warfighting, and the Army War College. He holds master's degrees in personnel management and strategic studies.

Daniel Moran is professor of international and military history at the Naval Postgraduate School, where he directs the programs in Middle Eastern and European security studies. He was educated at Yale and Stanford universities, and was formerly a member of the Institute for Advanced Study at Princeton, and a professor of strategy at the Naval War College. His recent books are *Wars of National Liberation* (2006) and an edited volume (with James Russell), *Energy Security and Global Politics: The Militarization of Resource Management* (2008). His current projects include an English edition of Carl von Clausewitz's *History of the Campaign of 1815* (with Christopher Bassford and Greg Pedlow) and an edited volume, *Climate Change and Regional Stability*.

Scott Moreland is a research associate at the Center for Civil-Military Relations at the Naval Postgraduate School and an Armor officer in the US Army Reserve. He served as a Civil-Military Operations Team leader and military liaison to the Babel Province Developmental Assistance Coordination Council during Operation Iraqi Freedom II. Captain Moreland has participated in multinational combat and civil-military operations with NATO Civil Military Integration Centers, the Iraqi and Panamanian National Police, and the El Salvadoran Special Forces. He holds a master's degree in international peace and conflict resolution from American Military University.

Mike Solomon is a senior analyst for the US Pacific Command's Joint Experimentation and Transformation program at Camp Smith, Hawaii, providing process and capability improvements for military response to emergencies and crises throughout Asia and the Pacific. Colonel Solomon served over thirty years in the US Air Force, and commanded squadrons in Germany and

Saudi Arabia and an Air Operations Group in South Korea. He earned a Master of Science degree in logistics and systems management from the University of Southern California. He is an associate faculty instructor for graduate and undergraduate business and management programs with the University of Phoenix.

Index

About the Book

In the face of today's security challenges, there is widespread recognition of the need to think and act in new ways to ensure both national and collective security interests. *Transforming Defense Capabilities* succinctly describes what transformation means in this context, why it is essential, and how to translate innovative concepts into relevant, feasible, and useful practice.

The authors define all aspects of the transformation process, offering useful insights and proven methods for developing integrated defense capabilities. Demonstrating how enabling technologies can be combined with personnel development, organizational improvements, and creative change, they present a comprehensive guide for implementing an essential, capabilities-based approach to international defense transformation.

Scott Jasper teaches in the National Security Affairs Department and the Center for Civil-Military Relations at the Naval Postgraduate School. As a captain in the US Navy, he served as deputy for Joint Experimentation at the US Pacific Command headquarters.